FORORGANS, PIANOS & ELECTRONIC KEYBOARDS

E-Z PLAY® TODAY

139

CROONERS

EIGHTY-FOUR SONGS BY TWENTY-EIGHT
MARVELOUS MALE VOCALISTS

2   CONTENTS

4   SINGER INDEX

6   THE CROONERS

16 THE SONGS

On the cover:
Bobby Darin, Billy Eckstine,
Brook Benton, Vic Damone,
Mel Tormé, Bing Crosby, Tony Martin

Photos of Vic Damone, Mel Tormé, Bing Crosby and
Tony Martin courtesy of Photofest

Photos of Brook Benton, Bobby Darin, Billy Eckstine,
courtesy of William "PoPsie" Randolph
www.PopsiePhotos.com

ISBN 978-1-4234-9368-6

HAL•LEONARD®
CORPORATION
7777 W. BLUEMOUND RD. P.O. BOX 13819 MILWAUKEE, WI 53213

Visit Hal Leonard Online at
www.halleonard.com

CONTENTS

16   Ac-cent-tchu-ate the Positive

18   Alright, Okay, You Win

24   Baby (You've Got What It Takes)

28   Baby, It's Cold Outside

21   Ballerina

30   Bewitched

32   Beyond the Sea

35   Blue Velvet

38   Body and Soul

40   Candy

42   Careless Hands

44   Chances Are

46   Change Partners

50   Cheek to Cheek

52   The Christmas Song (Chestnuts Roasting on an Open Fire)

54   Cold, Cold Heart

56   Come Rain or Come Shine

58   A Cottage for Sale

60   Cry

62   Dear Hearts and Gentle People

64   Didn't We

70   Do I Love You Because You're Beautiful?

67   Don't Let the Stars Get in Your Eyes

72   Dream Lover

78   Everyday I Have the Blues

84   (I Love You) For Sentimental Reasons

86   Friendly Persuasion

88   Georgia on My Mind

90   Gonna Build a Mountain

92   How Deep Is the Ocean (How High Is the Sky)

94   I Almost Lost My Mind

75   I Believe

96   I Get Ideas

99   I'm Walking Behind You (Look Over Your Shoulder)

102   I've Got the World on a String

110	I'Ve Got You under My Skin
114	If
105	The Impossible Dream (The Quest)
116	It's Just a Matter of Time
118	It's Not for Me to Say
124	Just in Time
126	Just Walking in the Rain
128	Lazy River
121	Learnin' the Blues
130	Lollipops and Roses
132	Love Letters in the Sand
134	Mr. Lonely
136	Misty
138	Mona Lisa
140	Moonlight Gambler
143	My Foolish Heart
146	My Kind of Girl
152	My One and Only Love
149	Nature Boy
154	The Nearness of You
156	Night Song
159	Oh! My Pa-Pa (O Mein Papa)
162	Oh! What It Seemed to Be
164	Ole Buttermilk Sky
168	On the Street Where You Live
170	Pistol Packin' Mama
172	A Rainy Night in Georgia
174	Red Roses for a Blue Lady
176	Return to Me
178	Rockin' Chair
180	Seems Like Old Times
182	She Loves Me
185	Stranger in Paradise
218	Sway (Quien será)
188	Teach Me Tonight
190	That's My Desire
192	There! I've Said It Again
194	There Is No Greater Love
196	There's No Tomorrow
198	They Say It's Wonderful
200	Till the End of Time
202	Walkin' My Baby Back Home
204	The Way You Look Tonight
206	What Kind of Fool Am I?
208	When I Fall in Love
210	Wish You Were Here
212	You're Breaking My Heart
214	You're Nobody 'til Somebody Loves You
216	Zip-A-Dee-Doo-Dah
221	REGISTRATION GUIDE

4

SINGER INDEX

FRED ASTAIRE

46   Change Partners
50   Cheek to Cheek
204   The Way You Look Tonight

TONY BENNETT

54   Cold, Cold Heart
56   Come Rain or Come Shine
124   Just in Time

BROOK BENTON

24   Baby (You've Got What It Takes)
116   It's Just a Matter of Time
172   A Rainy Night in Georgia

PAT BOONE

86   Friendly Persuasion
94   I Almost Lost My Mind
132   Love Letters in the Sand

HOAGY CARMICHAEL

88   Georgia on My Mind
164   Ole Buttermilk Sky
178   Rockin' Chair

NAT "KING" COLE

84   (I Love You)
    For Sentimental Reasons
138   Mona Lisa
149   Nature Boy

PERRY COMO

67   Don't Let the Stars
    Get in Your Eyes
114   If
200   Till the End of Time

BING CROSBY

16   Ac-cent-tchu-ate the Positive
62   Dear Hearts and
    Gentle People
170   Pistol Packin' Mama

VIC DAMONE

70   Do I Love You Because
    You're Beautiful?
168   On the Street Where You Live
212   You're Breaking My Heart

BOBBY DARIN

32   Beyond the Sea
72   Dream Lover
128   Lazy River

SAMMY DAVIS JR.

90   Gonna Build a Mountain
156   Night Song
206   What Kind of Fool Am I?

BILLY ECKSTINE

38   Body and Soul
58   A Cottage for Sale
143   My Foolish Heart

EDDIE FISHER

99   I'm Walking Behind You
    (Look Over Your Shoulder)
159   Oh! My Pa-Pa (O Mein Papa)
210   Wish You Were Here

JOHNNY HARTMAN

152 My One and Only Love
194 There Is No Greater Love
198 They Say It's Wonderful

DICK HAYMES

92 How Deep Is the Ocean (How High Is the Sky)
154 The Nearness of You
162 Oh! What It Seemed to Be

JACK JONES

105 The Impossible Dream (The Quest)
130 Lollipops and Roses
182 She Loves Me

FRANKIE LAINE

75 I Believe
140 Moonlight Gambler
190 That's My Desire

DEAN MARTIN

176 Return to Me
218 Sway (Quien será)
214 You're Nobody 'til Somebody Loves You

TONY MARTIN

96 I Get Ideas
185 Stranger in Paradise
196 There's No Tomorrow

JOHNNY MATHIS

44 Chances Are
118 It's Not for Me to Say
136 Misty

JOHNNY MERCER

28 Baby, It's Cold Outside
40 Candy
216 Zip-A-Dee-Doo-Dah

MATT MONROE

64 Didn't We
146 My Kind of Girl
208 When I Fall in Love

VAUGHN MONROE

21 Ballerina
180 Seems Like Old Times
192 There! I've Said It Again

JOHNNIE RAY

60 Cry
126 Just Walking in the Rain
202 Walkin' My Baby Back Home

FRANK SINATRA

102 I've Got the World on a String
110 I've Got You under My Skin
121 Learnin' the Blues

MEL TORMÉ

30 Bewitched
42 Careless Hands
52 The Christmas Song (Chestnuts Roasting on an Open Fire)

BOBBY VINTON

35 Blue Velvet
134 Mr. Lonely
174 Red Roses for a Blue Lady

JOE WILLIAMS

18 Alright, Okay, You Win
78 Everyday I Have the Blues
188 Teach Me Tonight

CROONERS
THE BIOGRAPHIES

FRED ASTAIRE
(1899-1987)

Over the course of his 76-year career as a dancer, choreographer, singer and actor, Fred Astaire became a household name in the United States. Born Frederick Austerlitz in Omaha, Astaire collected two Academy Awards®, two Emmy® Awards, three Golden Globes® and a long list of other honors and awards. The debonair Astaire was paired with elegant actress, dancer and singer Ginger Rogers in ten films. He introduced "Cheek to Cheek" while dancing with Rogers in *Top Hat* in 1935. He sang "The Way You Look Tonight," while sitting at a piano in the 1936 film *Swing Time*, only to turn and see Rogers with her hair covered in shampoo. Rogers was dancing with someone else when Astaire sang "Change Partners" in the 1938 film *Carefree*. Despite his unforgettable film performances and recordings, Astaire always claimed he couldn't sing.

TONY BENNETT
(B. 1926)

Born Anthony Dominick Benedetto in Queens, New York, Tony Bennett is the quintessential comeback kid. The World War II U.S. Army veteran got his big break in 1949 thanks to Pearl Bailey and Bob Hope. A life-long civil rights activist, Bennett developed a unique interpretive style that imitated the playing of some of the best jazz musicians of his day. He won his first GRAMMY® in 1962. When the Beatles and the groups that followed them took over the 1960s pop scene, Bennett's career faltered. After Bennett's drug overdose in 1979, his son Danny took over management of his father's career, creating a new image for him. The singer's class act found a new audience, winning him twelve GRAMMYs from 1992 to 2006, and a Lifetime Achievement GRAMMY in 2001. He made cameo appearances as himself in films and on television, and has won Emmy® Awards for his work on A&E and PBS. Bennett is also an accomplished visual artist, painting under the name Benedetto.

BROOK BENTON
(1931-1988)

Born in Camden, South Carolina, Benjamin Franklin Peay began singing gospel as a teenager. He established himself as a songwriter and record producer in the 1950s and recorded a few songs. His big break as a singer came in 1959 with the song "It's Just a Matter of Time," which made it to #3 on the *Billboard* Hot 100 chart and #1 on the R&B chart. In addition to solo hits, Benton put "Baby (You've Got What It Takes)" on the charts in a recording with singer Dinah Washington. His smooth baritone voice landed more than fifty songs on the rock, pop and R&B charts in the late 1950s and early 1960s, until the Beatles and other British Invasion bands took over the charts. Benton made a comeback in 1970 with the song "Rainy Night in Georgia."

PAT BOONE
(B. 1934)

Charles Eugene Boone has been tagged by *Billboard* magazine as the "second biggest-charting artist of the late 1950s," behind Elvis. Born in Jacksonville, Florida and raised in Nashville, Boone sported a clean-cut, wholesome image on and off the stage. A born-again Christian, he began recording gospel music in the late 1950s, turning his focus to this genre some years later. Boone is a member of the Gospel Music Hall of Fame. Over the course of his career, Boone put sixty hits on the U.S. charts, hitting #1 six times. He took "I Almost Lost My Mind" to #1 in 1956, and "Love Letters in the Sand" to the top spot in 1957, where it stayed for five weeks. Boone continued his public life as a preacher, motivational speaker and television personality.

HOAGY CARMICHAEL
(1899-1981)

Named for a circus act, Hoagland "Hoagy" Howard Carmichael was born in Bloomington, Indiana. He learned to play the piano from his mother, who played for silent films and parties. Carmichael earned a law degree but left it behind, moving to New York City in 1929 to become a musician. He had some success with "Rockin' Chair," for which he wrote music and lyrics, but was thinking of getting out of music when "Georgia on My Mind" changed his mind. Thought of as one of the most creative songwriters in the business, Carmichael moved to Hollywood in 1936, where he continued to write songs and launched an acting career. He was inducted into the Songwriters Hall of Fame in 1971. Despite many successful recordings, Carmichael often said he had "Wabash fog and sycamore twigs" in his throat.

NAT "KING" COLE
(1919-1965)

Born in Alabama and raised in Chicago, Nathaniel Adams Coles was nicknamed "King" in 1937 by a Los Angeles nightclub owner. Although Cole's smooth, mellow voice put sixty songs in the Top 30 between 1943 and 1954, he also led a jazz trio from the piano for many years. He fought for equal rights and became the first African-American performer to have his own radio program and later, to host a television show. In 1956, while playing in Montgomery, Cole was attacked onstage by a group of white supremacists. He never played in the South again. Cole received a GRAMMY in 1959 and a posthumous Lifetime Achievement GRAMMY in 1990. He was inducted posthumously into the Rock and Roll Hall of Fame in 2000, in the "Early Influence" category.

PERRY COMO
(1912-2001)

Born near Pittsburgh, Pierino Ronald Como ran a barbershop while attending high school. He sang at weddings and parties on the side. In 1933 he won a job with Freddie Carlone's band and married his high school sweetheart. Both music and the marriage proved lifelong commitments. Como became one of the best-loved American singers and television personalities of his era. He put 127 songs into the Top 30, thirteen of them hitting the #1 spot, during his six-decade career. He took music to television (NBC) in 1948, moving to CBS two years later with a fifteen-minute show seen after the evening news three nights per week. He became the highest paid television performer of the time, winning a ratings battle with Jackie Gleason. Como won a GRAMMY in 1958, the first year of the awards, and a posthumous Lifetime Achievement GRAMMY in 2002.

BING CROSBY
(1903-1977)

Born in Tacoma, Washington, Harry Lillis Crosby spent twenty years as the reigning king of three entertainment genres: recordings, radio and film. He is remembered as the most often electronically recorded voice in history. Known by his childhood nickname, he became one of the most popular musical acts in history, and was voted the most admired man alive in the late 1940s. Crosby, who wanted to be a lawyer, was led into show business by a mail-order drum set. After his big break in 1926, from bandleader Paul Whiteman, Crosby worked with Bix Beiderbecke, Jack Teagarden, Hoagy Carmichael and the Dorseys, among others. His smooth-as-silk sound put four hundred songs on the pop charts. In 1962, Crosby, whose hits predated the GRAMMY awards, became the first recipient of a Lifetime Achievement GRAMMY. He won an Academy Award® in 1944.

VIC DAMONE
(B. 1928)

Born in Brooklyn, Vito Rocco Farinola was working as a theater usher in Manhattan when he got a chance to sing for Perry Como. Como became a mentor to the young singer, introducing and referring him to people in the business. Taking his mother's maiden name as his stage name, a nineteen-year-old Damone won a talent search on *Arthur Godfrey's Talent Scouts* in 1947. Within a few months he had a recording contract, and just a year later he had a weekly radio show. Over the years he appeared in movies and on television, released numerous recordings on several labels, and became a Vegas nightclub regular. Frank Sinatra once commented on Damone's velvety sound, saying he had "the best set of pipes in the business."

BOBBY DARIN
(1936-1973)

Bronx-born Walden Robert Cassotto lost his father as an infant and was raised on welfare by his British mother. Rheumatic fever, at age eight, weakened Darin's heart and caused his death at age thirty-seven. The singer/songwriter launched his career after one year of college, scoring a multi-million-selling hit in 1959 with his ballad "Dream Lover." Darin developed a close friendship with comedian, actor and writer George Burns, referring to him as the father he never had. In the course of his short life, Darin appeared in thirteen films, owned a publishing business, recorded with Johnny Mercer, had his own television variety show and was married to Sandra Dee for several years. He won two GRAMMY awards in 1959, was inducted into the Rock & Roll Hall of Fame in 1990 and the Songwriters Hall of Fame in 1999.

SAMMY DAVIS JR.
(1925-1990)

Born in New York City, Samuel George Davis, Jr. began his entertaining career playing vaudeville with his father. Davis, who lost his left eye in a 1954 car accident, was known as a dancer, singer and all-around entertainer. He was the only African-American in Frank Sinatra's Rat Pack. Davis' recordings climbed high on several charts, including "What Kind of Fool Am I?" which hit #6 on the Billboard Easy Listening chart and #17 on the Billboard Hot 100 chart. He appeared in films and on television, played nightclubs and made hit records. Davis was nominated for a Golden Globe® and for several Emmy® Awards, including one for an appearance on *The Cosby Show* and one for *The Sammy Davis Jr.'s 60th Anniversary Celebration* in 1990. Davis was awarded a posthumous GRAMMY Lifetime Achievement Award in 2001.

BILLY ECKSTINE
(1914-1993)

Known by many in the business as "Mr. B.," Billy Eckstine launched his career when he won an amateur singing contest in 1930. He was born William Clarence Eckstein in Pittsburg, and was raised in Washington, D.C. He changed the spelling of his last name because a club owner thought it looked "too Jewish." He was committed to bebop and helped build the careers of Charlie Parker, Sarah Vaughan, Dizzy Gillespie, Miles Davis and others. Although he was also a trumpeter and a snappy dresser who patented the Mr. B. Collar, he is best remembered for his rich, seamless, baritone voice and polished deliveries. That smooth sound, and the ballad singing he turned to when popular taste swung away from big bands, made him the first African-American romantic male in the pop music industry. He was a favorite guest on late night and variety television shows like *The Tonight Show* and *The Dean Martin Show.*

EDDIE FISHER
(1928-2010)

The son of Russian, Jewish immigrants, Edwin Jack Fisher was born in Philadelphia. A talented child, he entered, and often won, amateur contests. He left high school during his senior year to chase his dream of singing. He was drafted and spent a year in Korea before becoming the official vocal soloist for Pershing's Own United States Army Band. A close friend and protégé of performer Eddie Cantor, Fisher became a nightclub performer after his Army stint and hosted television variety shows. He was married five times, once to Elizabeth Taylor and once to Debbie Reynolds. He and Reynolds are the parents of actress Carrie Fisher (Princess Leia in the original *Star Wars* trilogy). He took "Oh! My Pa-pa" to the top of the pop charts in 1953, shortly before rock took over.

JOHNNY HARTMAN
(1923-1983)

Chicago native John Maurice Hartman was dubbed the "quintessential romantic balladeer" in a National Public Radio profile. He sang with Dizzy Gillespie's big band, recorded with Earl Hines, made numerous recordings and did spectacular work with John Coltrane's quartet. He sang with an exceptionally rich, polished, baritone voice, creating an absolutely distinctive, smooth sound and conveying tremendous emotion through elegant nuances. But Hartman's name and sound were largely unknown outside jazz circles during his lifetime. His 1980 album *Once in Every Life* earned him a GRAMMY nomination. Hartman was inducted into the Big Band Hall of Fame three years after his death. His music found a new, much broader audience twelve years after his death, when director Clint Eastwood included several of his songs in his 1995 film *The Bridges of Madison County*.

DICK HAYMES
(1916-1980)

One of the most popular pop singers of the 1940s, Dick Haymes was born in Buenos Aires to parents of Scottish and Irish descent. He lived in Paris for a time as a child, moving to New York with his mother during the Depression. Haymes set out for Hollywood in 1933, where he tried songwriting and formed a short-lived band. In 1939 he was hired to sing with Harry James' band, a job he kept for nearly a decade. He also sang with the Benny Goodman and Tommy Dorsey bands, building a successful career that included radio, film and recordings. The calm, satin sound of Haymes' baritone voice gave no clue to the turmoil that filled his personal life, including financial troubles and six marriages.

JACK JONES
(B. 1938)

Born in Hollywood to the show business family of actor Allan Jones and actress Irene Hervey, singer Jack Jones was just nineteen when he began his career in his father's Vegas act. After only three weeks Jones struck out on his own, working odd jobs to support his singing ambitions. He made a couple of recordings, but was still working as a filling station attendant when he first heard one of his own songs on the radio of a stranger's car. Mel Tormé called Jones "one of the greatest 'pure' singers in the world." Jones' smooth, tenor voice is familiar to millions, thanks to his recording of the theme song for the television series *The Love Boat*. Jones won two GRAMMY Awards, in 1961 and 1963, one of them for his recording of "Lollipops and Roses."

FRANKIE LAINE
(1913-2007)

Starting out as a marathon dancer at age seventeen, Francesco Paolo LoVecchio set the all-time marathon dance record in Atlantic City, dancing 3,501 hours over 145 consecutive days. The son of Sicilian immigrants, he then tried his luck at singing, capturing the interest and assistance of jazz musician and songwriter Hoagy Carmichael. His big break came in 1947, with a cover recording of "That's My Desire." He scored twenty-one gold records and performed in several films, including Mel Brooks' Blazing Saddles. His recording of the theme song for the television series Rawhide became one of the most popular television theme songs of all time. Laine's recording of "I Believe" was at #1 on the U.K. singles chart three times, for a total of eighteen weeks, more weeks than any other single before or since.

DEAN MARTIN
(1917-1995)

Dino Paul Crocetti dropped out of an Ohio high school to work in illegal gambling and bootlegging establishments on his way to becoming one of the most famous entertainers of the 1950s and '60s. Although Martin did well on the nightclub circuit, his big break came when he appeared as a duo with Jerry Lewis in 1946. The pair's improvised slapstick act was an enormous hit that led to a ten-year partnership. Martin went on to become a Vegas fixture and a part of the famed Rat Pack. The singer had the business savvy to control rights to his recordings and performances, which eventually made him a very wealthy man. He appeared in several films, recorded more than six hundred songs and created a hard-drinking, womanizing image that became the centerpiece of his television variety series.

TONY MARTIN
(1913-2012)

Born Alvin Morris in San Francisco, Tony Martin had dreams of becoming an actor. After moving to Hollywood, he appeared frequently on the radio program of George Burns and Gracie Allen. He landed bit parts in several films before he began appearing as himself in a long string of films and television specials and shows. Serving in the military in World War II, he sang with Captain Glenn Miller's band. In addition to maintaining a long career, which found him performing in San Francisco in 2009, at age 95, Martin was married to Cyd Charisse for sixty years — one of Hollywood's longest marriages. Martin's recording of "There's No Tomorrow," based on the Italian song, "O sole mio," spent twenty-seven weeks on the charts, reaching the #2 spot. His recording of "I Get Ideas" hit #3, spending thirty weeks on the charts.

JOHNNY MATHIS
(B. 1935)

Born in Gilmer, Texas, John Royce Mathis spent most of his childhood in San Francisco. Mathis began voice lessons at age thirteen, studying vocal technique, classical music and opera. A strong athlete, he entered college as an English and Physical Education major and was invited to trials for the 1956 Olympic games. But a Columbia Records contract arrived at the same time as the Olympic invitation, changing his path. His 1957 recording of "Chances Are" took him to the top of the charts. His Ed Sullivan show appearance that same year made him a household name in the U.S. In 1958 his *Johnny's Greatest Hits* album hit the *Billboard* Top Albums chart, where it stayed for four hundred and ninety continuous weeks — just short of ten years. It remains one of the most popular albums of all time.

JOHNNY MERCER
(1909-1976)

John Herndon Mercer wrote lyrics to more than 1,000 songs, in musicals, films and popular music. Born into old money in Savannah, Georgia, he is also remembered as a singer, songwriter and co-founder of Capitol Records. Mercer left the South in 1928, when his father's fortune evaporated. After moving to New York City he tried his hand at acting but found work writing lyrics and songs. When a Hollywood job offer came from RKO in 1933, he took it. Over the course of his career, Mercer created hits with such greats as Harold Arlen, Henry Mancini, Harry Warren, Jerome Kern, Marvin Hamlisch and others. Mercer received two "Song of the Year" GRAMMY Awards and four Academy Awards®. He was inducted into the Songwriters Hall of Fame in 1971.

MATT MONRO
(1930-1985)

London-born Terence Edward Parsons sang under the names Terry Fitzgerald and Al Jordan before settling on a stage name. He dropped out of school at age fourteen and worked odd jobs, enlisting in the British Army at seventeen. After twelve years in the service, he returned to London and worked as a bus driver, singing band gigs in his off hours. He did some recording with Decca in those years, recording more than forty commercial jingles in Britain to make ends meet. A Sinatra imitation done for a demo disc, under the name Fred Flange, brought the singer his big break. Before long he had his own television series in Britain and was scoring hits there and in the U.S. He toured the U.S. and appeared on popular American variety shows of the 1960s. Later, Monro released entire albums in Spanish, and enjoyed global fame.

VAUGHN MONROE
(1911-1973)

Born in Akron, Ohio, baritone Vaughn Wilton Monroe's enormous, baritone voice won him nicknames like "old leather tonsils" and "the baritone with muscles" during the big band era. Raised in Wisconsin, Pennsylvania and Massachusetts, he was also a noted trumpeter, trombonist and bandleader, forming a band in Boston in 1940 as lead vocalist. He put a number of hits on the charts in the 1940s, including "There! I've Said It Again," in 1945. In later years, Monroe would say that "Ballerina" was his best recorded performance. As popular taste in music shifted from swing to rock, Monroe tried his hand at singing cowboy films for a time. He worked in television and radio, hosting the *Camel Caravan* for years. An avid pilot, he was known for flying himself to engagements.

JOHNNIE RAY
(1927-1990)

John Alvin Ray lost most of the hearing in one ear as a child, but still built a singing career that took him around the world. Born in Hopewell, Oregon, the singer, songwriter and pianist was one of the pivotal transition singers between the era of the crooners and era of the rockers. His jazz- and blues-flavored style and on-stage theatrics influenced the likes of Elvis, Jerry Lee Lewis and others. His recording of "Cry" spent eleven weeks at #1 on the charts. Ray made numerous television appearances and performed at the Tropicana in Las Vegas. He developed a huge following in Europe and Australia and was honored with a star on the Hollywood Walk of Fame. Called the most popular singer of the pre-Elvis era, he suffered the effects of a tumultuous personal life.

FRANK SINATRA
(1915-1998)

Whether he was called "Ol' Blue Eyes," "The Chairman of the Board," or "The Voice," Francis Albert Sinatra was undeniably one of the most important entertainers of the 20th century. He dropped out of a New Jersey high school to sing, landing gigs with bands led by Harry James and Tommy Dorsey, striking out on his own in the early 1940s. Sinatra was a heartthrob – women swooned when he sang. He was also a tough character, the rattiest of the "Rat Pack." Men emulated his macho image. Meanwhile, Sinatra sang, acted and built an entertainment empire. He won three Academy Awards®, nine GRAMMY Awards and a Lifetime Achievement GRAMMY. He was an enormous star before rock 'n' roll hit the airwaves in the early 1950s, and put out his best-selling album a half-century later.

MEL TORMÉ
(1925-1999)

Melvin Howard Tormé hated the nickname "The Velvet Fog." Raised in Chicago, Tormé was a child actor in radio days and worked the vaudeville circuit as a child as well. He and Frank Sinatra made their film debuts in *Higher and Higher*, in 1943. Tormé formed a vocal quintet called the Mel-Tones, going solo in 1947 with a crooning, pop style. During the 1950s he brought his laid-back style to several jazz recordings, a dream come true for him, and he continued recording jazz throughout his life. Tormé had his own television show for a short time and appeared in more than twenty films. He also appeared on numerous television shows, including the series *Night Court* and *Seinfeld*. Although Tormé wrote more than three hundred songs and won two GRAMMY Awards, as well as a Lifetime Achievement GRAMMY, he scored only one #1 hit in his long career.

BOBBY VINTON
(B. 1935)

Known by fans as the "Polish Prince," Stanley Robert Vinton, Jr. was born in Canonsburg, Pennsylvania, the son of a local bandleader. Singing in his first band at age sixteen, Vinton earned a degree in composition from Duquesne University, where he learned to play quite a few musical instruments. But he is remembered, according to *Billboard* magazine, as "the all-time most successful love singer of the Rock era." His big break came on Guy Lombardo's *TV Talent Scouts* in 1960. Three years later he took the song "Blue Velvet" to the top of the charts. Although Vinton scored more #1 hits between 1962 and 1972 than any other male solo singer, "Blue Velvet" remains his most famous song. He had his own television variety show for three years and was honored with a star on the Hollywood Walk of Fame.

JOE WILLIAMS
(1918-1999)

Born Joseph Goreed in Cordele, Georgia, baritone jazz singer Joe Williams grew up with his mother, grandmother and aunt in Chicago. He sang in a Gospel quartet, The Jubilee Boys, and with Chicago-area bands in his teens, dropping out of school at sixteen. Although he sang with Jimmy Noone's band, Lionel Hampton's band, and Coleman Hawkins, he first found fame singing with Count Basie's orchestra in 1954. He scored the biggest hit of his career with Basie, "Every Day I Have the Blues," in 1955 and was inducted into the GRAMMY Hall of Fame in 1992 for his recording of the song. In his later years he had a recurring television role as Grandpa Al on *The Cosby Show*. In 1983 he was honored with a star on the Hollywood Walk of Fame and received a GRAMMY in 1984.

Ac-cent-tchu-ate the Positive
from the Motion Picture HERE COME THE WAVES

Registration 1
Rhythm: Swing

Lyric by Johnny Mercer
Music by Harold Arlen

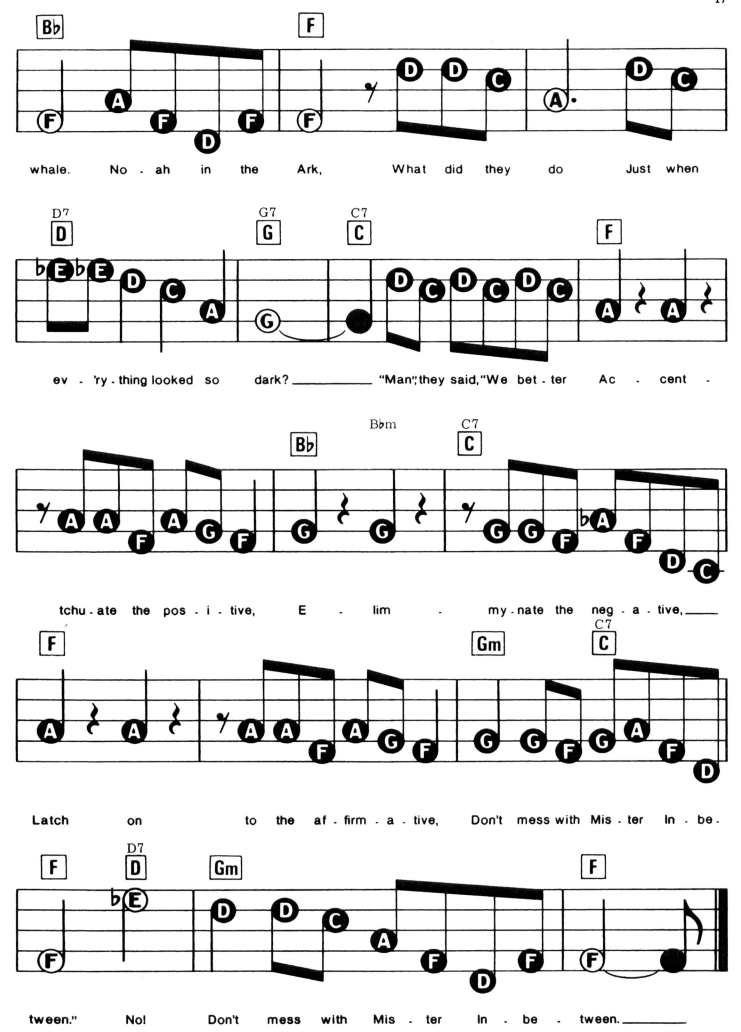

Alright, Okay, You Win

Registration 7
Rhythm: Swing

Words and Music by Sid Wyche
and Mayme Watts

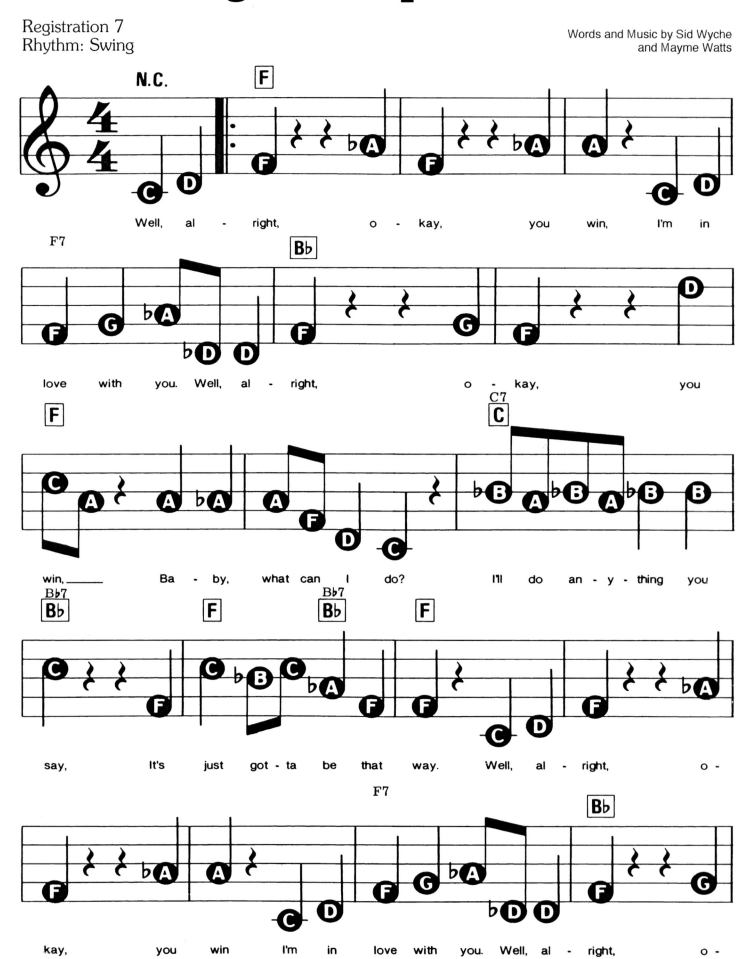

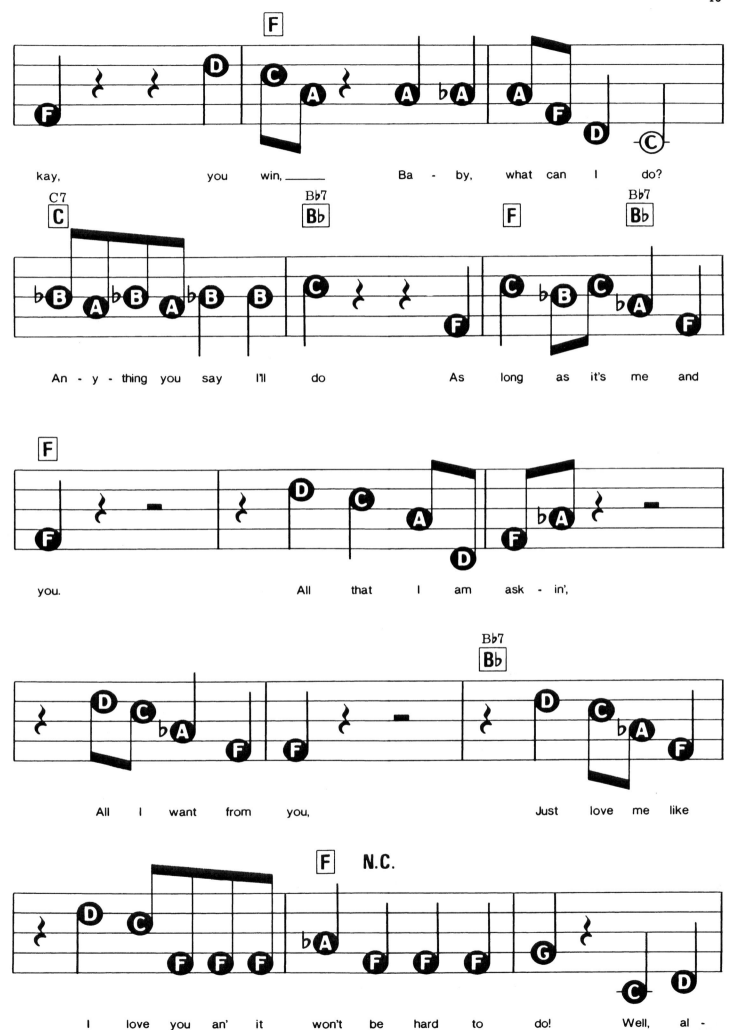

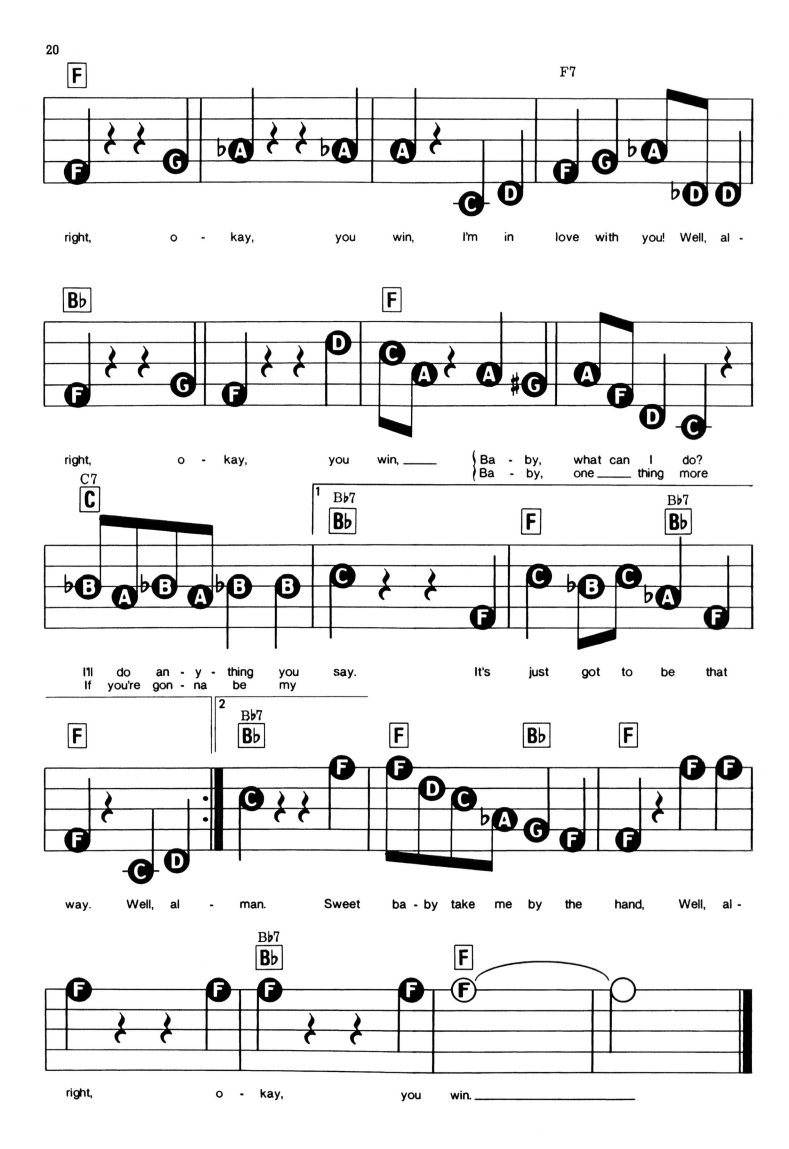

Ballerina

Registration 7
Rhythm: Fox Trot

Words and Music by Bob Russell
and Carl Sigman

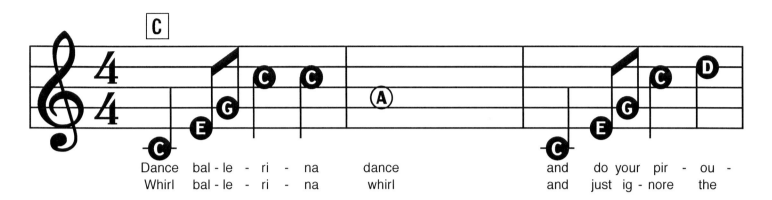

Dance bal - le - ri - na   dance   and   do your pir - ou -
Whirl bal - le - ri - na   whirl   and   just ig - nore the

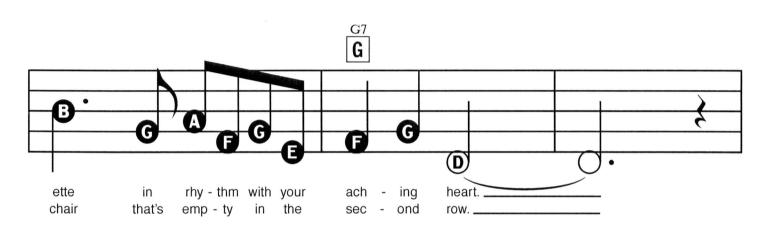

ette   in   rhy - thm with your ach - ing heart. _____
chair   that's emp - ty in the sec - ond row. _____

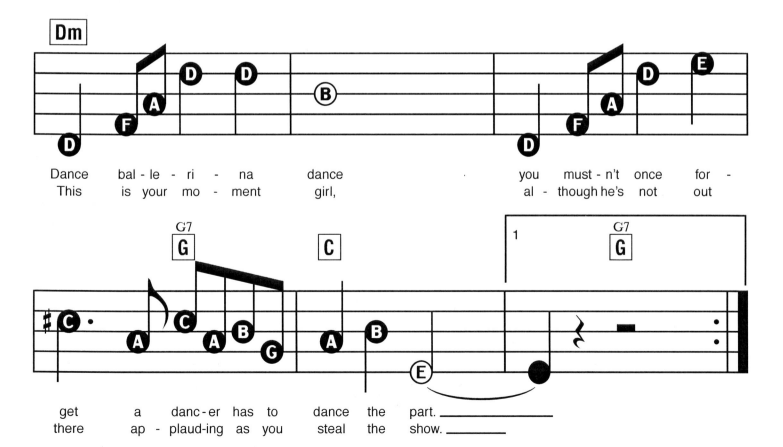

Dance bal - le - ri - na   dance   you must - n't once for -
This   is your mo - ment dance girl,   al - though he's not out

get   a   danc - er has to   dance the part. _____
there   ap - plaud-ing as you steal the show. _____

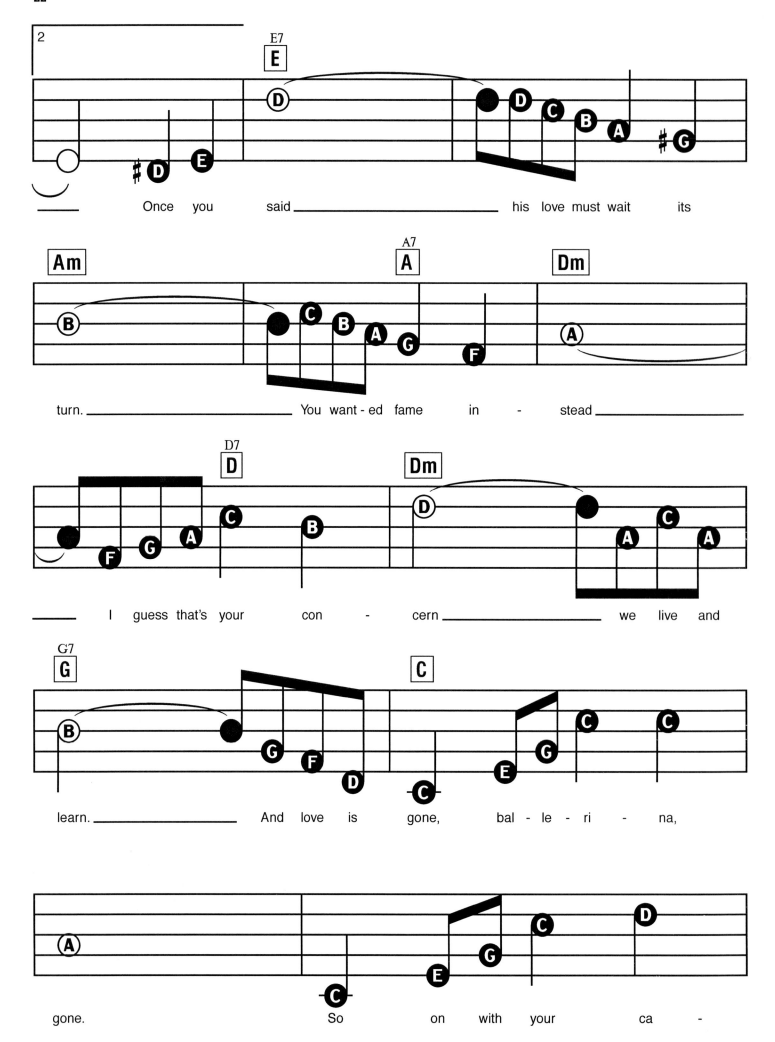

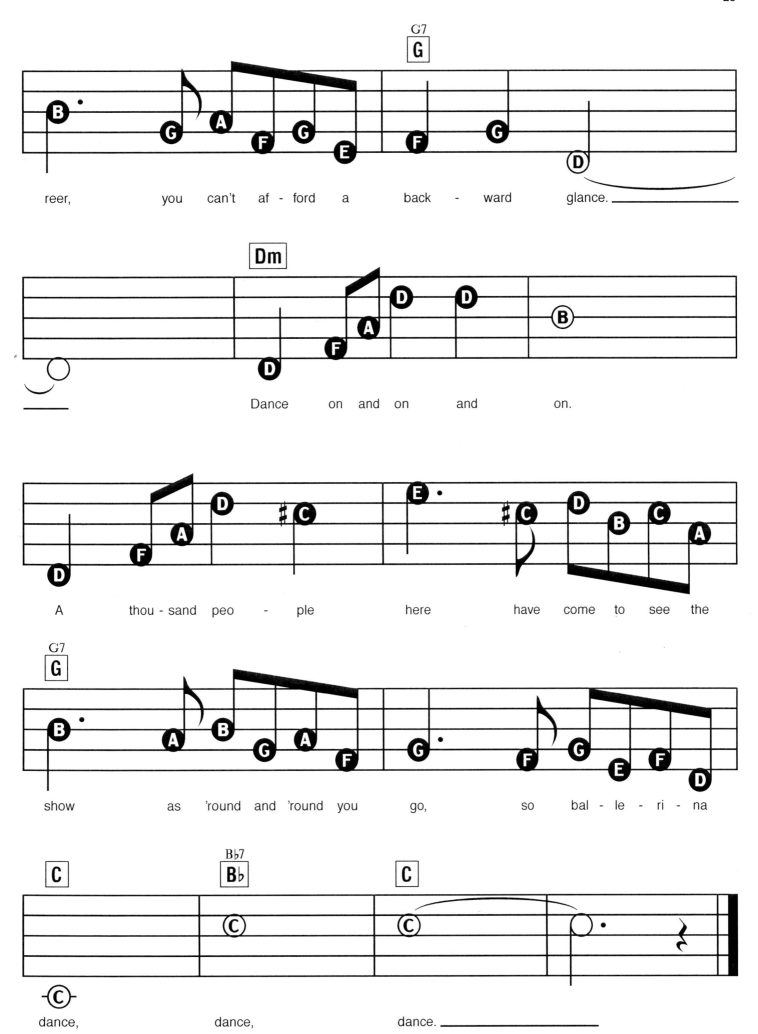

Baby
(You've Got What It Takes)

Registration 5
Rhythm: Shuffle or Swing

Words and Music by Clyde Otis
and Murray Stein

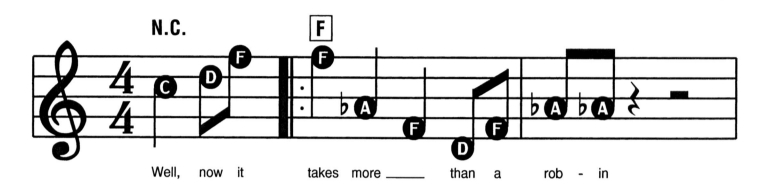

Well, now it takes more _____ than a rob - in

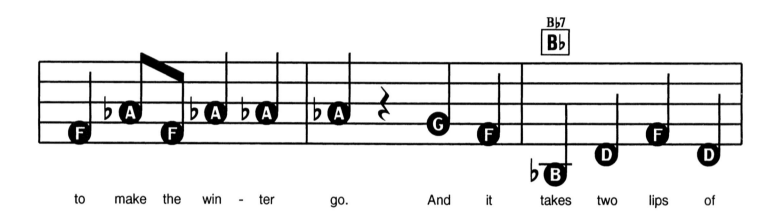

to make the win - ter go. And it takes two lips of

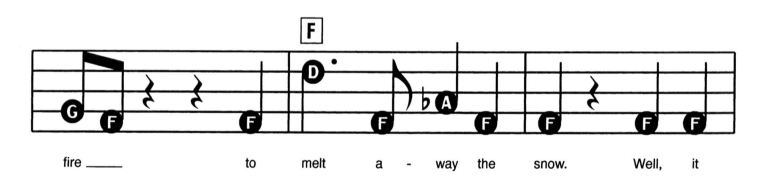

fire _____ to melt a - way the snow. Well, it

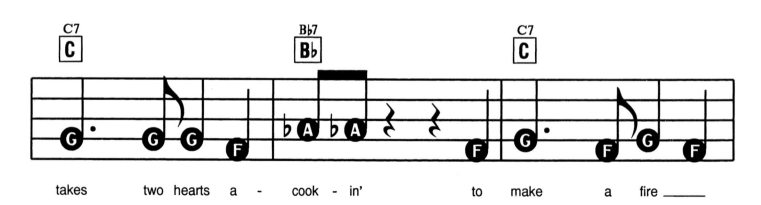

takes two hearts a - cook - in' to make a fire _____

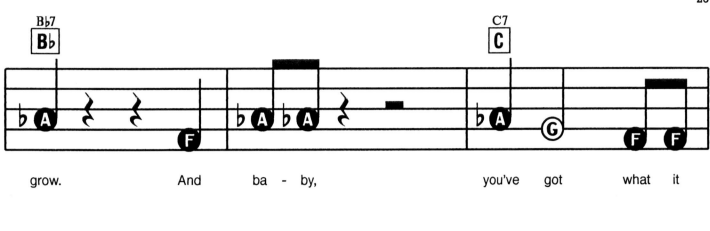

grow. And ba - by, you've got what it

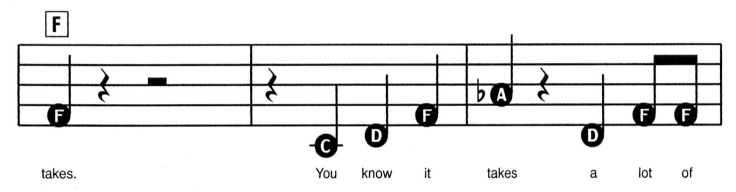

takes. You know it takes a lot of

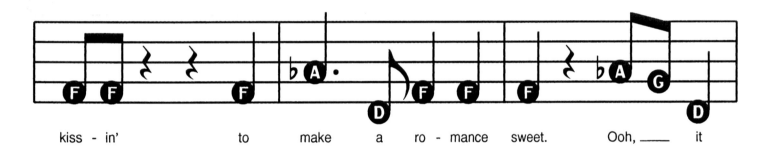

kiss - in' to make a ro - mance sweet. Ooh, ____ it

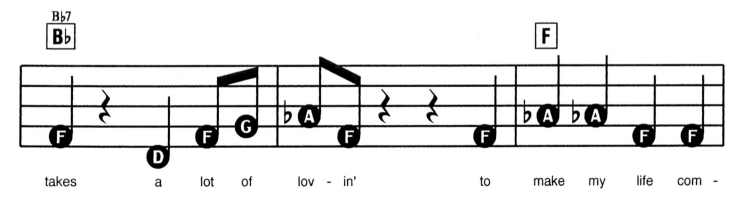

takes a lot of lov - in' to make my life com -

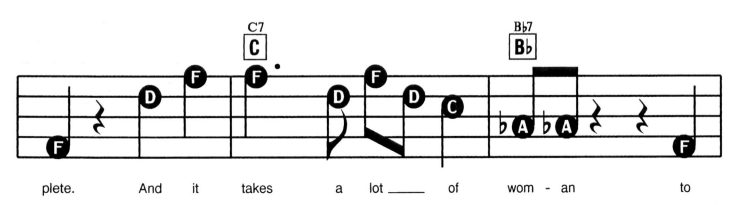

plete. And it takes a lot ____ of wom - an to

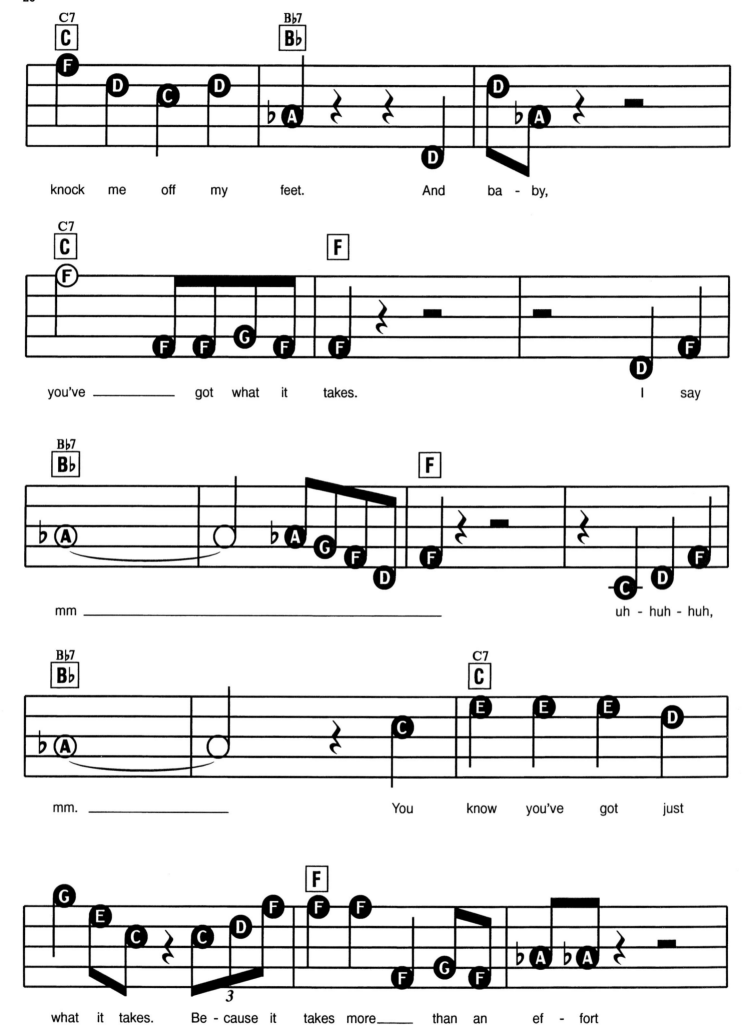

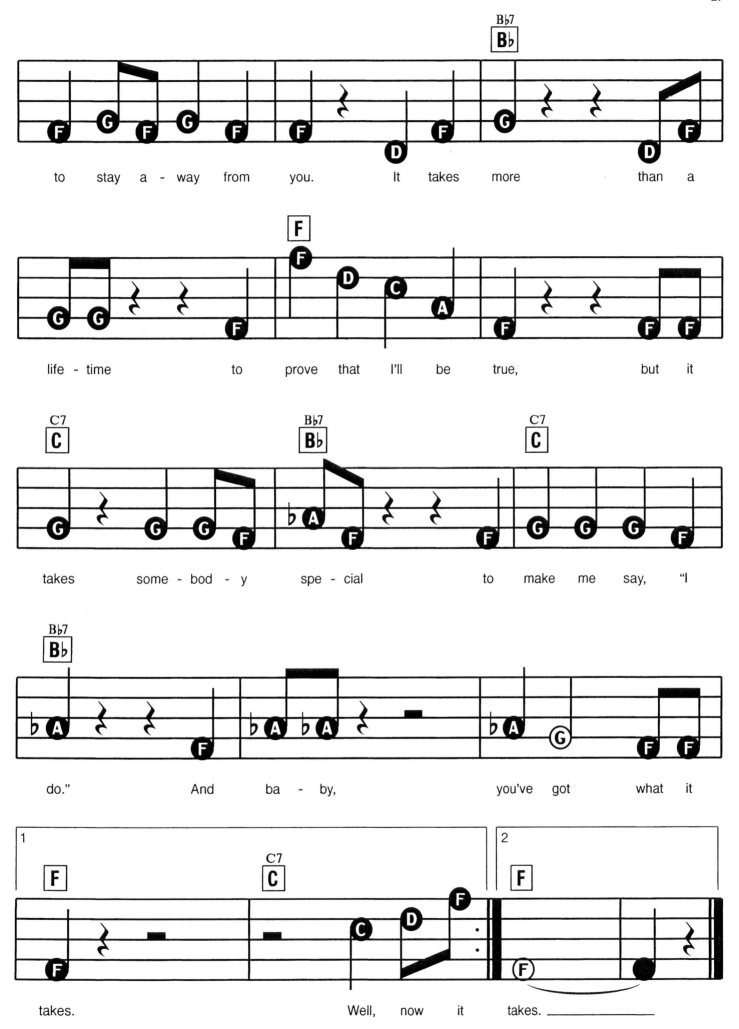

Baby, It's Cold Outside
from the Motion Picture NEPTUNE'S DAUGHTER

Registration 1
Rhythm: Fox Trot

By Frank Loesser

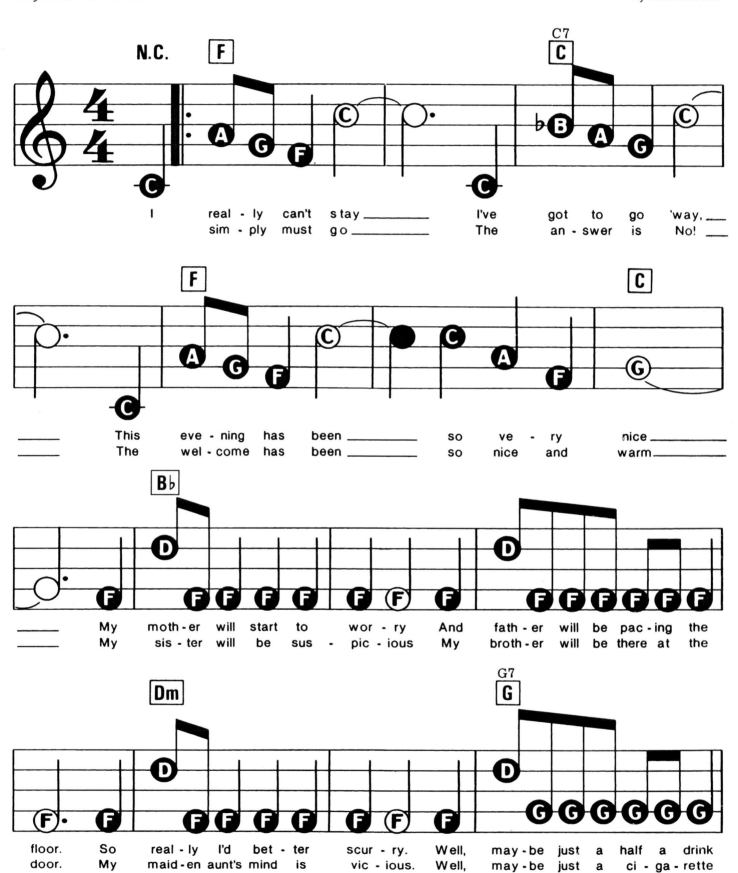

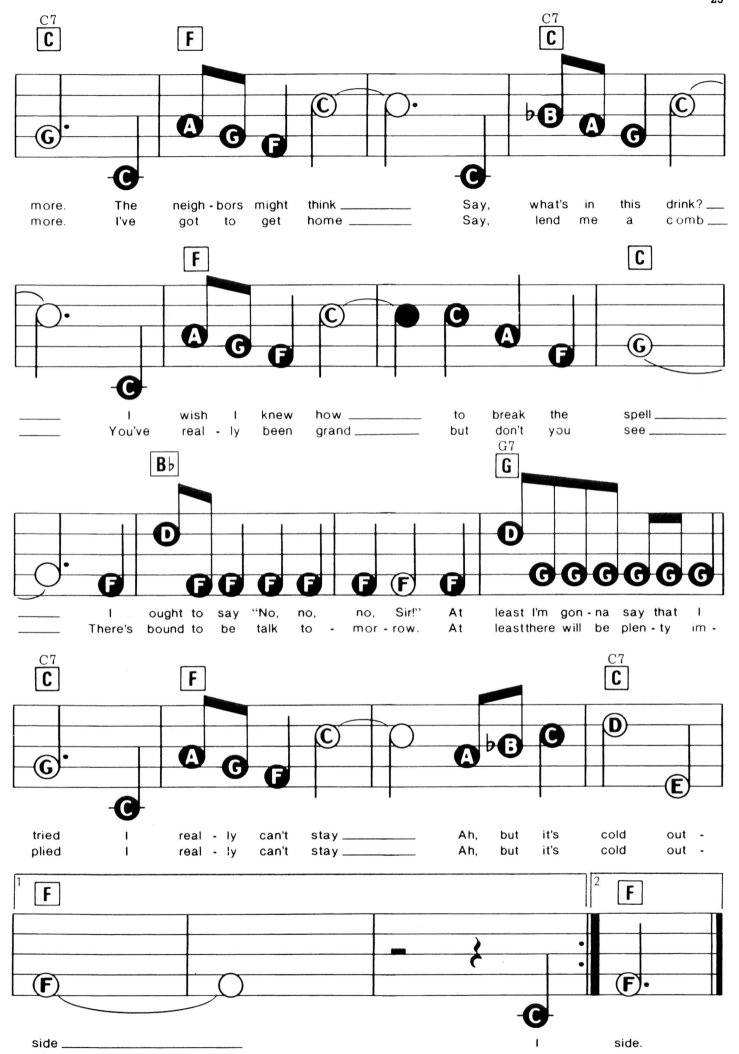

Bewitched
from PAL JOEY

Registration 10
Rhythm: Ballad or Fox Trot

Words by Lorenz Hart
Music by Richard Rodgers

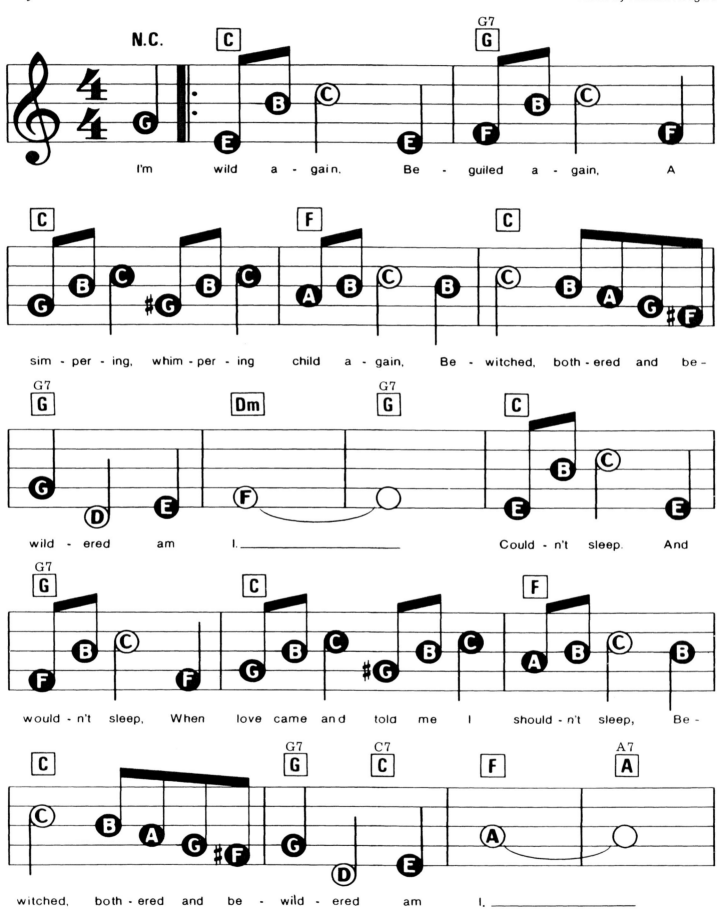

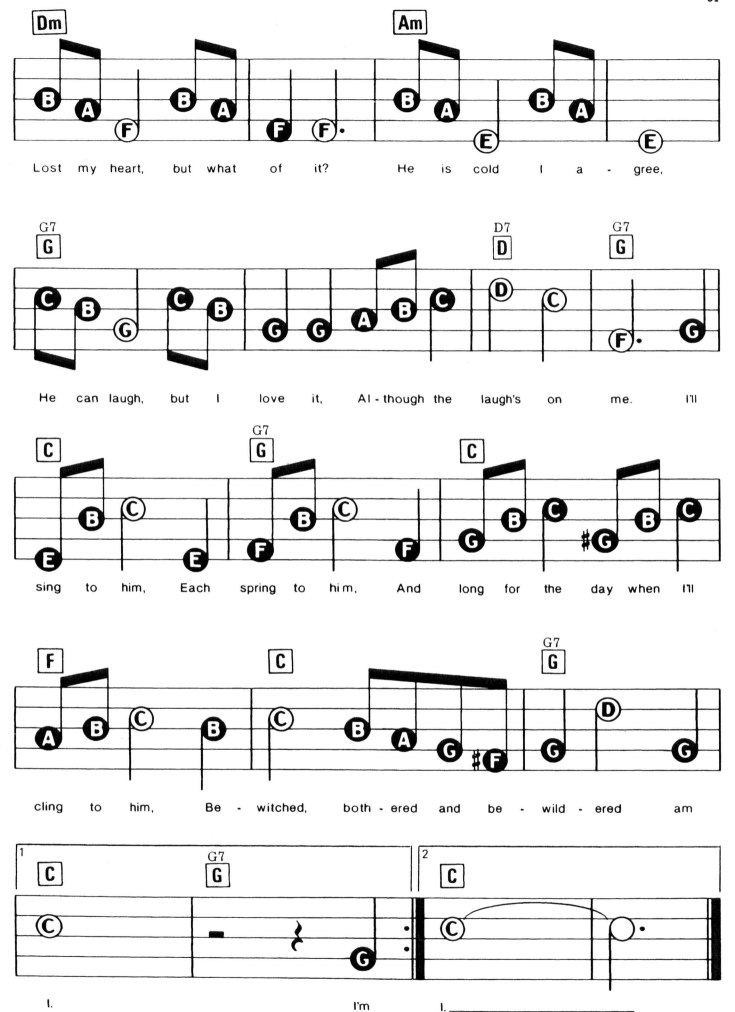

Beyond the Sea

Registration 7
Rhythm: Slow Ballad or Rock

Lyrics by Jack Lawrence
Music by Charles Trenet and Albert Lasry
Original French Lyric to "La Mer" by Charles Trenet

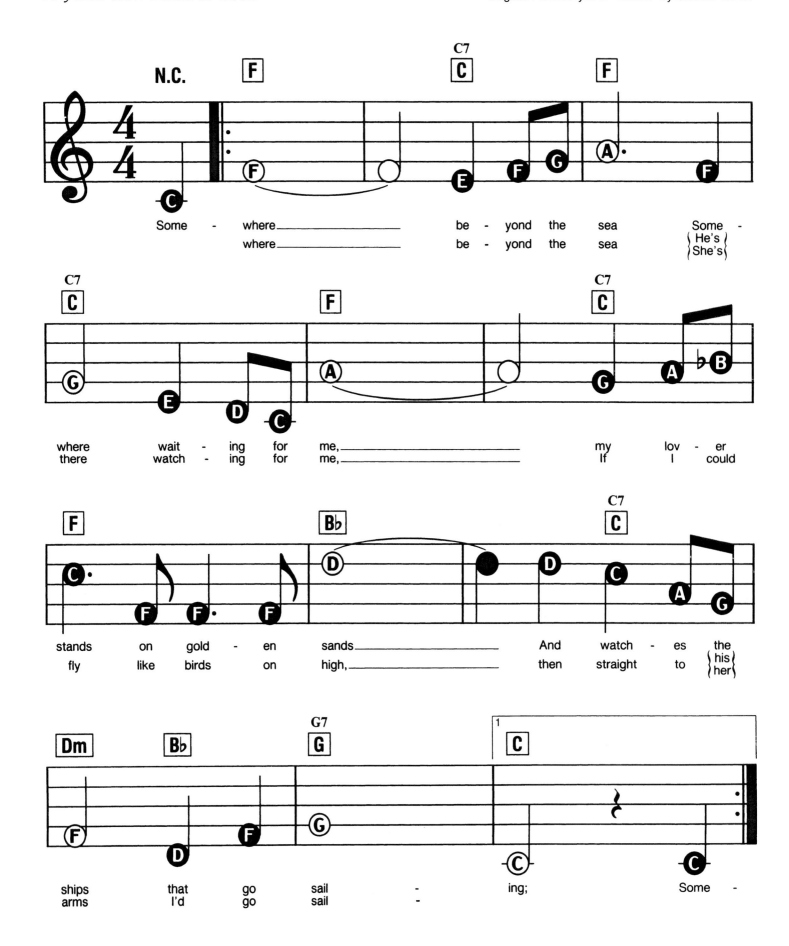

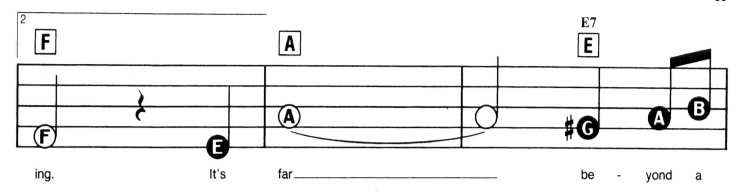

ing. It's far_____ be - yond a

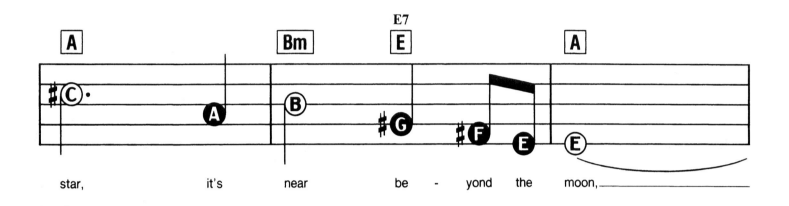

star, it's near be - yond the moon,_____

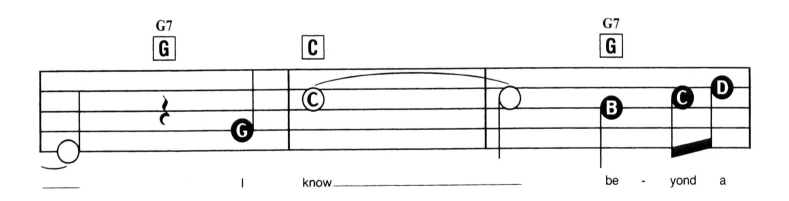

_____ I know_____ be - yond a

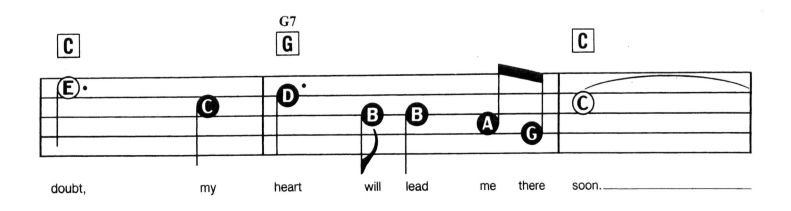

doubt, my heart will lead me there soon._____

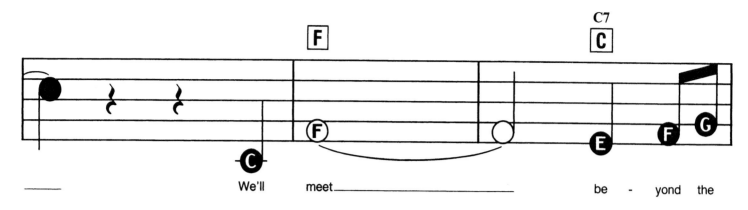

We'll meet _____ be - yond the

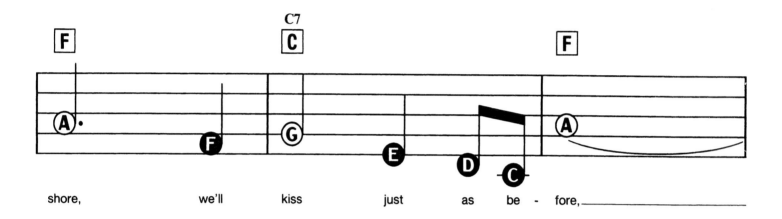

shore, we'll kiss just as be - fore, _____

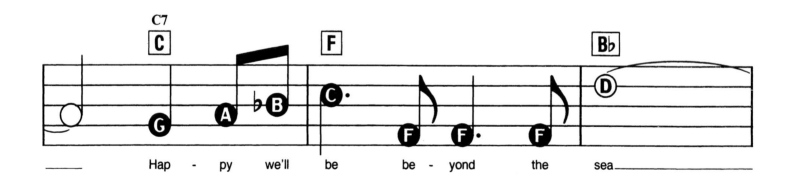

Hap - py we'll be be - yond the sea _____

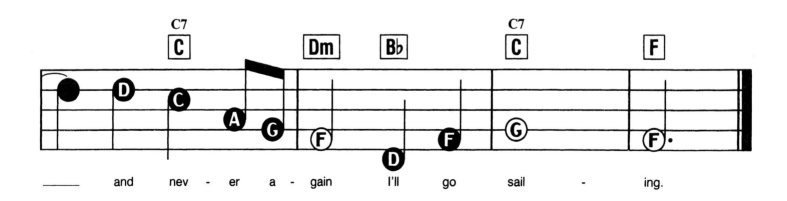

___ and nev - er a - gain I'll go sail - ing.

Blue Velvet

Registration 1
Rhythm: Fox Trot or Swing

Words and Music by Bernie Wayne
and Lee Morris

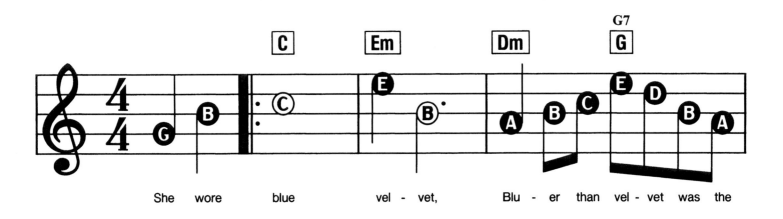

She wore blue vel - vet, Blu - er than vel - vet was the

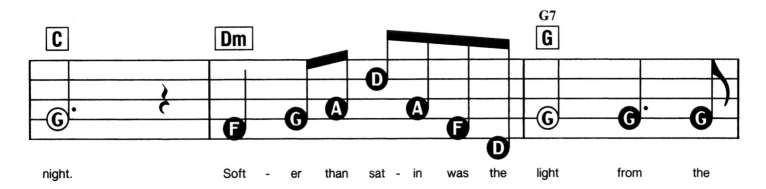

night. Soft - er than sat - in was the light from the

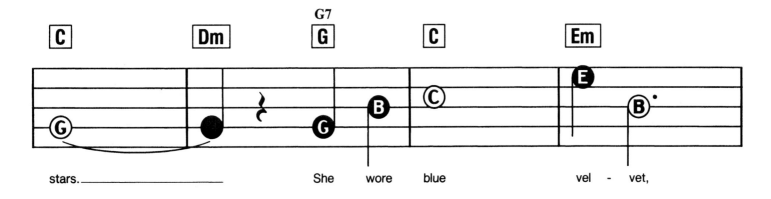

stars._____ She wore blue vel - vet,

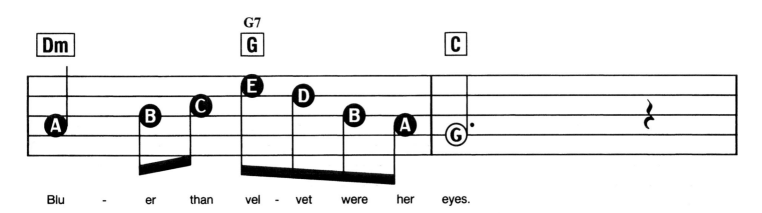

Blu - er than vel - vet were her eyes.

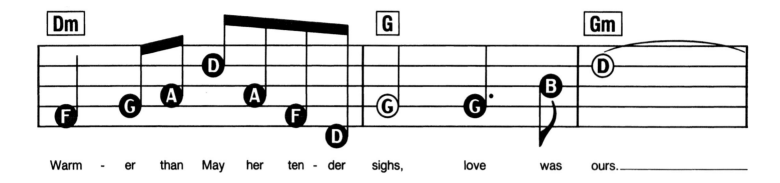

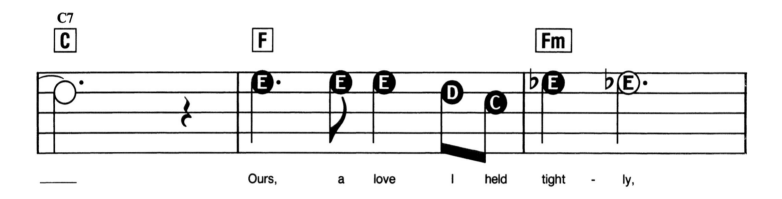

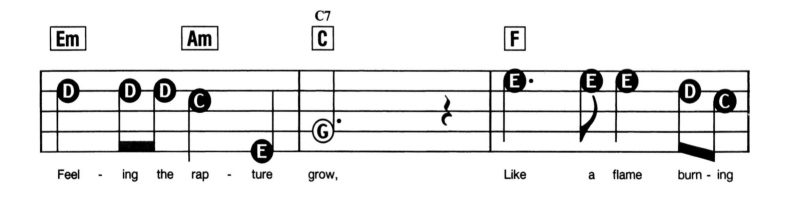

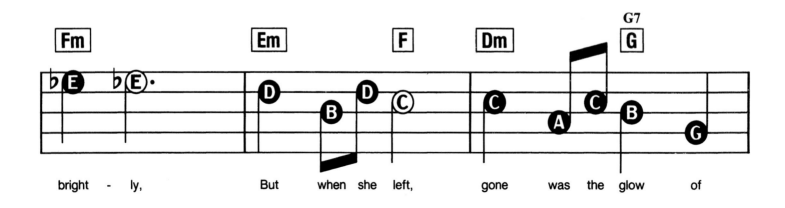

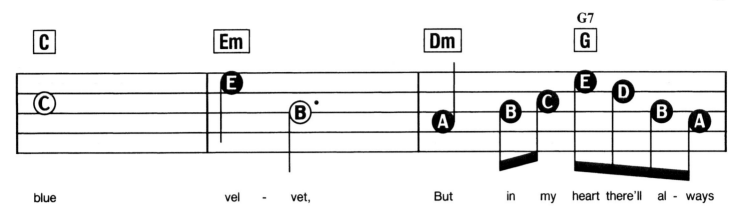

blue   vel - vet,   But   in   my   heart there'll al - ways

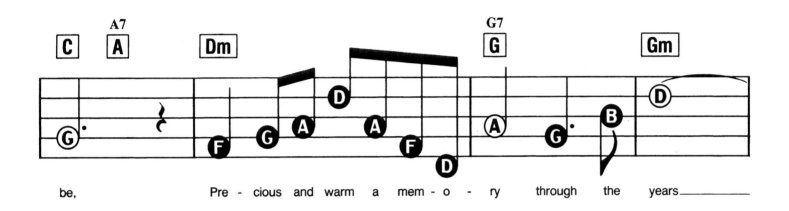

be,   Pre - cious and warm a mem - o - ry   through   the   years

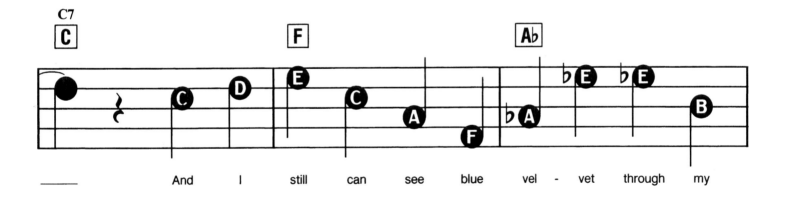

          And   I   still   can   see   blue   vel - vet through   my

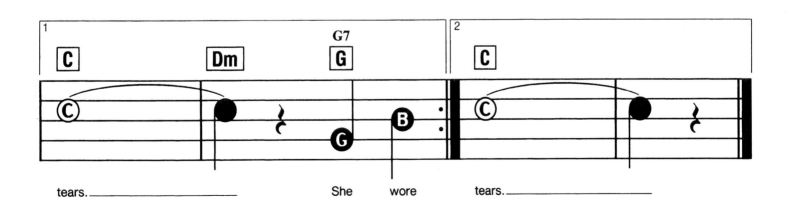

tears.   She   wore   tears.

Body and Soul

Registration 1
Rhythm: Fox Trot or Swing

Words by Edward Heyman,
Robert Sour and Frank Eyton
Music by John Green

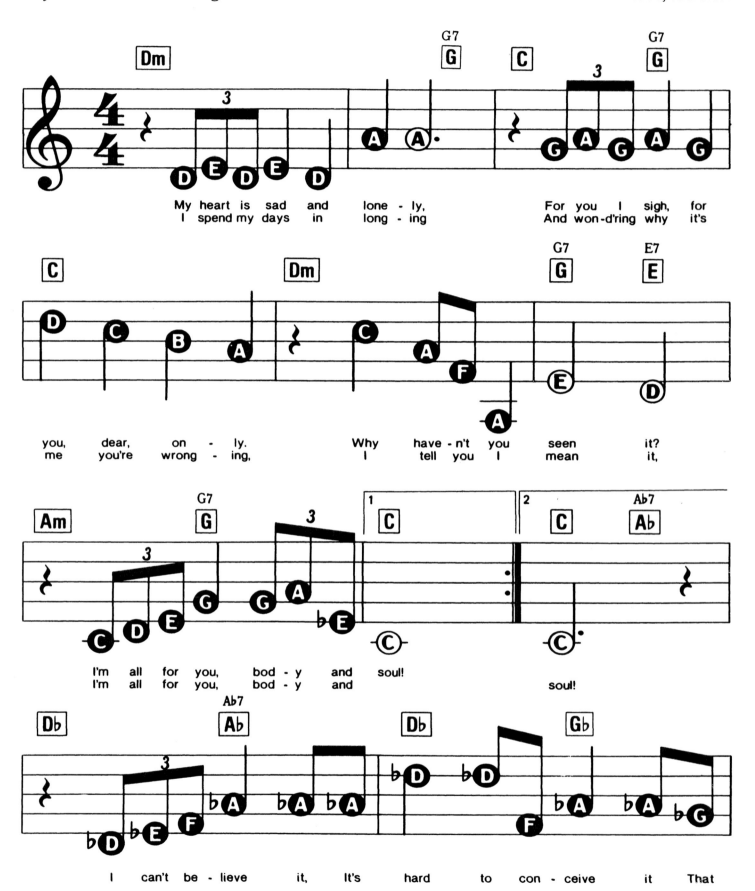

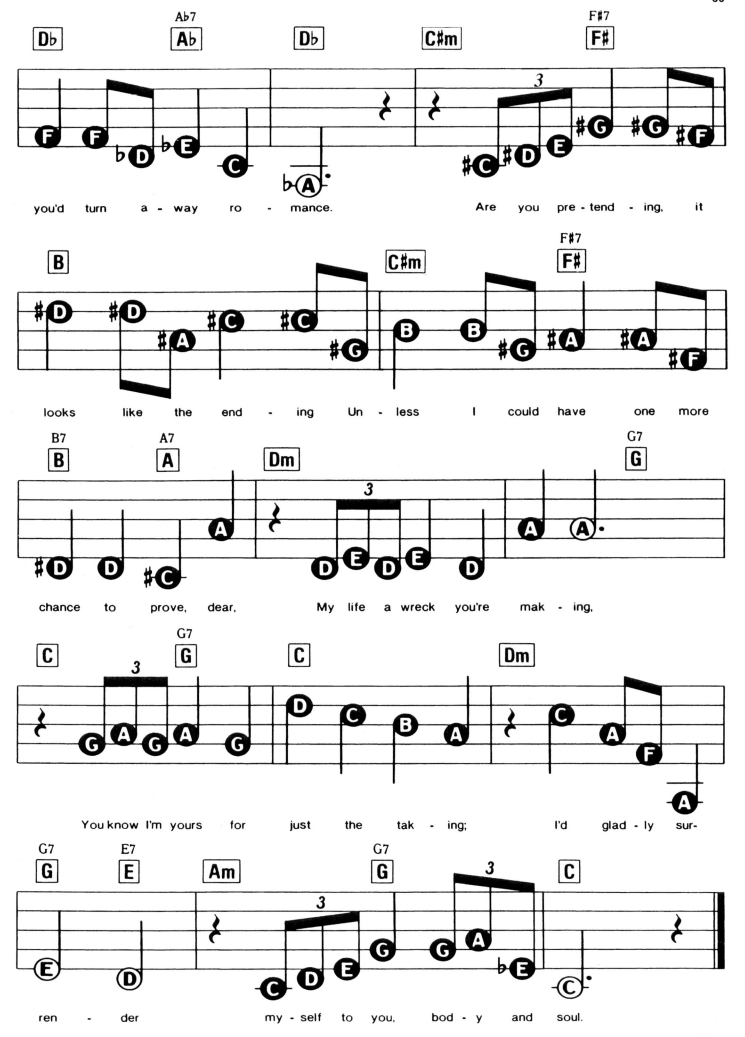

Candy

Registration 4
Rhythm: Fox Trot or Swing

Words and Music by Mack David,
Alex Kramer and Joan Whitney

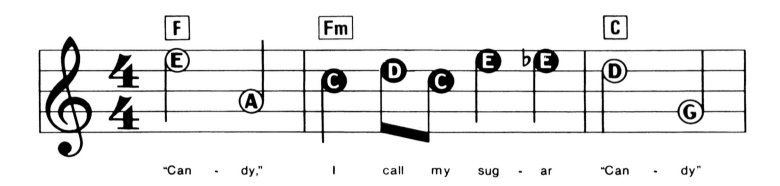

"Can - dy," I call my sug - ar "Can - dy"

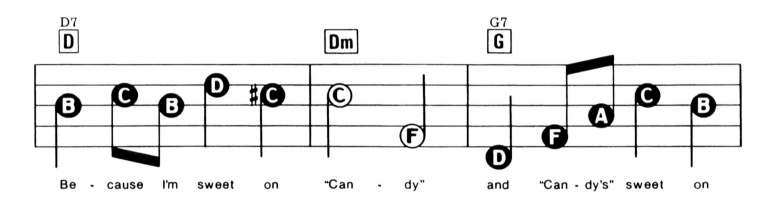

Be - cause I'm sweet on "Can - dy" and "Can - dy's" sweet on

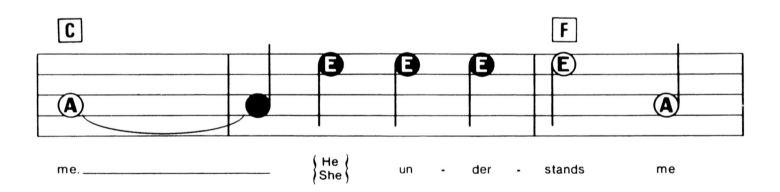

me. _____ {He} {She} un - der - stands me

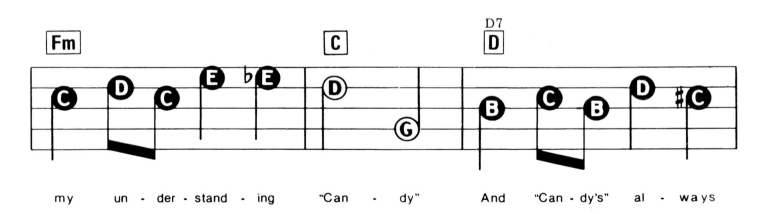

my un - der - stand - ing "Can - dy" And "Can - dy's" al - ways

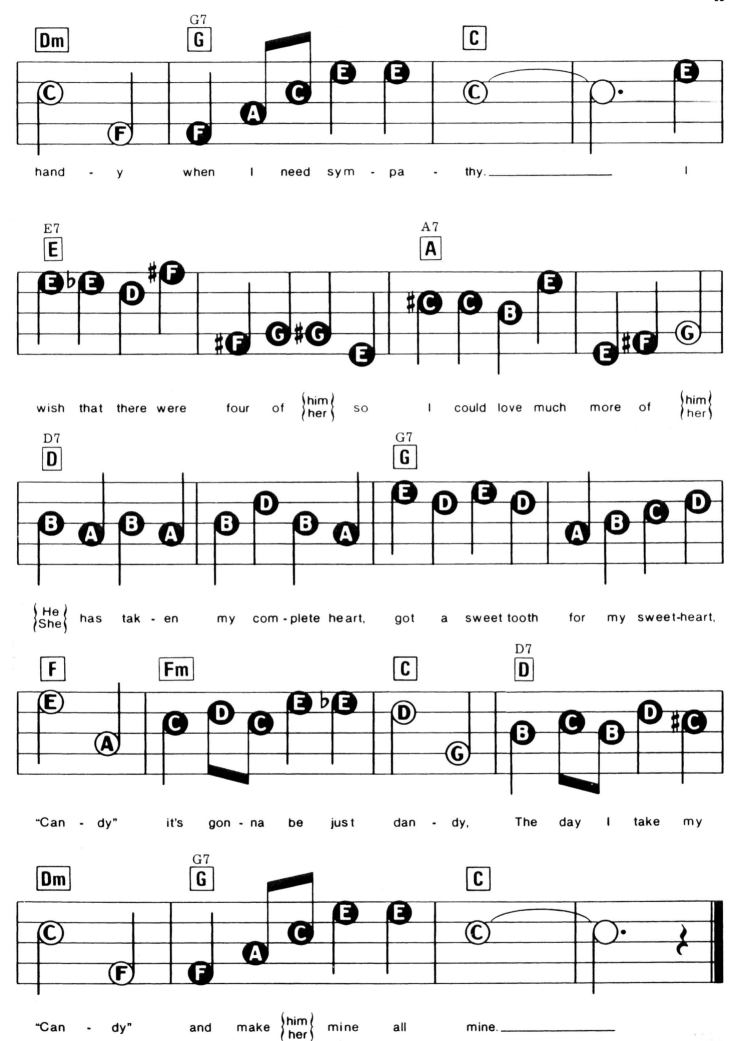

Careless Hands

Registration 2
Rhythm: Ballad or Fox Trot

Words and Music by Carl Sigman
and Bob Hilliard

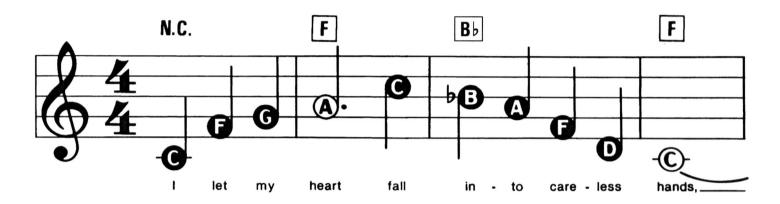

I let my heart fall in - to care - less hands,

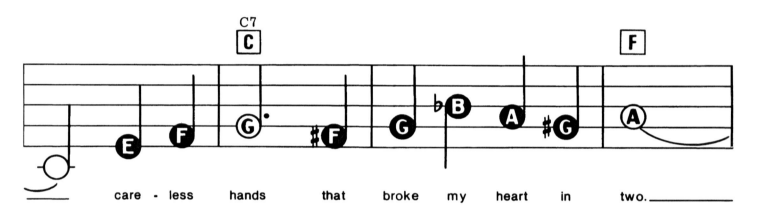

care - less hands that broke my heart in two.

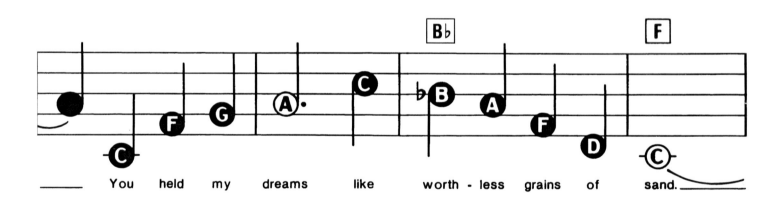

You held my dreams like worth - less grains of sand.

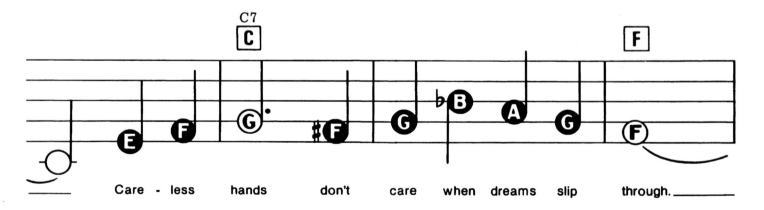

Care - less hands don't care when dreams slip through.

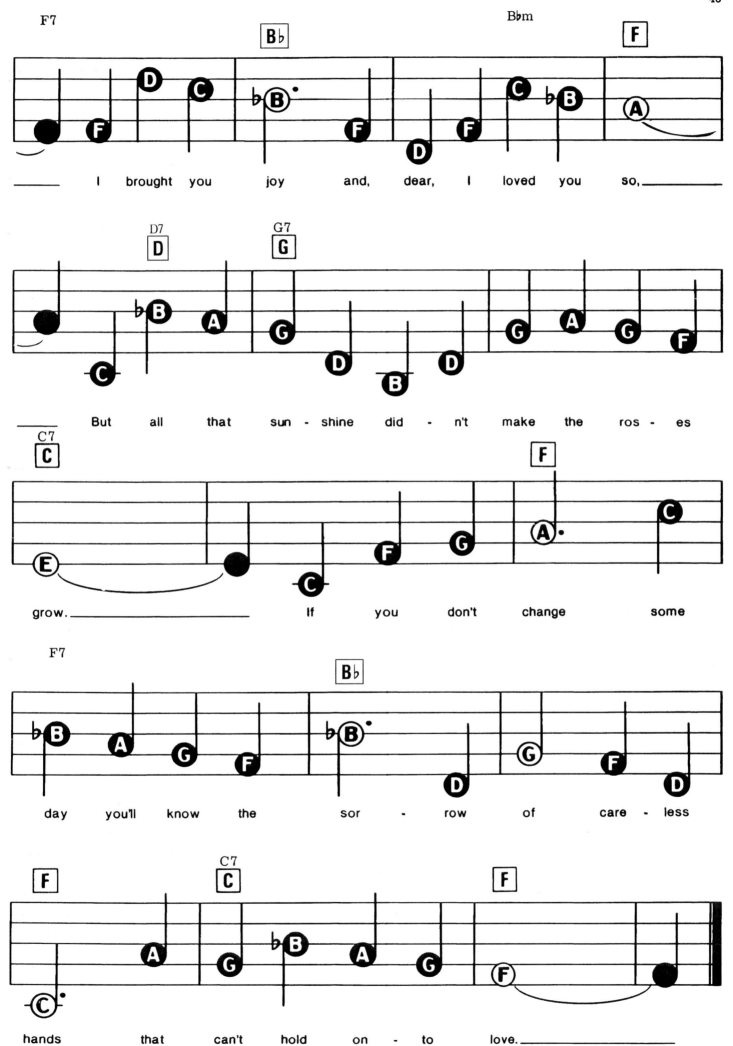

Chances Are

Registration 3
Rhythm: Swing or Jazz

Words by Al Stillman
Music by Robert Allen

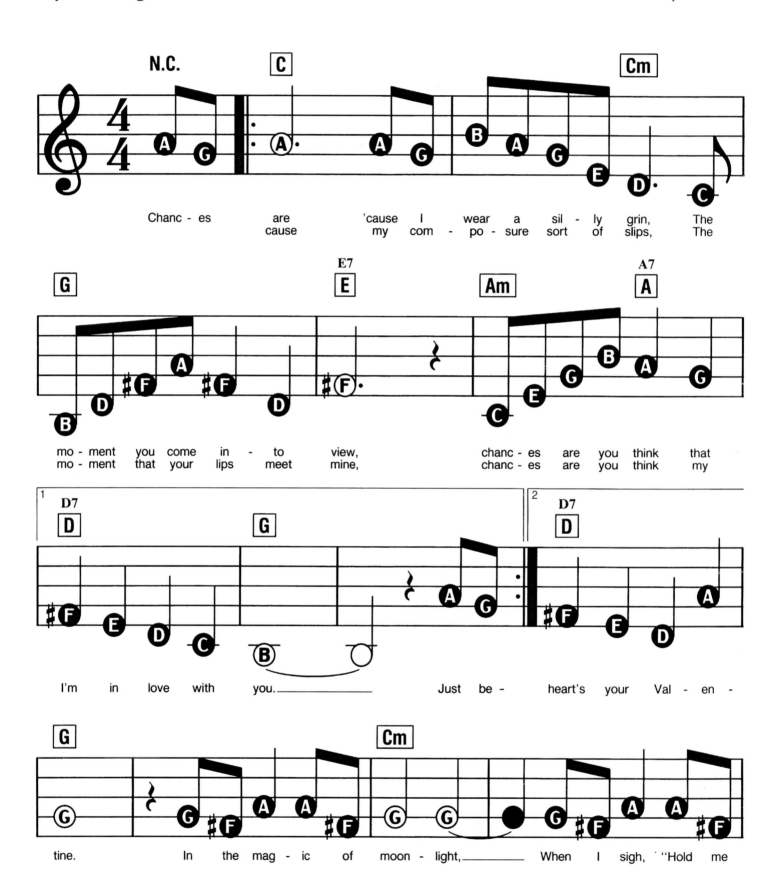

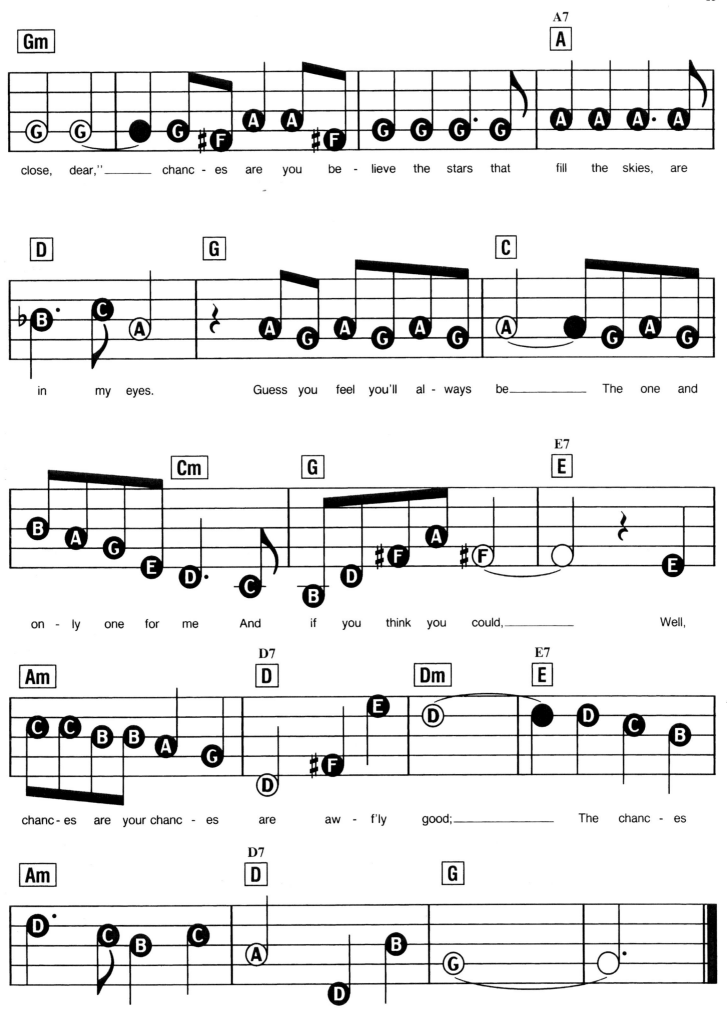

Change Partners
from the RKO Radio Motion Picture CAREFREE

Registration 2
Rhythm: Swing

Words and Music by
Irving Berlin

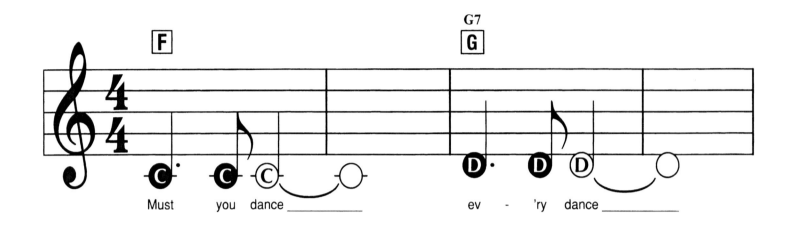

Must you dance _____ ev - 'ry dance _____

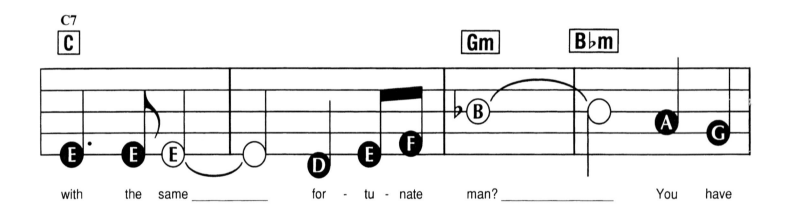

with the same _____ for - tu - nate man? _____ You have

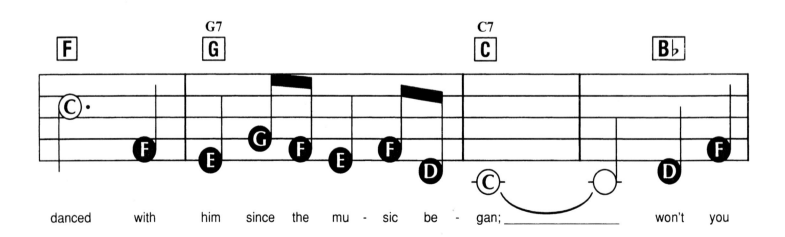

danced with him since the mu - sic be - gan; _____ won't you

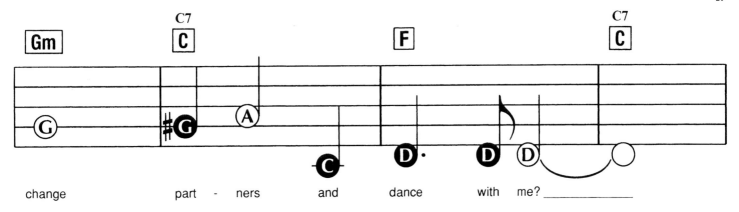

change part - ners and dance with me? _____

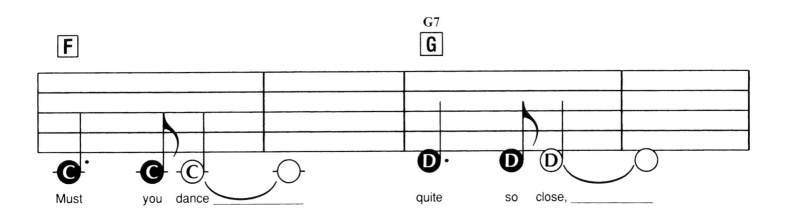

Must you dance _____ quite so close, _____

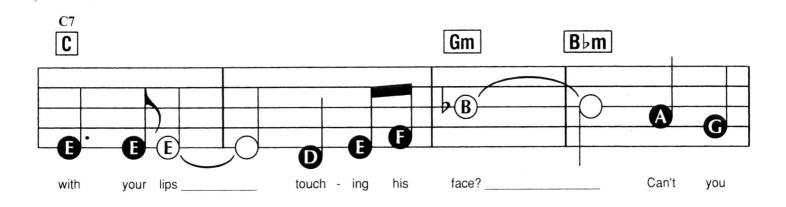

with your lips _____ touch - ing his face? _____ Can't you

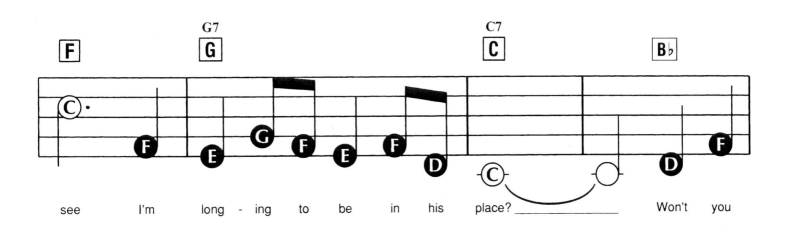

see I'm long - ing to be in his place? _____ Won't you

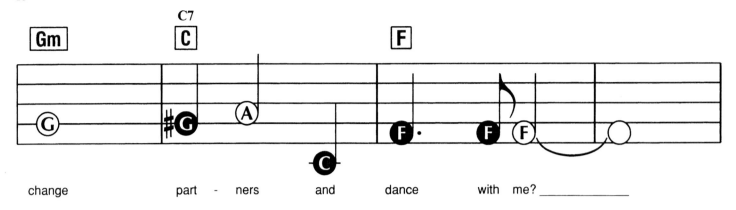

change   part - ners   and   dance   with me? _____

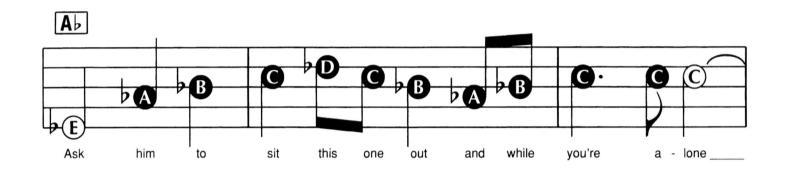

Ask   him   to   sit   this   one   out   and   while   you're   a - lone ____

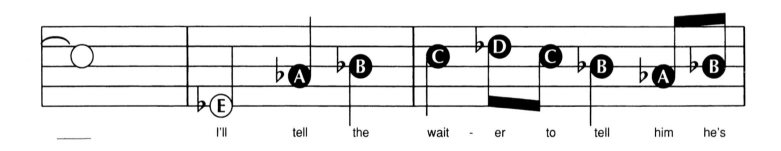

____   I'll   tell   the   wait - er   to   tell   him   he's

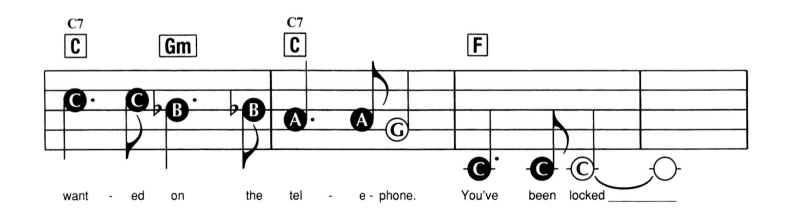

want - ed   on   the   tel - e - phone.   You've   been   locked _____

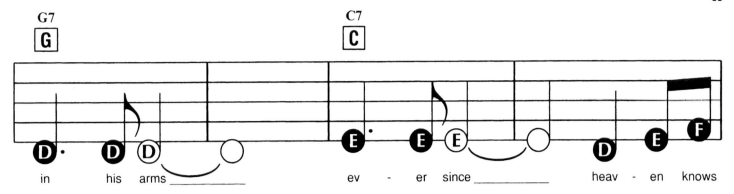

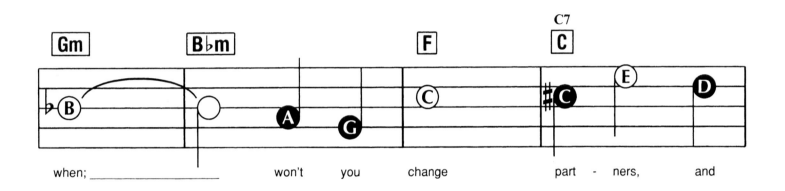

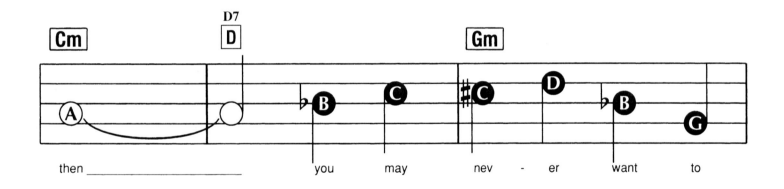

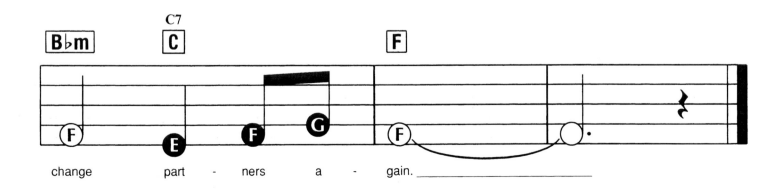

Cheek to Cheek
from the RKO Radio Motion Picture TOP HAT

Registration 1
Rhythm: Fox Trot or Swing

Words and Music by
Irving Berlin

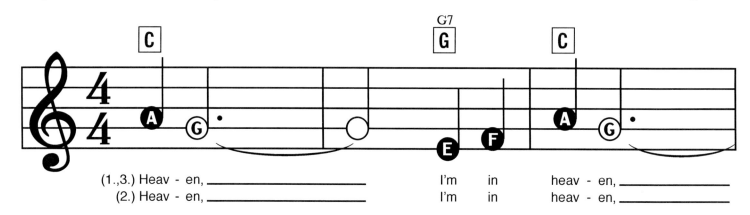

(1.,3.) Heav - en, _____ I'm in heav - en, _____
(2.) Heav - en, _____ I'm in heav - en, _____

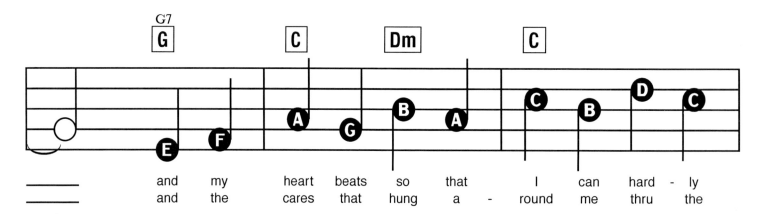

_____ and my heart beats so that I can hard - ly
_____ and the cares beats that hung a - round me thru the

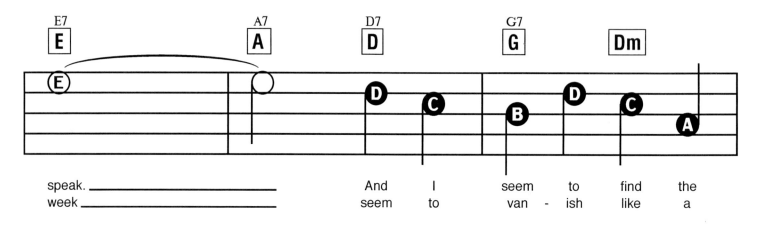

speak. _____ And I seem to find the
week _____ seem to van - ish like a

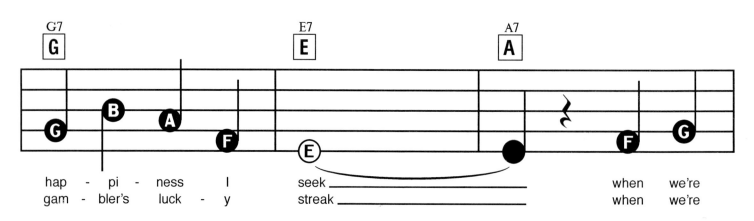

hap - pi - ness I seek _____ when we're
gam - bler's luck - y streak _____ when we're

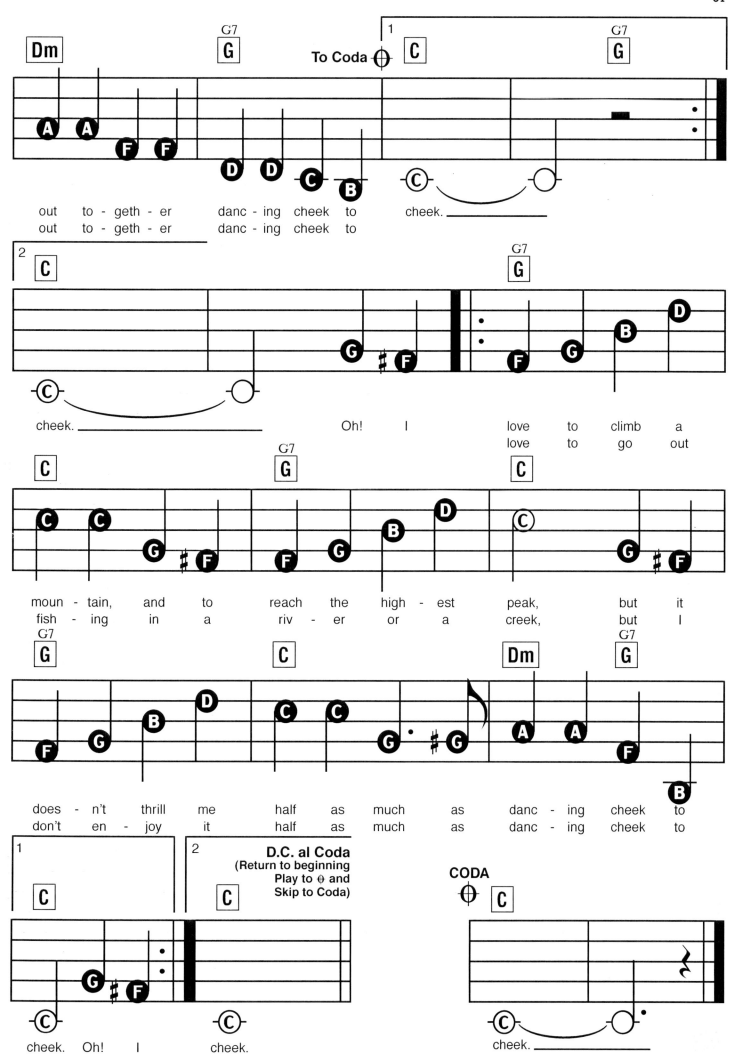

The Christmas Song
(Chestnuts Roasting on an Open Fire)

Registration 2
Rhythm: Ballad or Fox Trot

Music and Lyric by Mel Torme
and Robert Wells

Chest-nuts roast-ing on an op-en fire, Jack Frost nip-ping at your nose, Yule-tide car-ols be-ing sung by a choir And folks dressed up like Es-ki-mos. Ev-'ry-bod-y knows a tur-key and some mis-tle-toe Help to make the sea-son bright. Ti-ny tots with their eyes all a-glow Will find it hard to sleep to-night. They know that

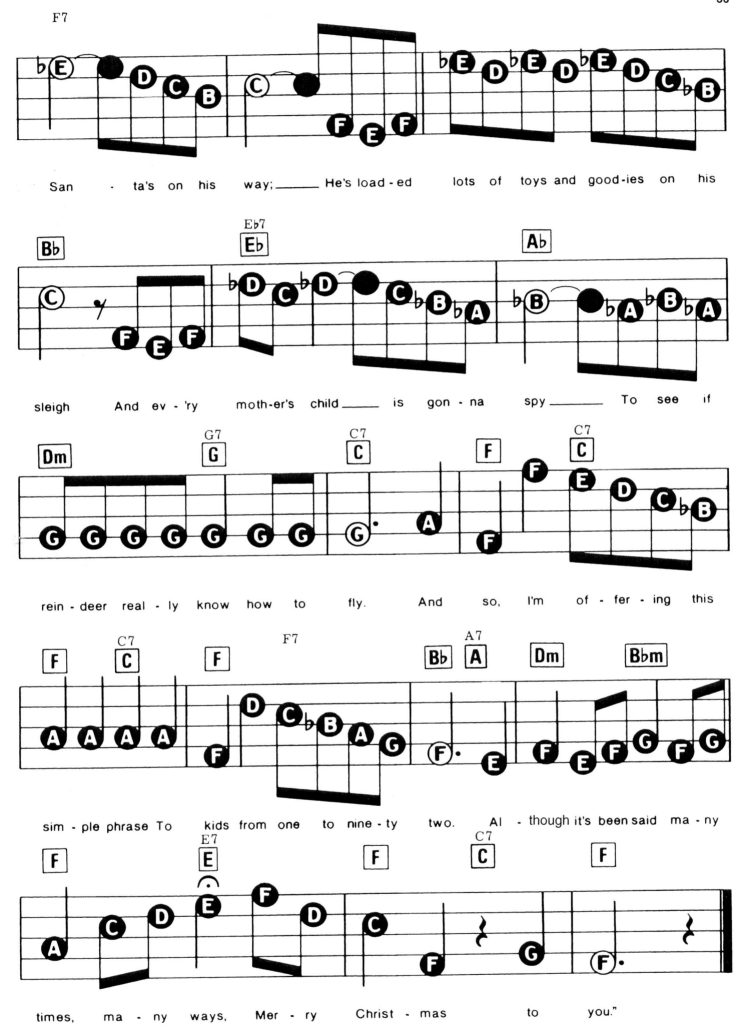

Cold, Cold Heart

Registration 4
Rhythm: Country

Words and Music by
Hank Williams

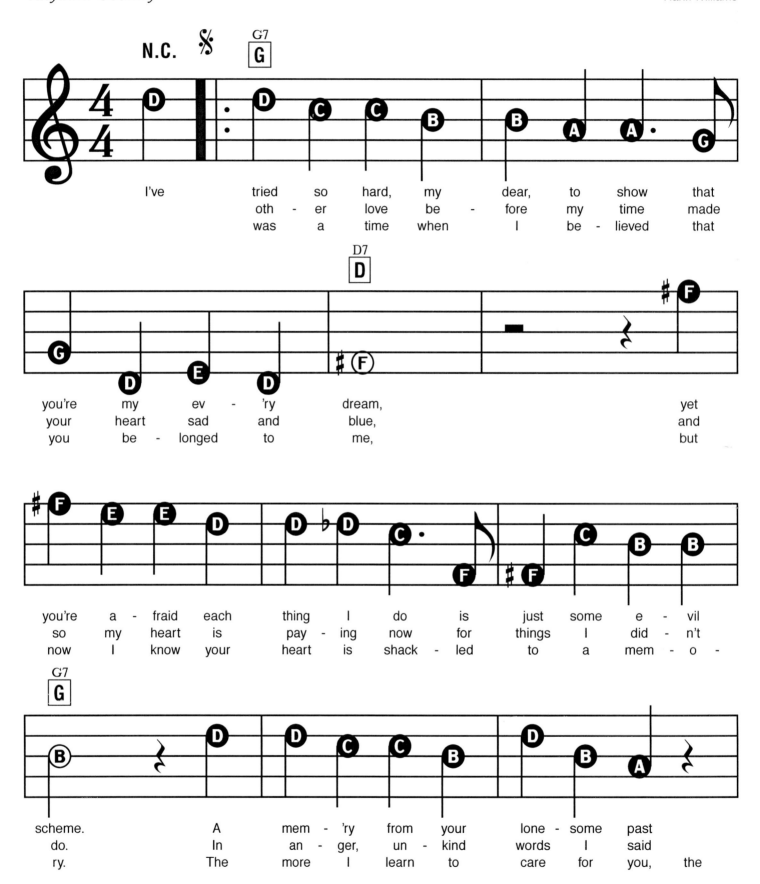

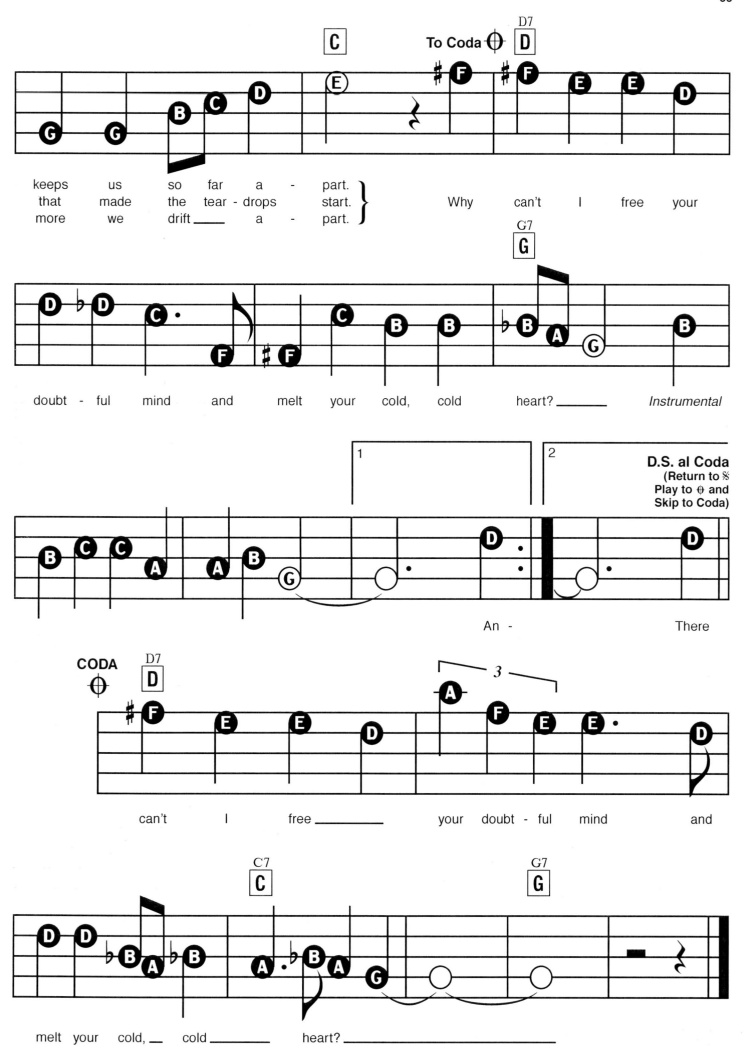

Come Rain or Come Shine
from ST. LOUIS WOMAN

Registration 7
Rhythm: Ballad or Swing

Words by Johnny Mercer
Music by Harold Arlen

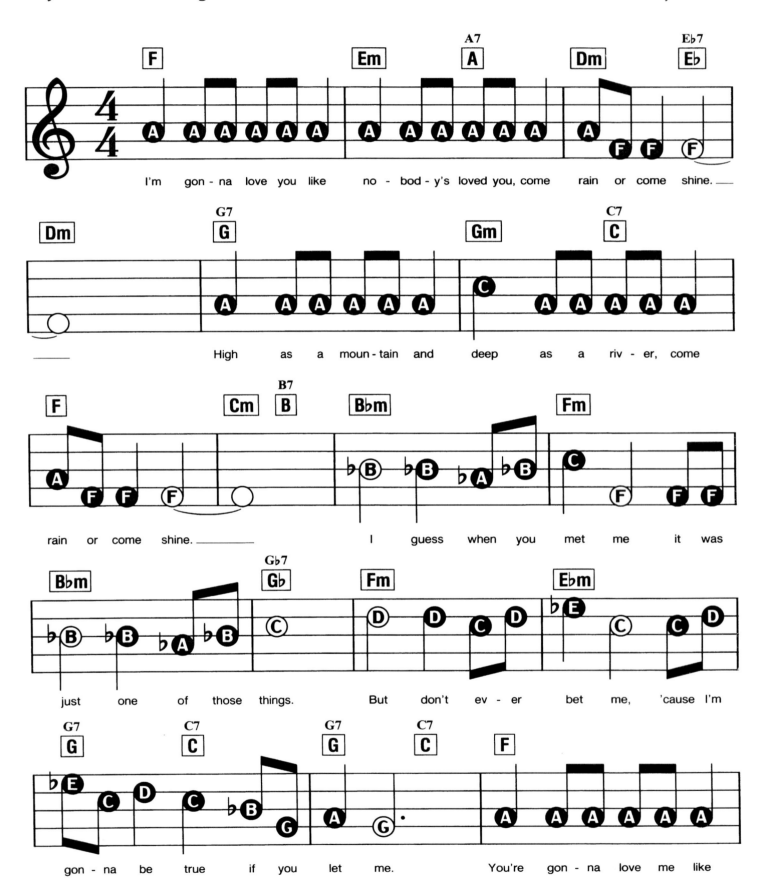

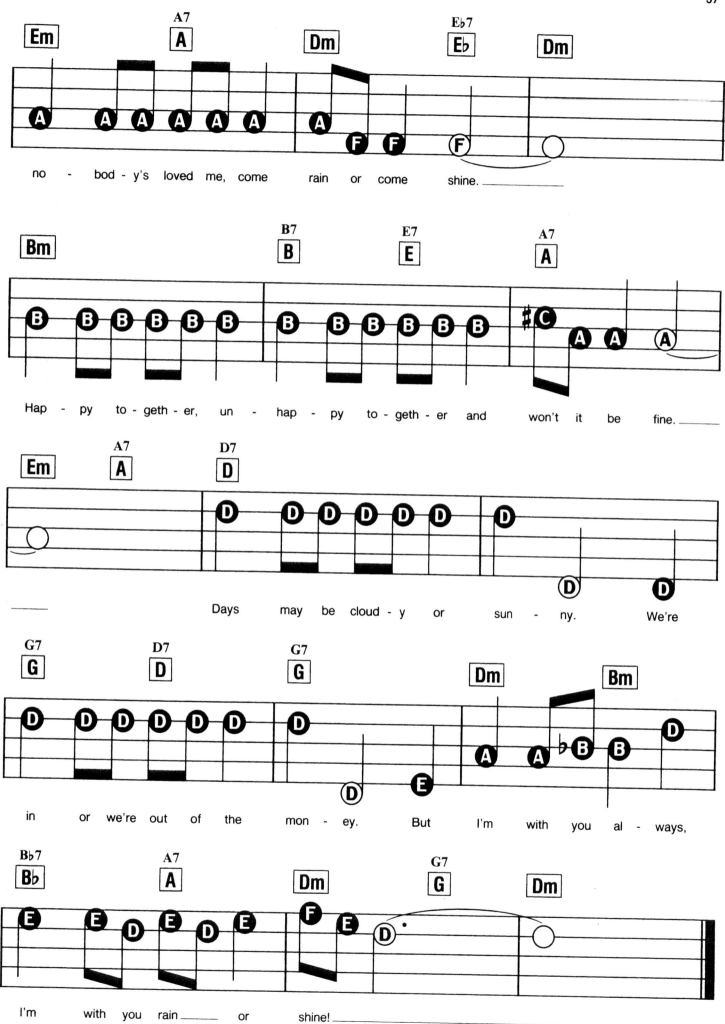

A Cottage for Sale

Registration 2
Rhythm: Ballad

Words by Larry Conley
Music by Willard Robison

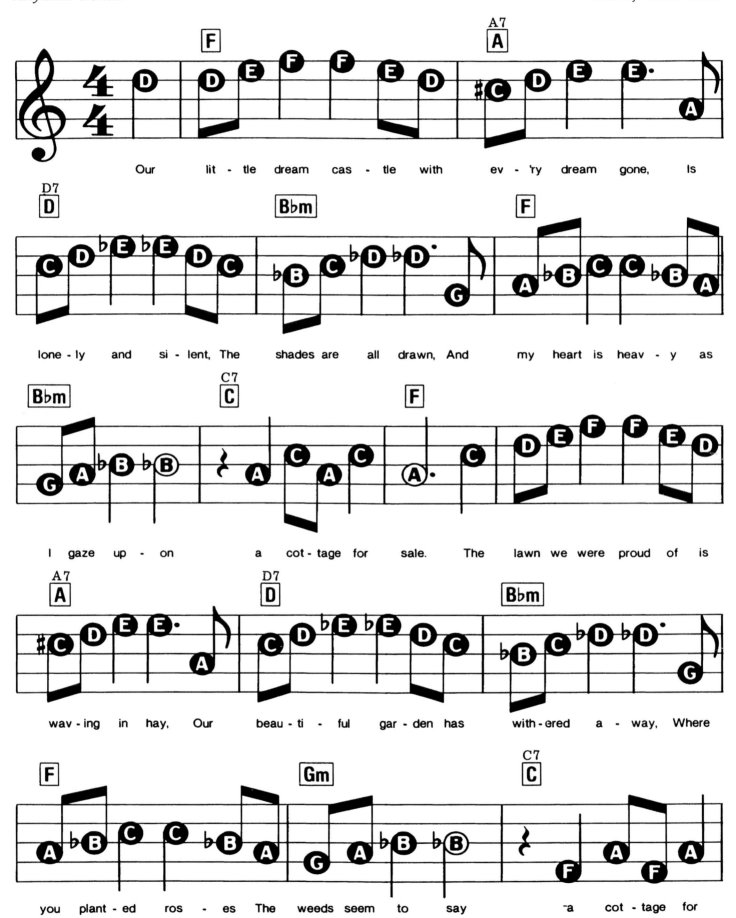

59

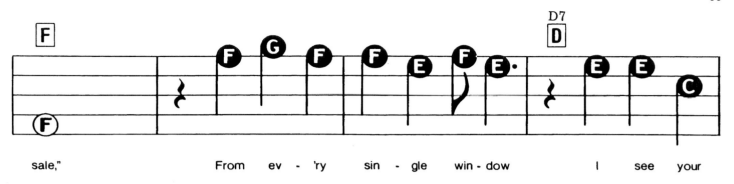

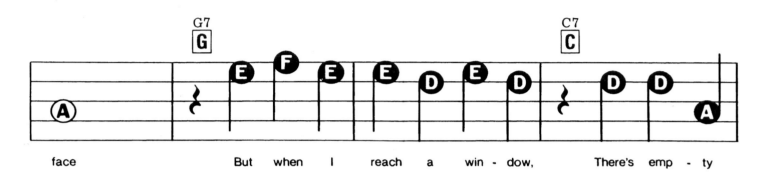

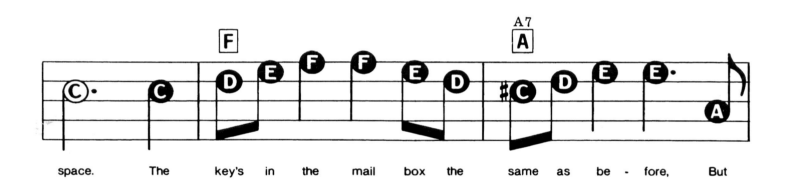

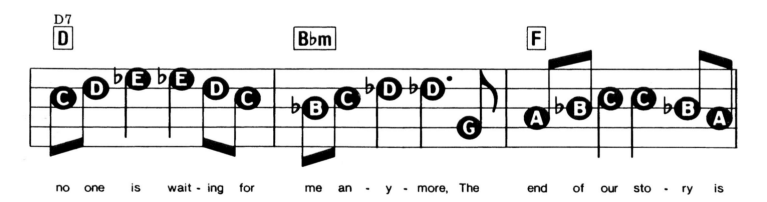

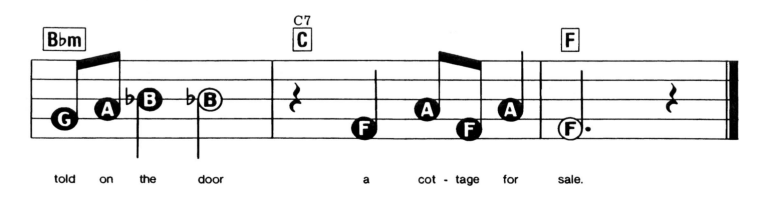

Cry

Registration 1
Rhythm: Swing

Words and Music by
Churchill Kohlman

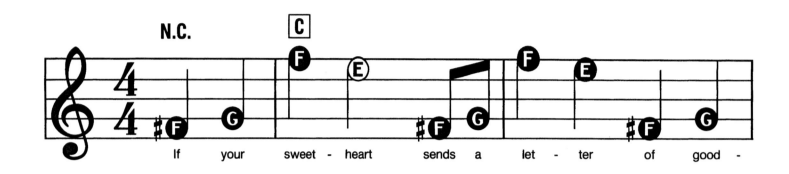

If your sweet - heart sends a let - ter of good -

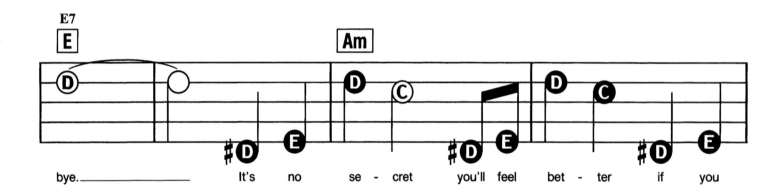

bye.___ It's no se - cret you'll feel bet - ter if you

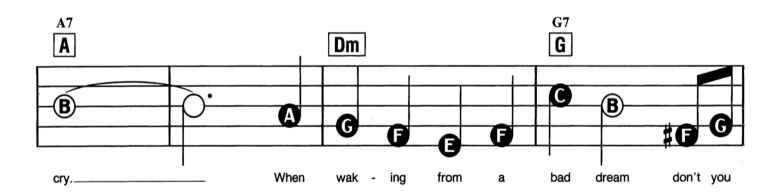

cry.___ When wak - ing from a bad dream don't you

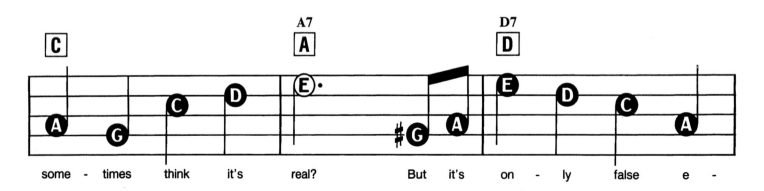

some - times think it's real? But it's on - ly false e -

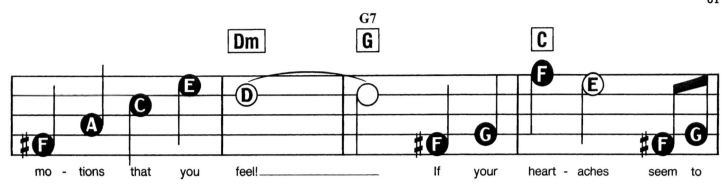

mo - tions that you feel!_____ If your heart - aches seem to

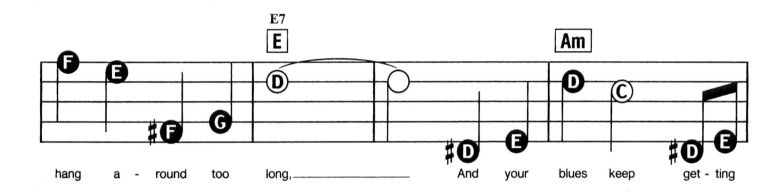

hang a - round too long,_____ And your blues keep get - ting

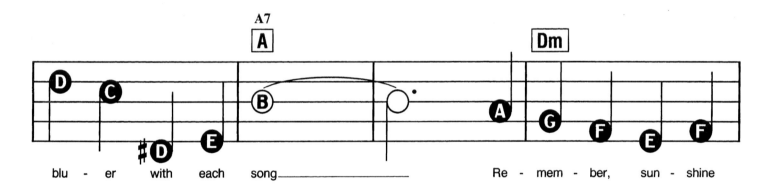

blu - er with each song_____ Re - mem - ber, sun - shine

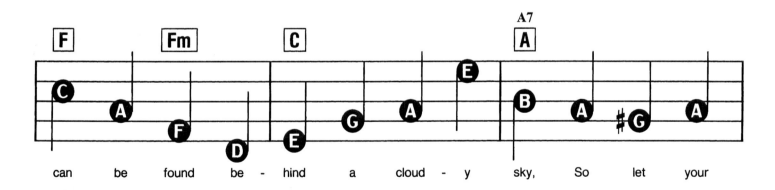

can be found be - hind a cloud - y sky, So let your

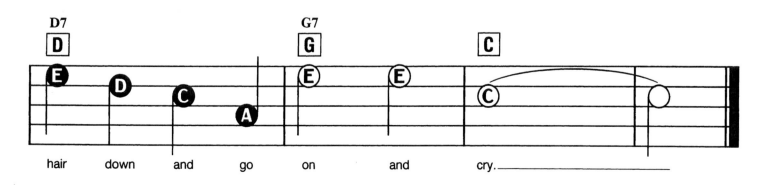

hair down and go on and cry._____

Dear Hearts and Gentle People

Registration 8
Rhythm: Fox Trot

Words by Bob Hilliard
Music by Sammy Fain

63

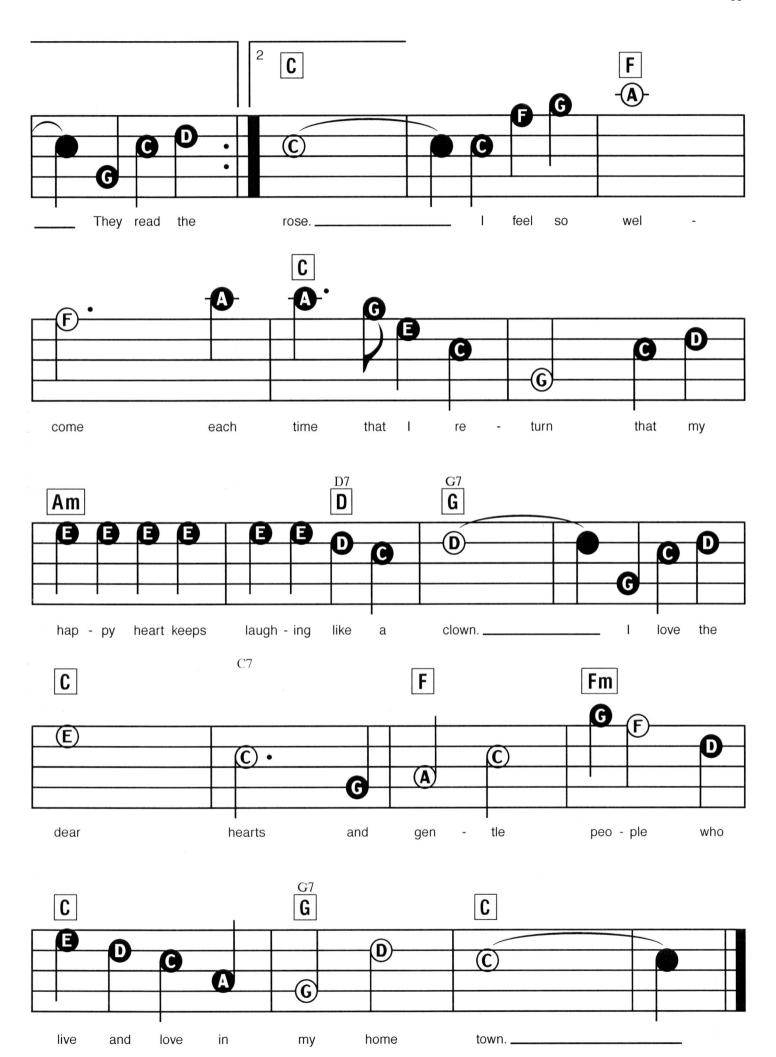

Didn't We

Registration 3
Rhythm: Pops or 8-Beat

Words and Music by
Jim Webb

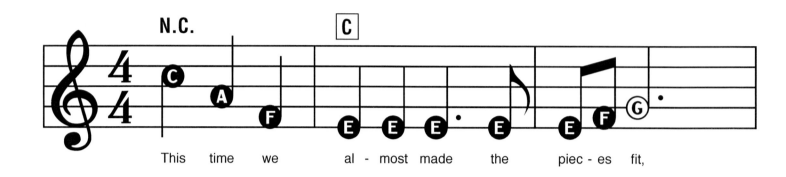

This time we al - most made the piec - es fit,

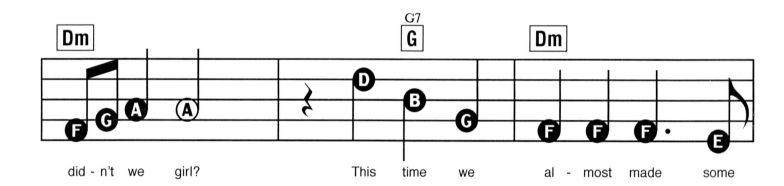

did - n't we girl? This time we al - most made some

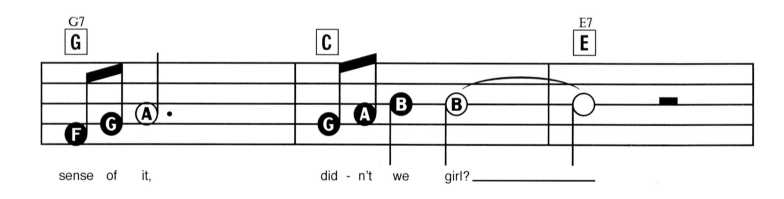

sense of it, did - n't we girl?

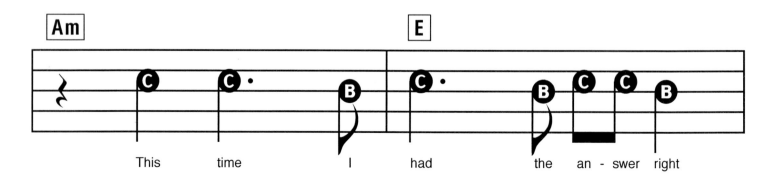

This time I had the an - swer right

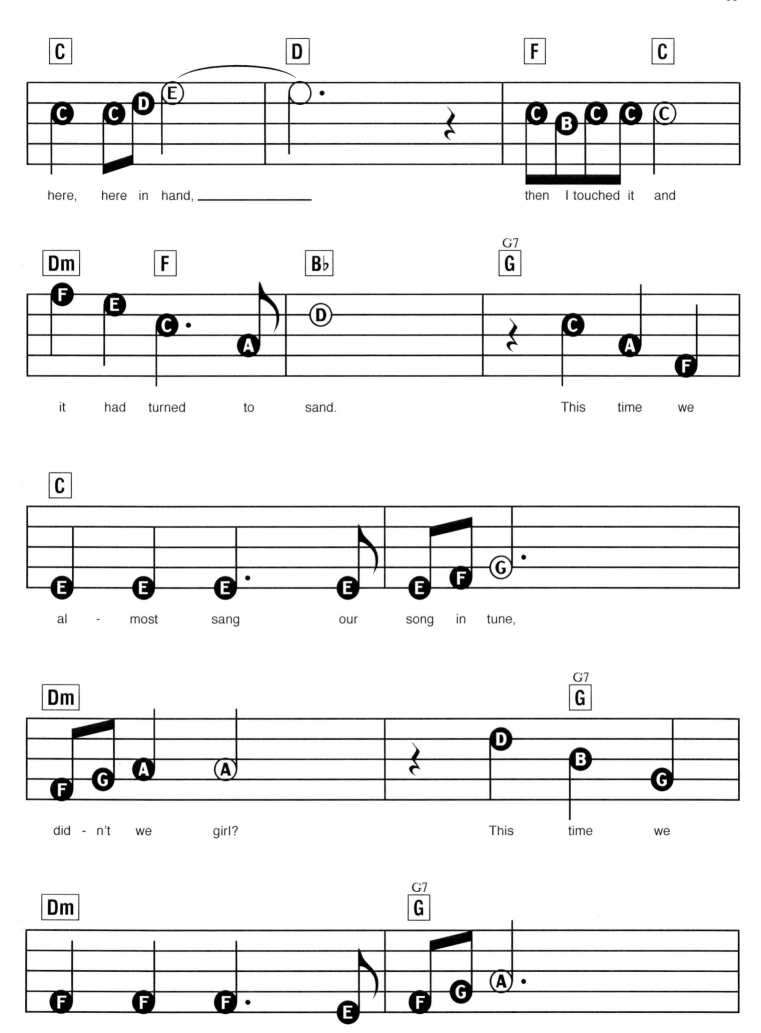

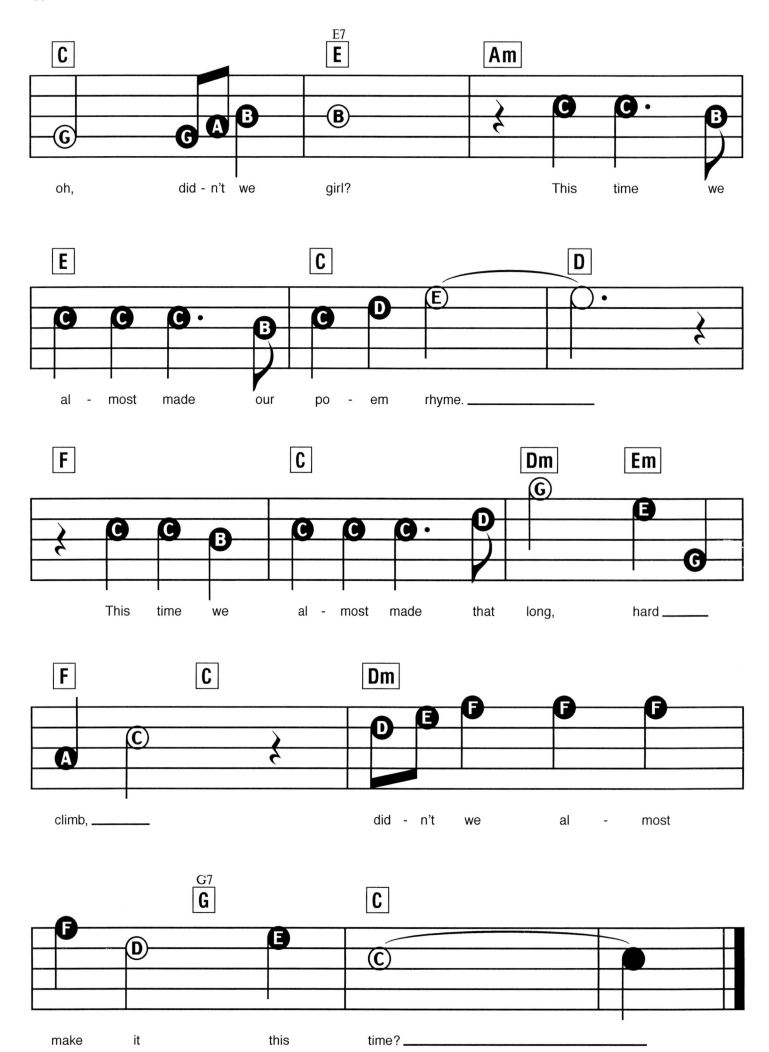

Don't Let the Stars Get in Your Eyes

Registration 2
Rhythm: Fox Trot or Swing

Words and Music by
Slim Willet

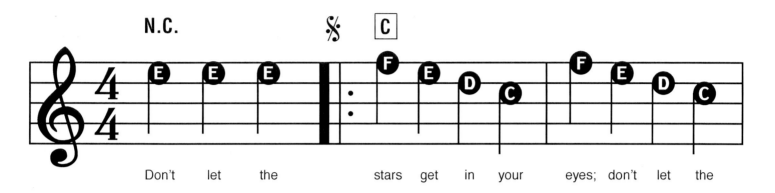

Don't let the stars get in your eyes; don't let the

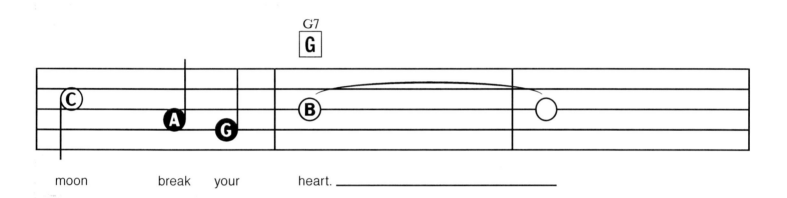

moon break your heart.

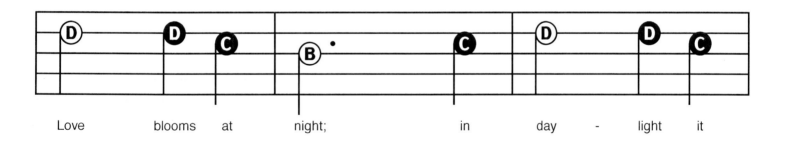

Love blooms at night; in day - light it

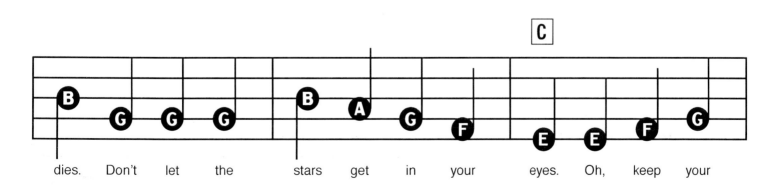

dies. Don't let the stars get in your eyes. Oh, keep your

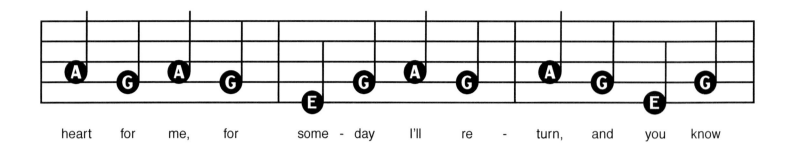

heart   for   me,   for   some - day   I'll   re   -   turn,   and   you   know

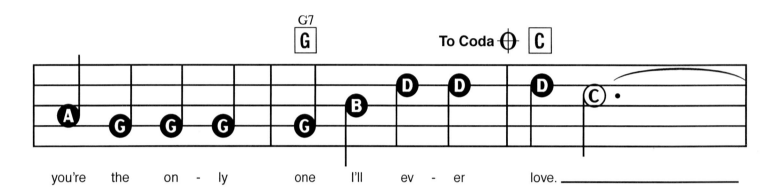

you're   the   on   -   ly   one   I'll   ev   -   er   love. _____

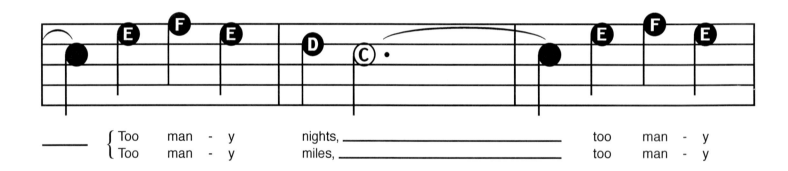

_____   Too   man - y   nights, _____   too   man - y
        Too   man - y   miles, _____   too   man - y

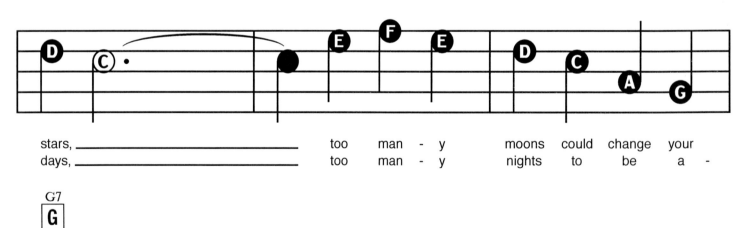

stars, _____   too   man - y   moons   could   change   your
days, _____   too   man - y   nights   to   be   a -

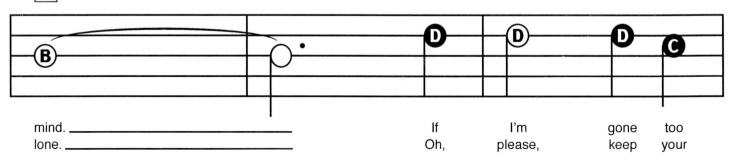

mind. _____   If   I'm   gone   too
lone. _____   Oh,   please,   keep   your

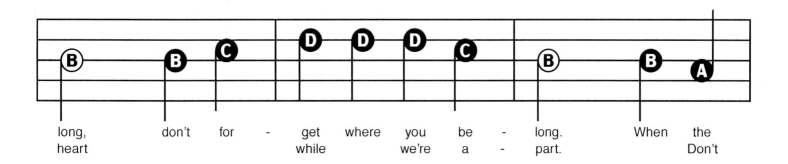

long, don't for - get where you be - long. When the
heart while we're a - part. Don't

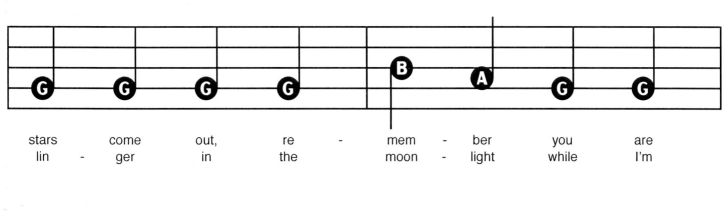

stars come out, re - mem - ber you are
lin - ger in the moon - light while I'm

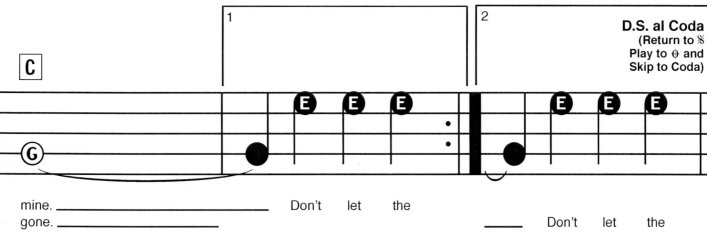

mine. _____ Don't let the
gone. _____ Don't let the

CODA

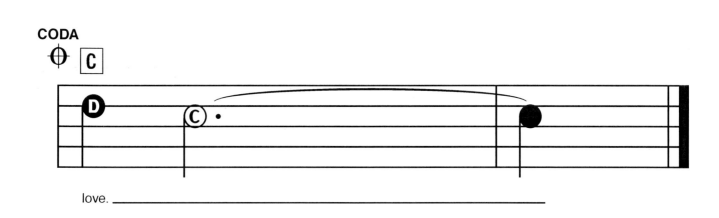

love. _____

Do I Love You Because You're Beautiful?

from CINDERELLA

Registration 2
Rhythm: Ballad or Slow Rock

Lyrics by Oscar Hammerstein II
Music by Richard Rodgers

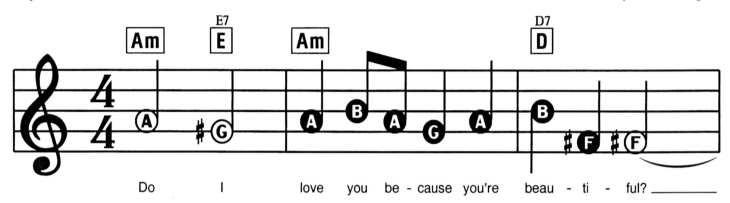

Do I love you be - cause you're beau - ti - ful? _____

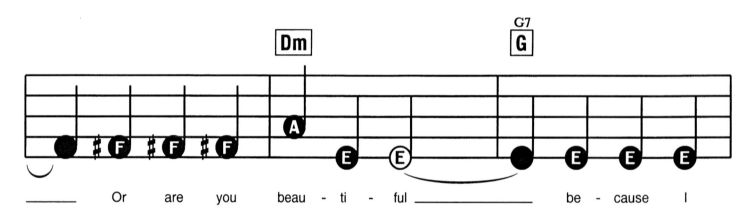

_____ Or are you beau - ti - ful _____ be - cause I

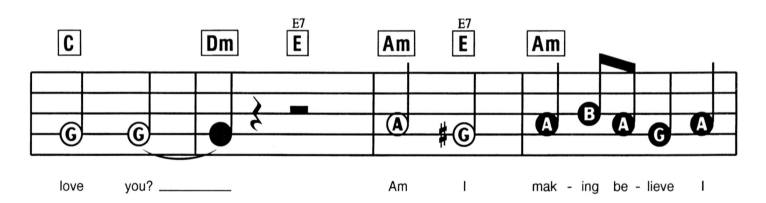

love you? _____ Am I mak - ing be - lieve I

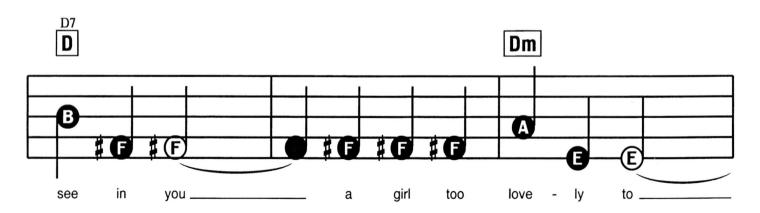

see in you _____ a girl too love - ly to _____

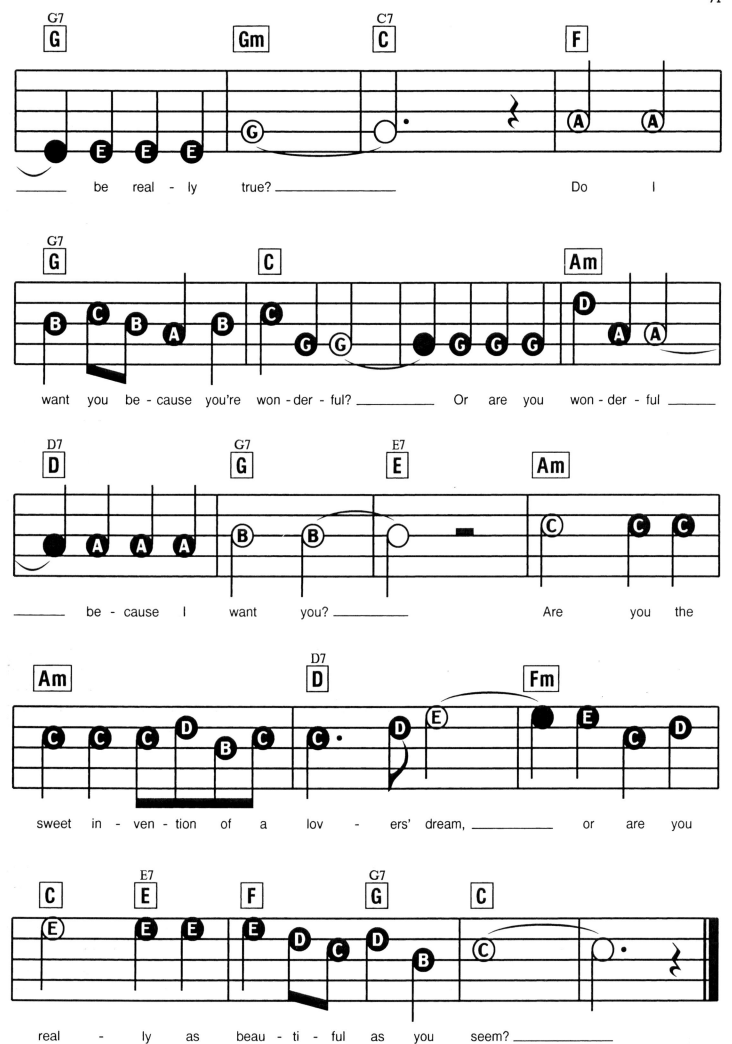

Dream Lover

Registration 4
Rhythm: Rock

Words and Music by
Bobby Darin

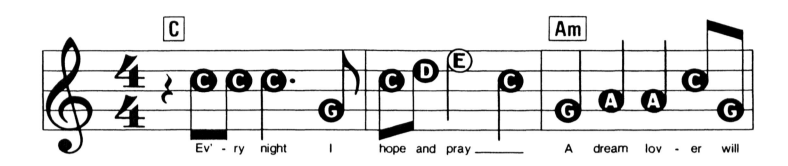

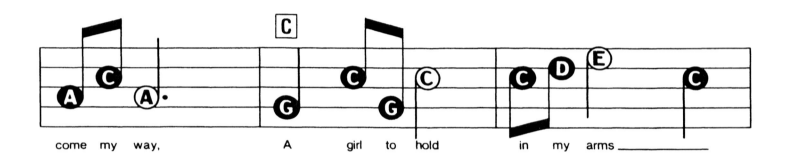

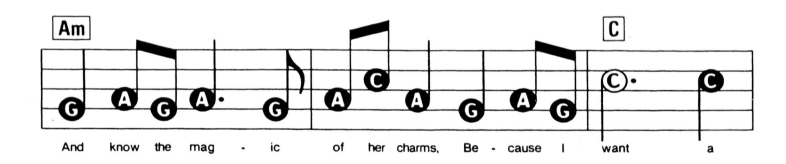

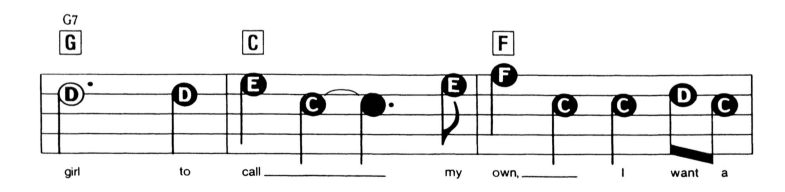

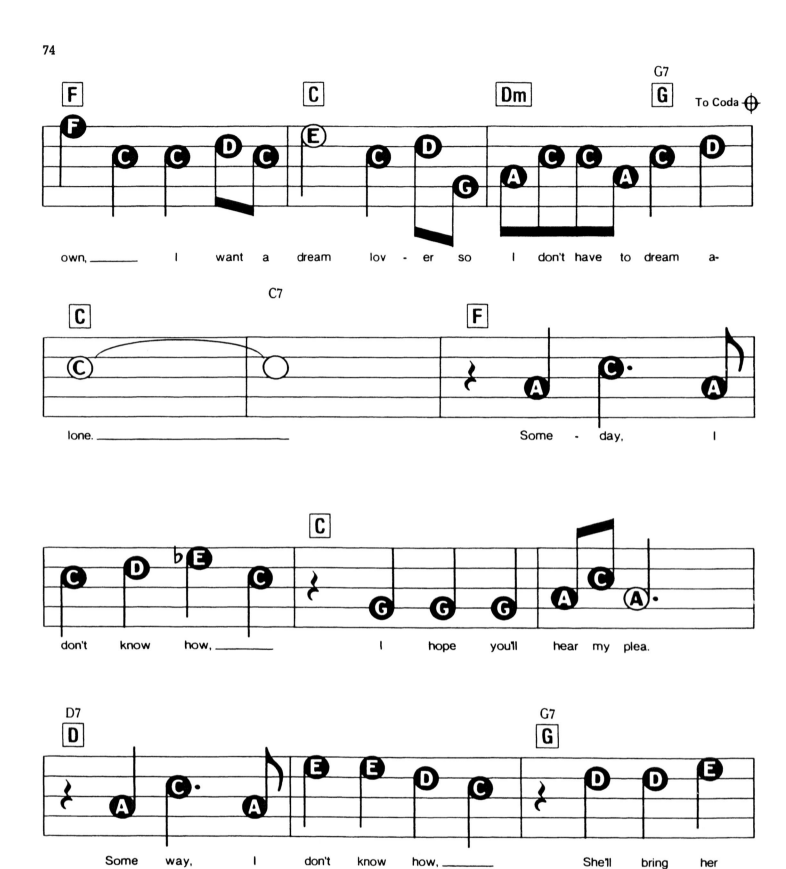

own, _____ I want a dream lov - er so I don't have to dream a-

lone. _____ Some - day, I

don't know how, _____ I hope you'll hear my plea.

Some way, I don't know how, _____ She'll bring her

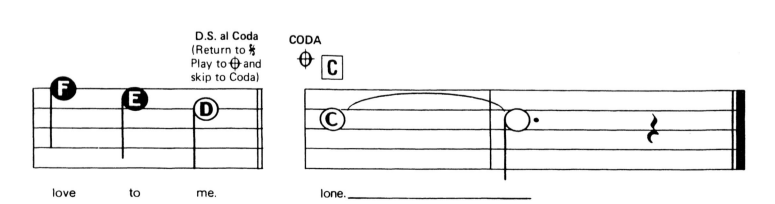

D.S. al Coda
(Return to 𝄋
Play to ⨁ and
skip to Coda)

CODA

love to me.

lone. _____

I Believe

Registration 2
Rhythm: Ballad or Slow Rock

Words and Music by Ervin Drake,
Irvin Graham, Jimmy Shirl and Al Stillman

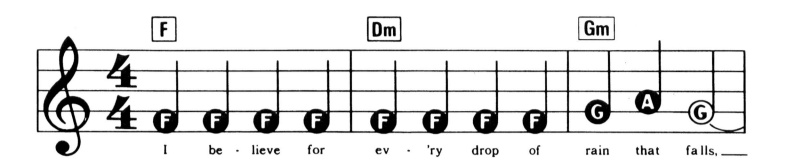

I be-lieve for ev-'ry drop of rain that falls,

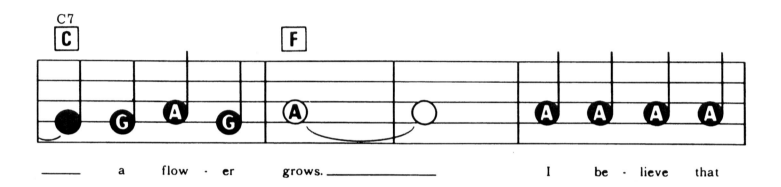

a flow-er grows. I be-lieve that

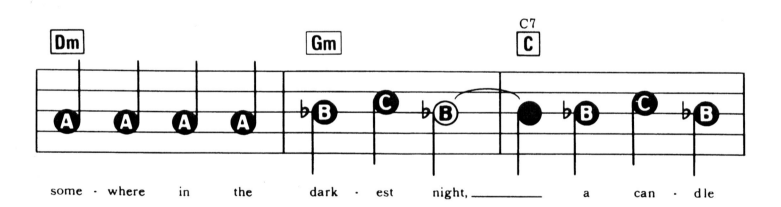

some-where in the dark-est night, a can-dle

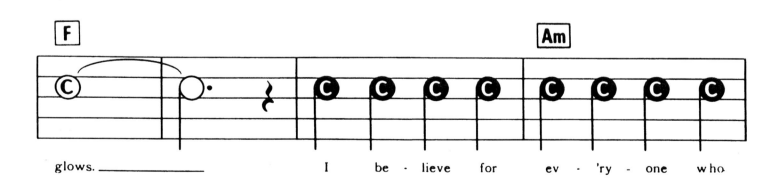

glows. I be-lieve for ev-'ry-one who

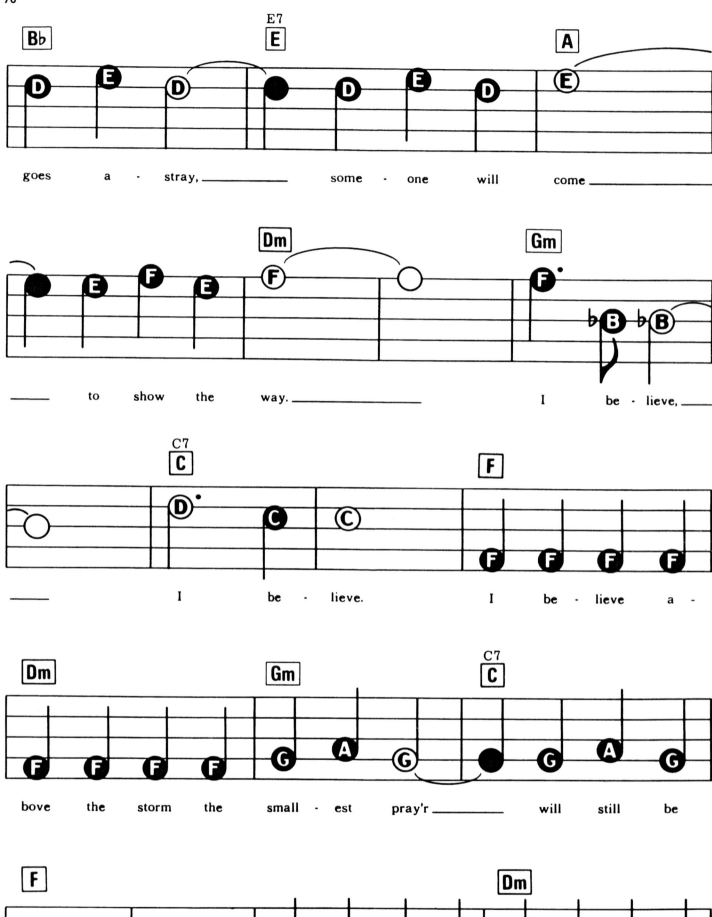

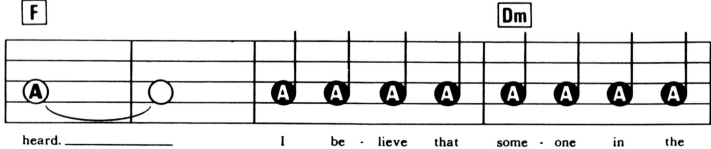

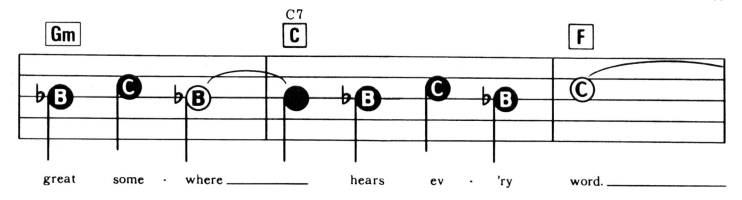

great some · where _____ hears ev · 'ry word. _____

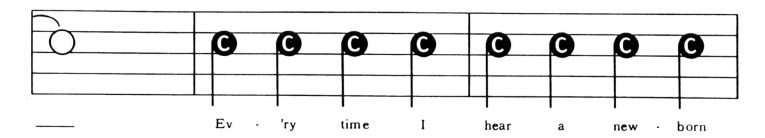

_____ Ev · 'ry time I hear a new · born

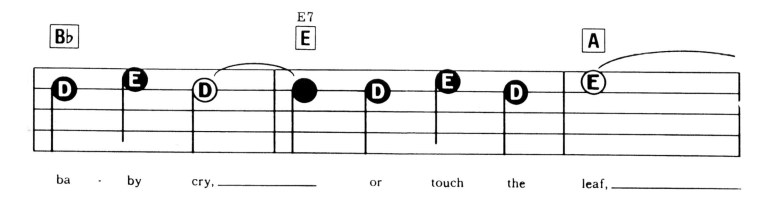

ba · by cry, _____ or touch the leaf, _____

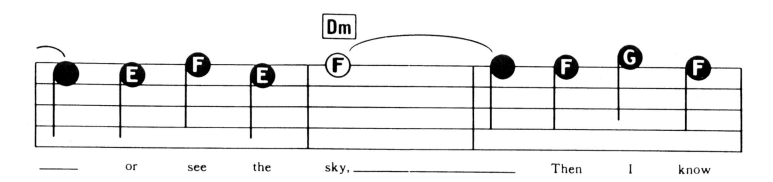

_____ or see the sky, _____ Then I know

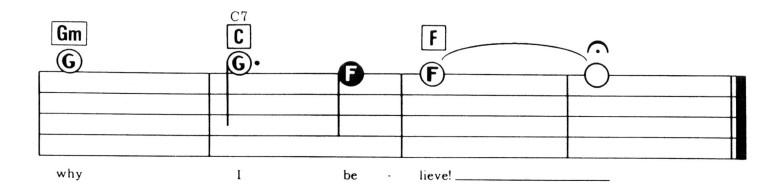

why I be · lieve! _____

Everyday I Have the Blues

Registration 2
Rhythm: Fox Trot or Swing

Words and Music by
Peter Chatman

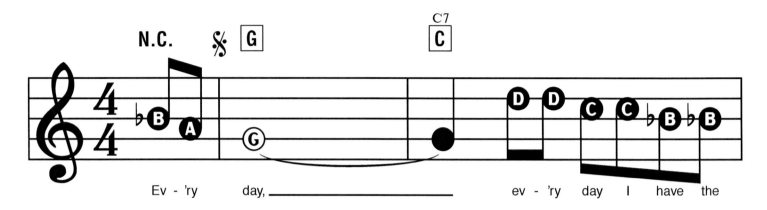

Ev - 'ry   day, _____   ev - 'ry day I have the

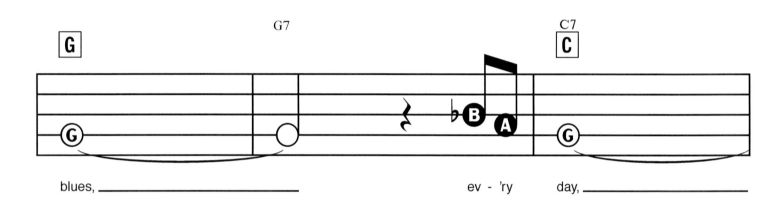

blues, _____   ev - 'ry   day, _____

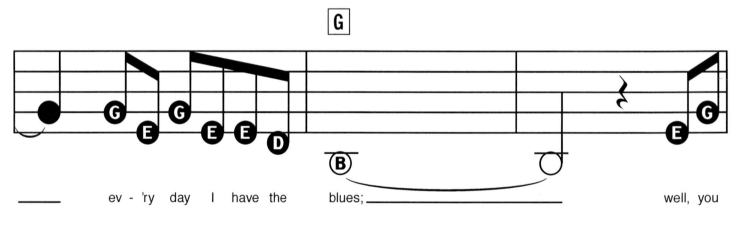

_____   ev - 'ry day I have the   blues; _____   well, you

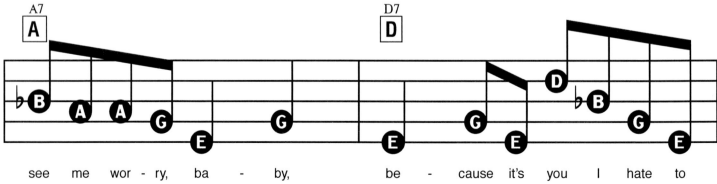

see me wor - ry, ba - by,   be - cause it's you I hate to

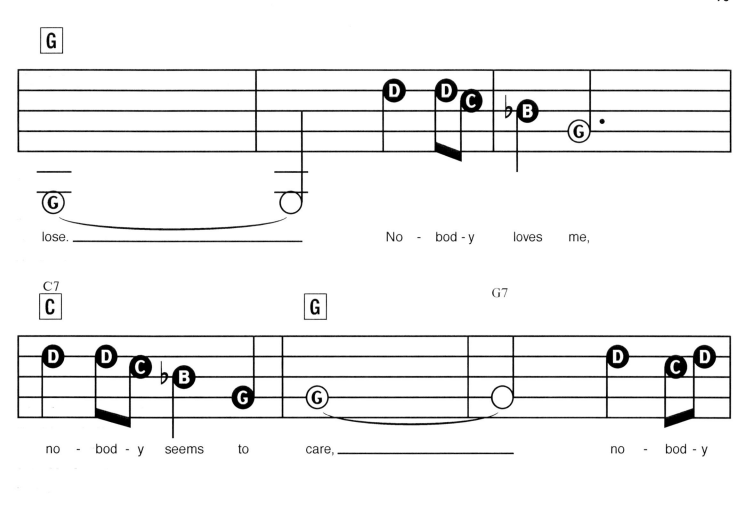

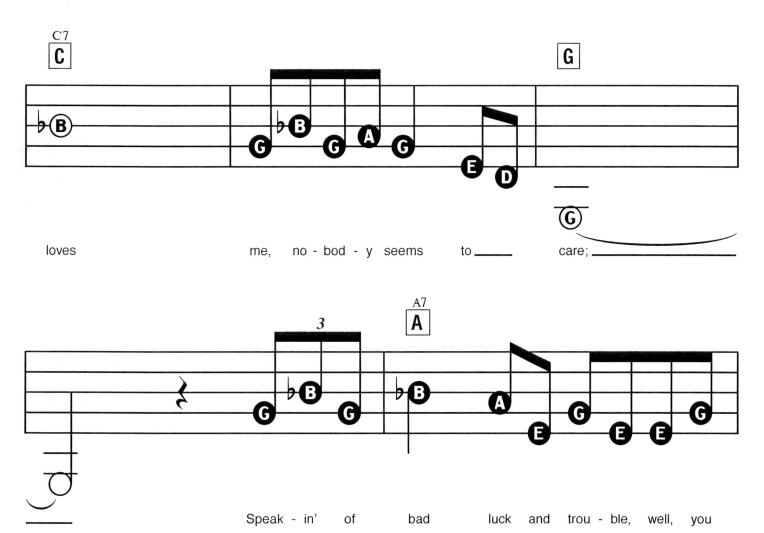

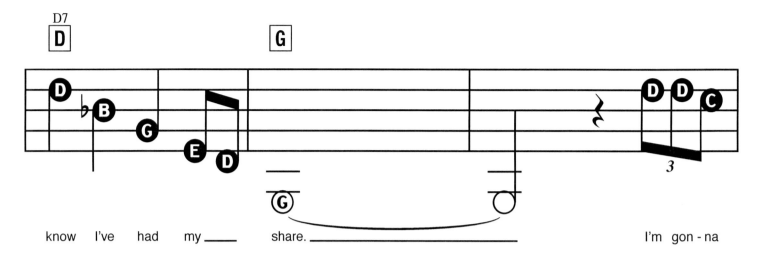

know I've had my ____ share. _____ I'm gon - na

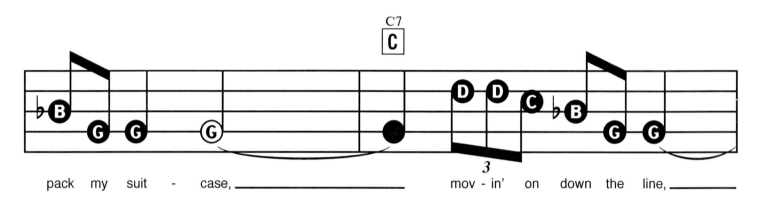

pack my suit - case, _____ mov - in' on down the line, _____

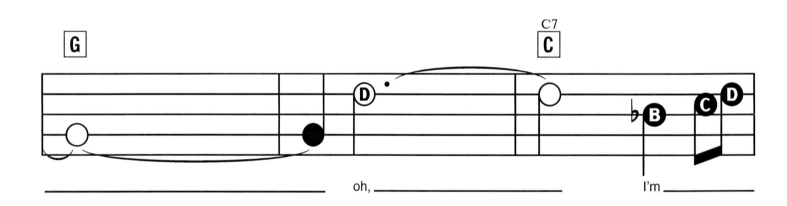

_____ oh, _____ I'm ____

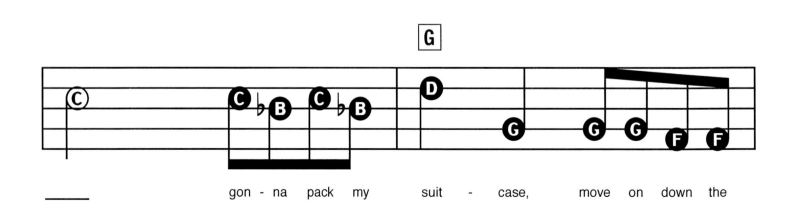

____ gon - na pack my suit - case, move on down the

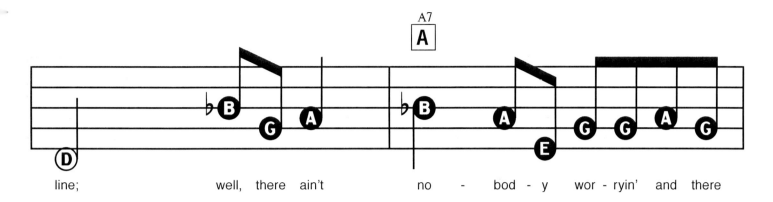

line;   well, there ain't   no - bod - y wor - ryin' and there

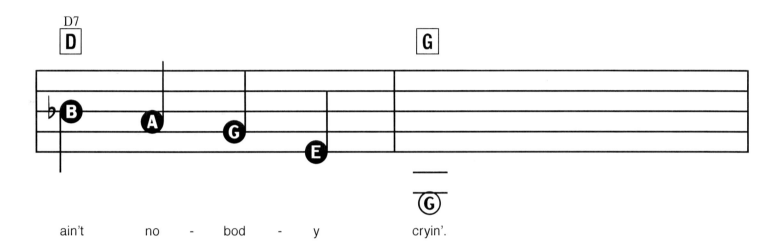

ain't   no - bod - y   cryin'.

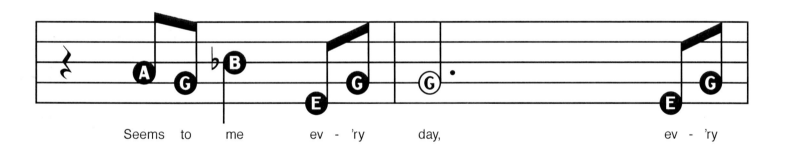

Seems to me ev - 'ry day,   ev - 'ry

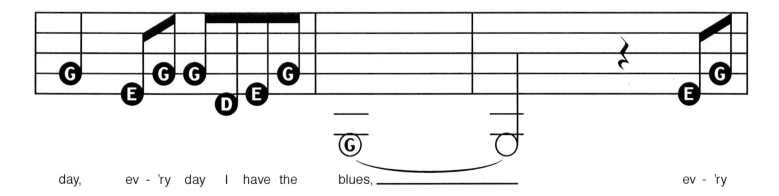

day, ev - 'ry day I have the blues, _____ ev - 'ry

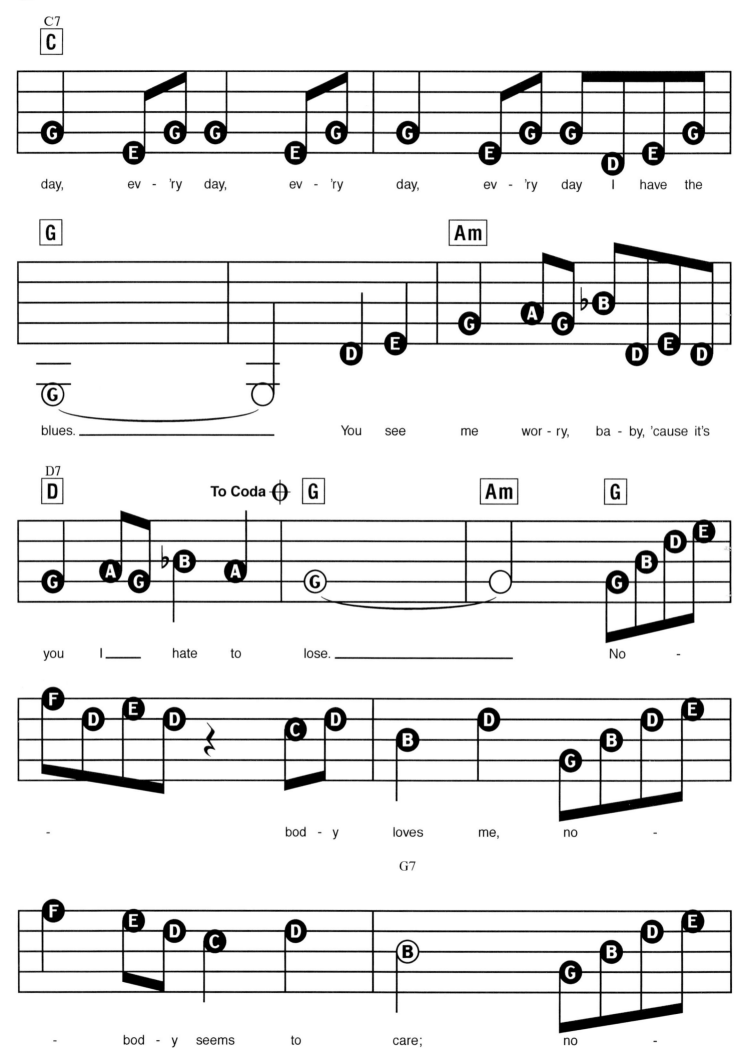

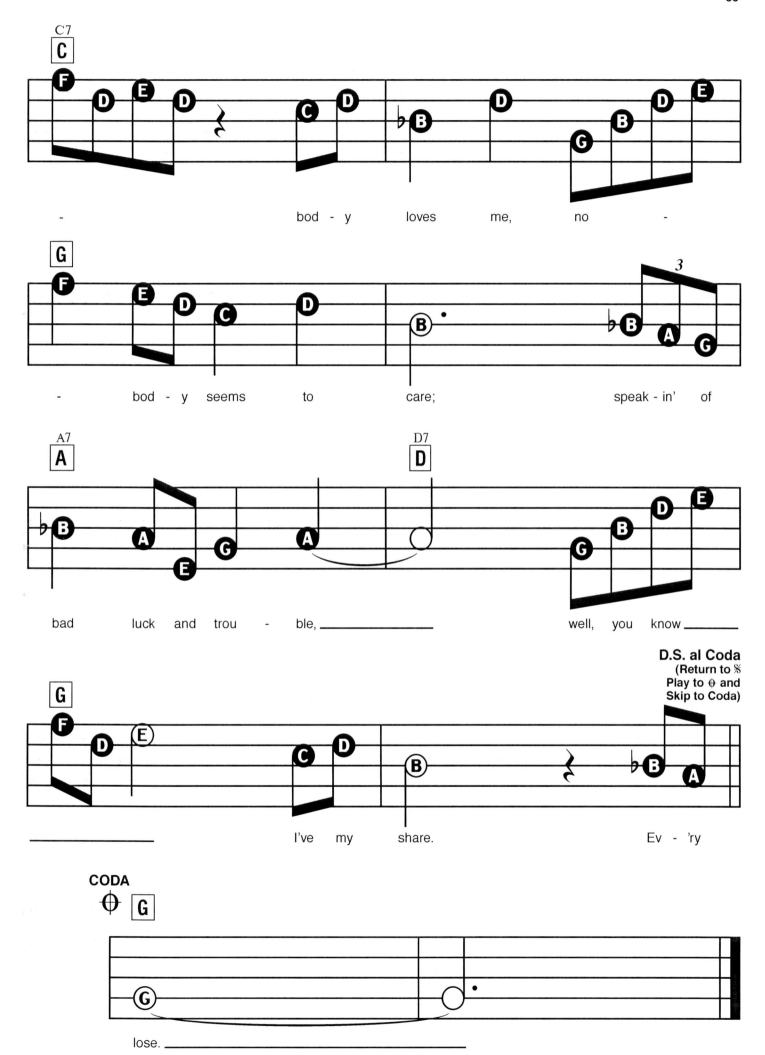

(I Love You)
For Sentimental Reasons

Registration 1
Rhythm: Fox Trot or Swing

Words by Deek Watson
Music by William Best

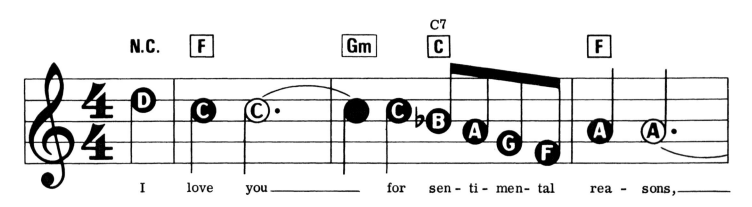

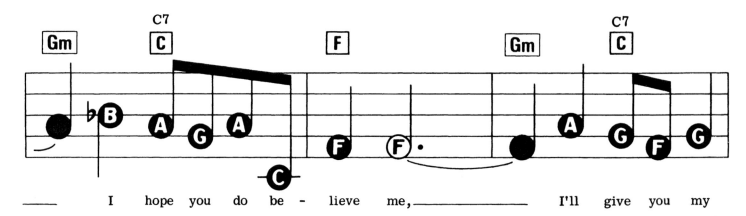

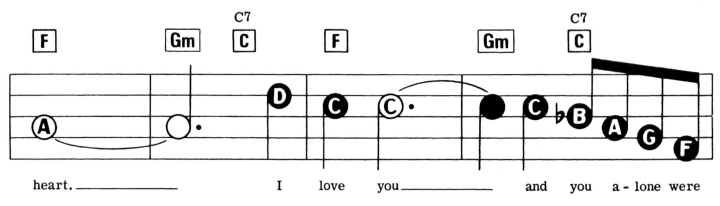

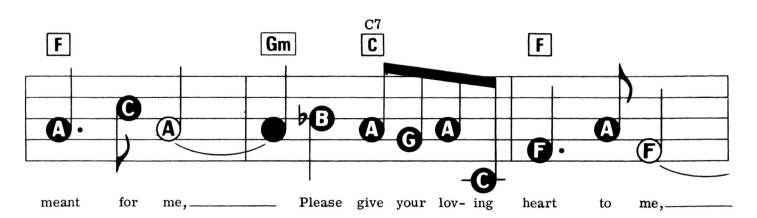

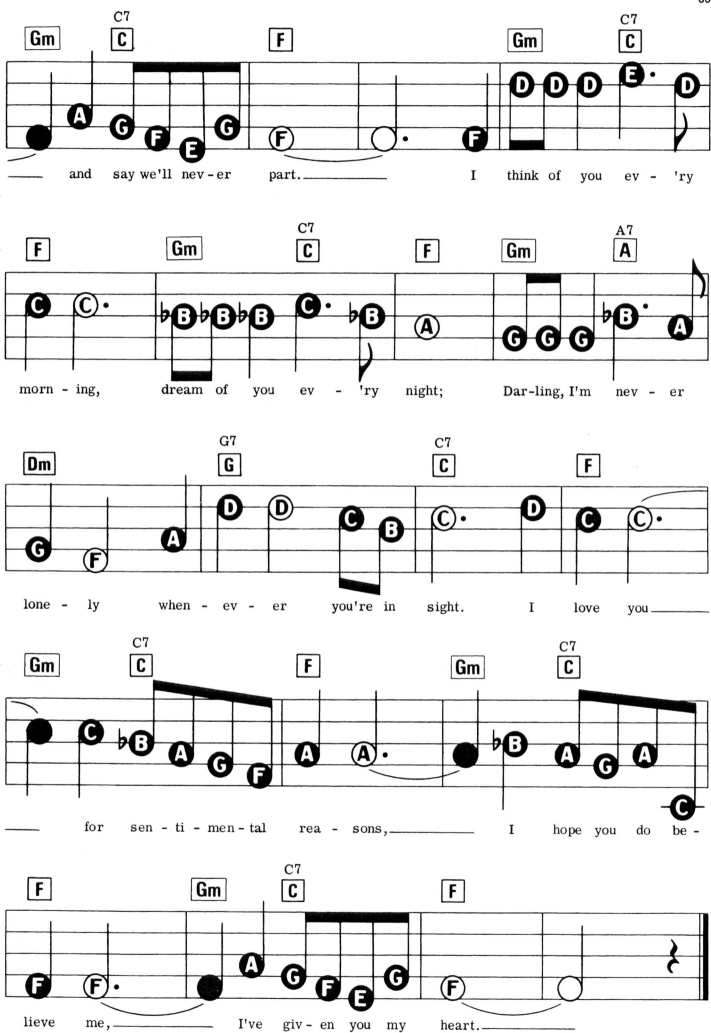

Friendly Persuasion

Registration 10
Rhythm: Ballad or Fox Trot

Words by Paul Francis Webster
Music by Dimitri Tiomkin

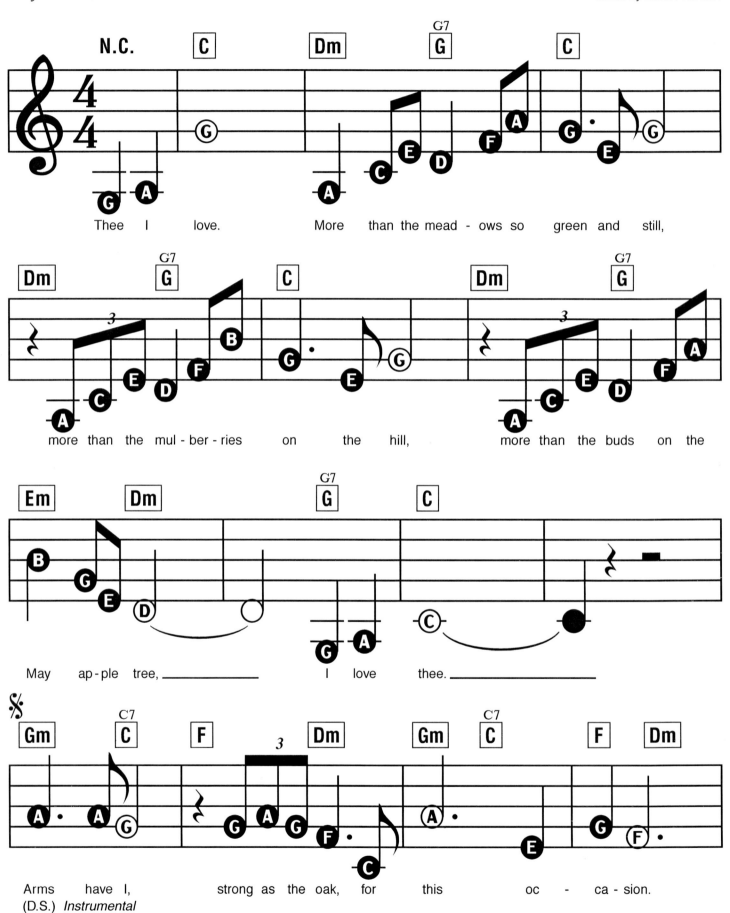

Georgia on My Mind

Registration 4
Rhythm: Swing

Words by Stuart Gorrell
Music by Hoagy Carmichael

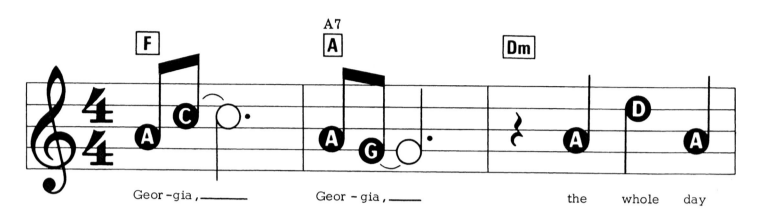

Geor-gia,_____ Geor - gia,_____ the whole day

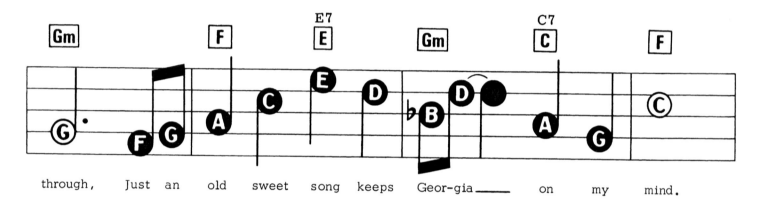

through, Just an old sweet song keeps Geor-gia_____ on my mind.

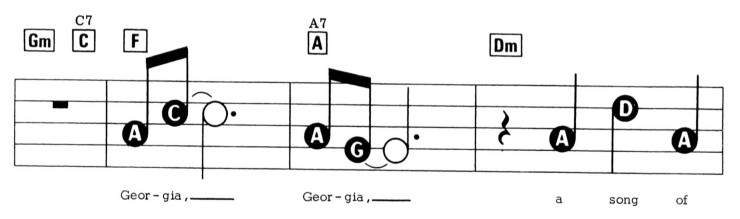

Geor - gia,_____ Geor - gia,_____ a song of

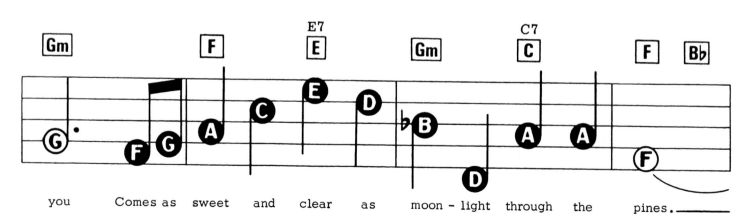

you Comes as sweet and clear as moon - light through the pines._____

89

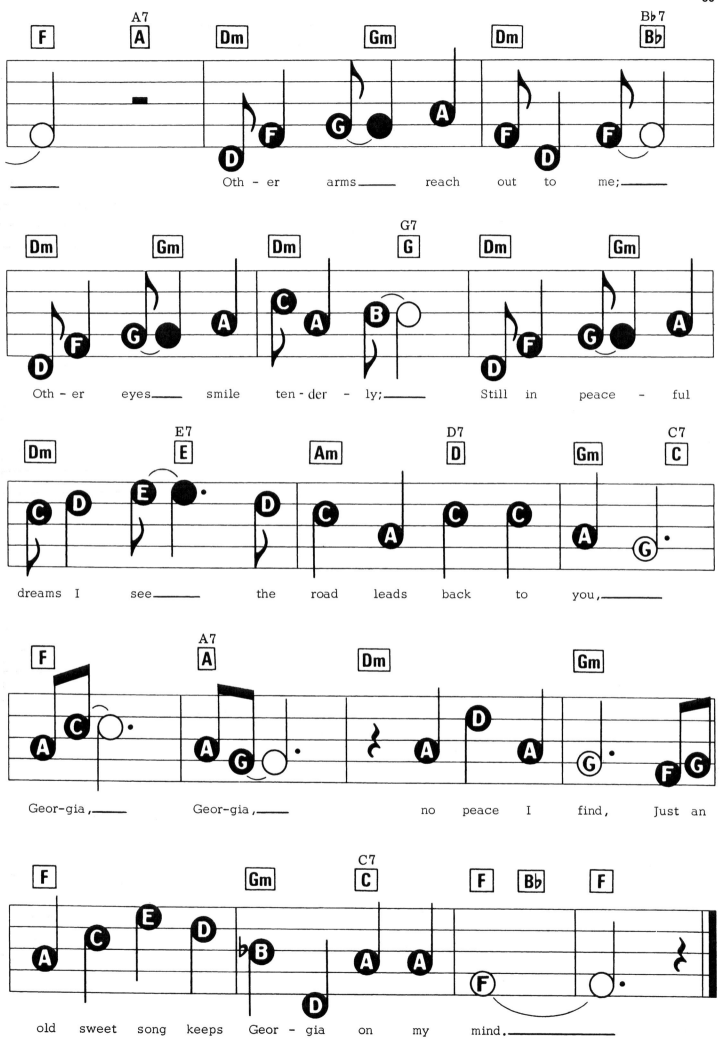

Gonna Build a Mountain

from the Musical Production STOP THE WORLD – I WANT TO GET OFF

Registration 4
Rhythm: Fox Trot

Words and Music by Leslie Bricusse
and Anthony Newley

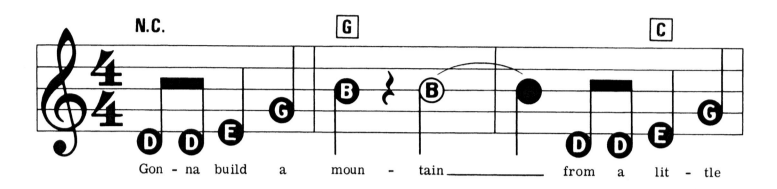

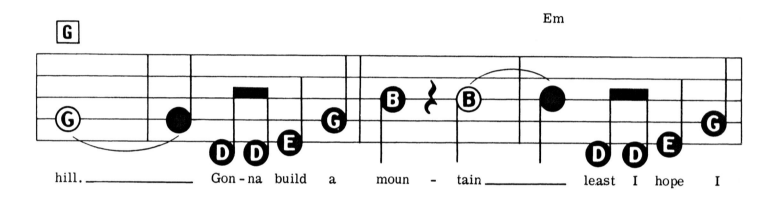

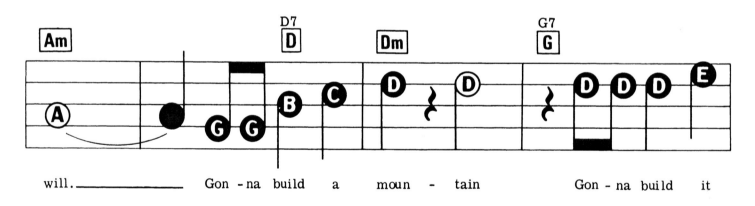

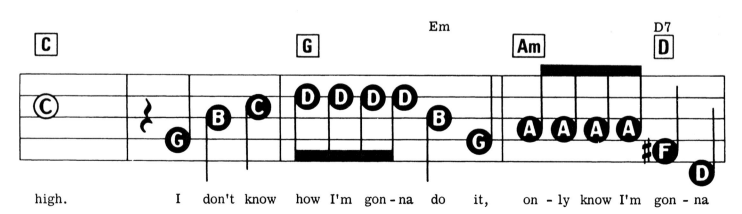

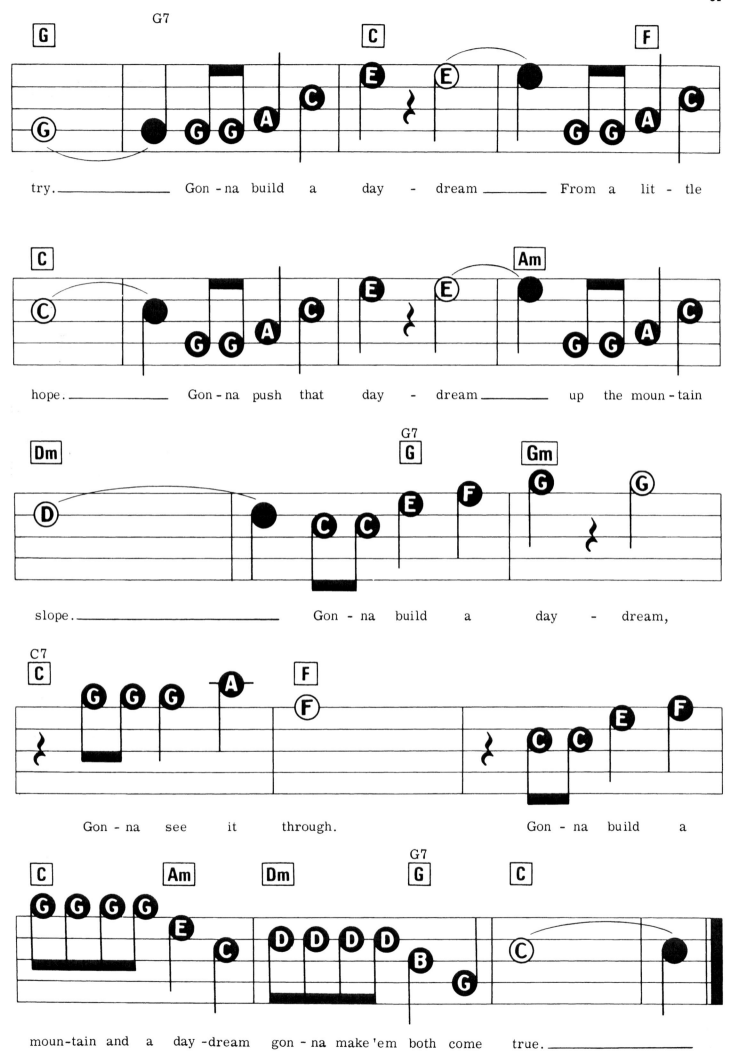

How Deep Is the Ocean
(How High Is the Sky)

Registration 4
Rhythm: Fox Trot or Swing

Words and Music by
Irving Berlin

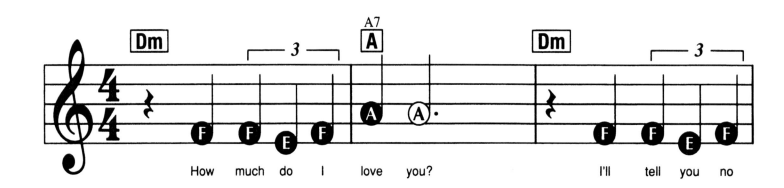

How much do I love you? I'll tell you no

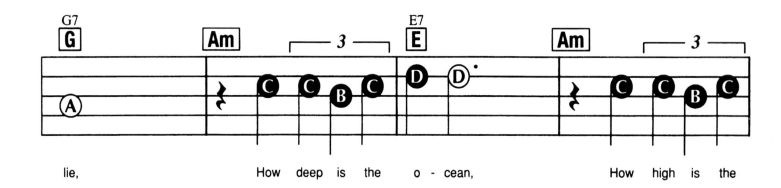

lie, How deep is the o - cean, How high is the

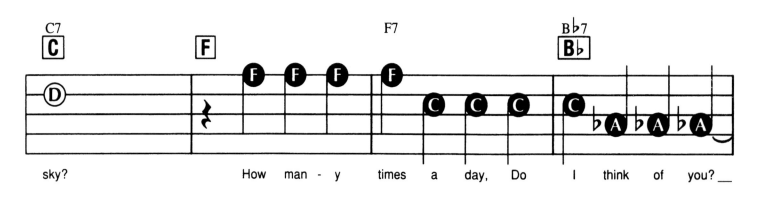

sky? How man - y times a day, Do I think of you? __

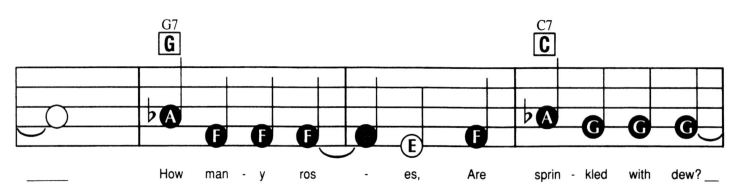

_____ How man - y ros - es, Are sprin - kled with dew? __

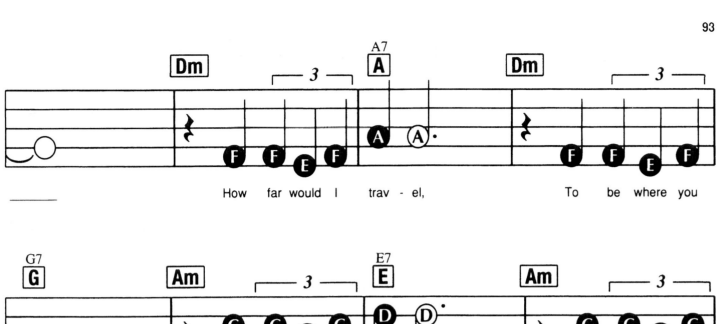

How far would I trav-el, To be where you

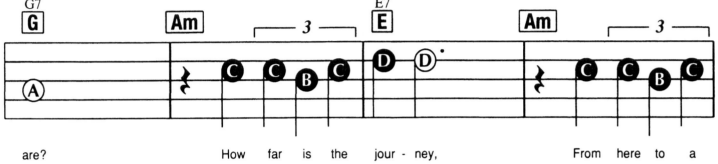

are? How far is the jour-ney, From here to a

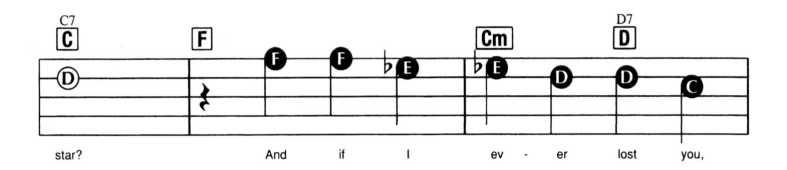

star? And if I ev-er lost you,

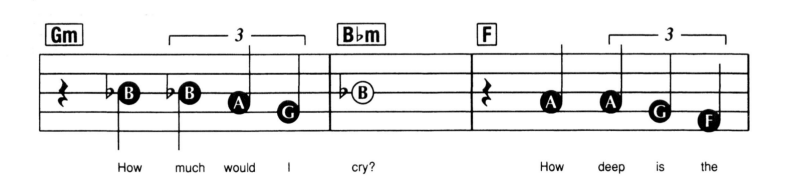

How much would I cry? How deep is the

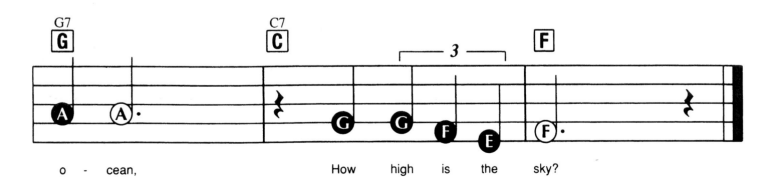

o-cean, How high is the sky?

I Almost Lost My Mind

Registration 4
Rhythm: Slow Rock or Rock

Words and Music by
Ivory Joe Hunter

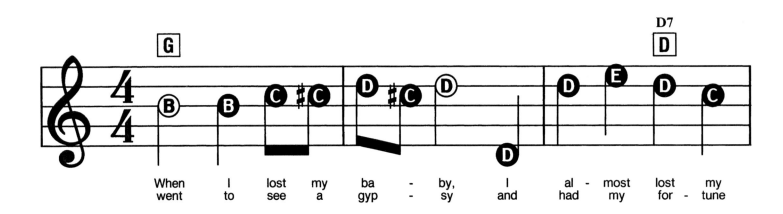

When I lost my ba - by, I al - most lost my
went to see a gyp - sy and had my for - tune

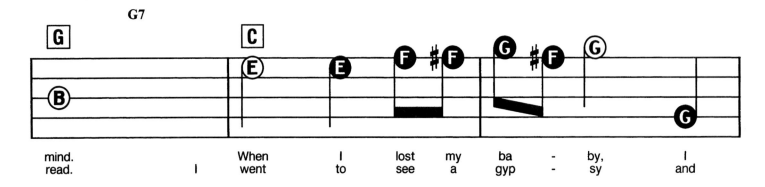

mind. When I lost my ba - by, I
read. I went to see a gyp - sy and

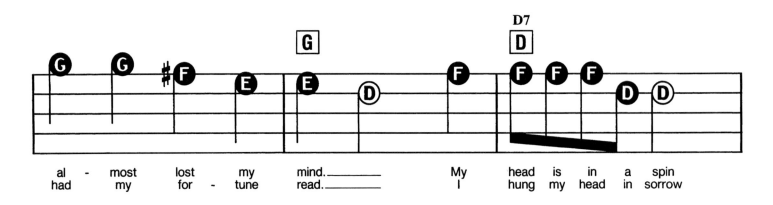

al - most lost my mind._____ My head is in a spin
had my for - tune read._____ I hung my head in sorrow

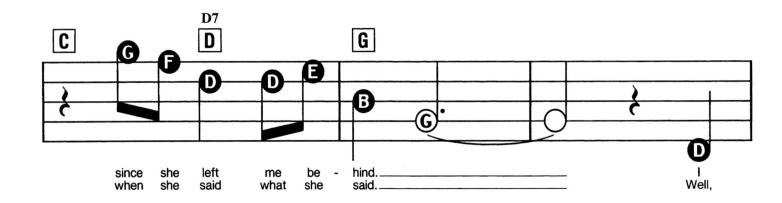

since she left me be - hind._____ I
when she said what she said._____ Well,

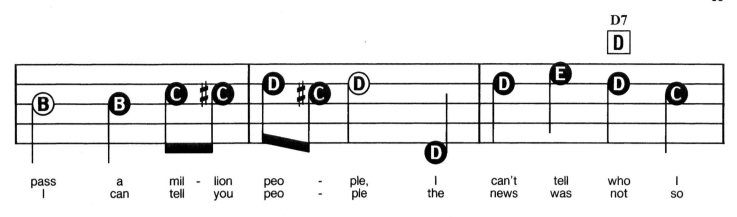

pass   a   mil - lion peo - ple,   I   can't   tell   who   I
I   can   tell you peo - ple   the   news was not   so

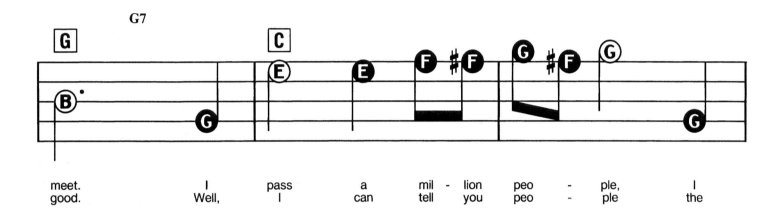

meet.   I   pass   a   mil - lion peo - ple,   I
good.   Well,   I   can   tell you peo - ple   the

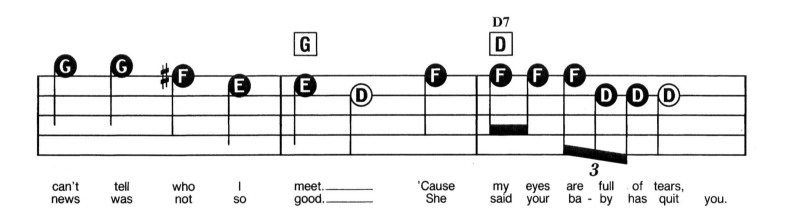

can't tell who   I   meet._____ 'Cause my eyes are full of tears,
news was not so   good._____ She   said your ba - by has quit you.

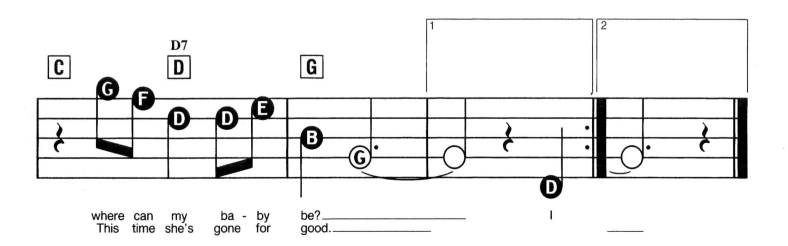

where can my   ba - by be?_____   I
This time she's gone for good._____

I Get Ideas

Registration 1
Rhythm: Tango or Latin

Words by Dorcas Cochran
Music by Julio C. Sanders

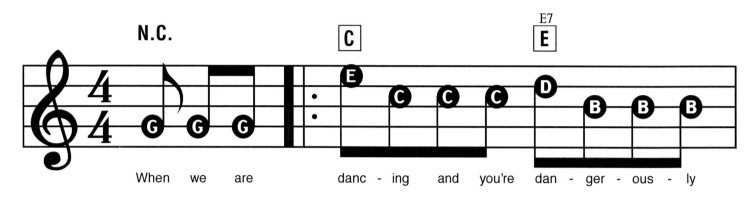

When we are danc - ing and you're dan - ger - ous - ly

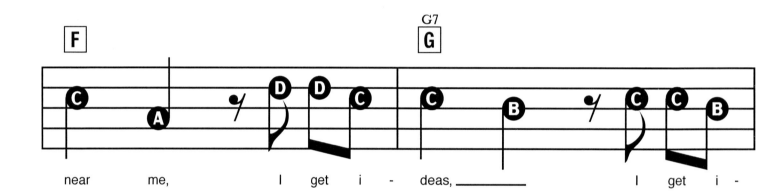

near me, I get i - deas, _____ I get i -

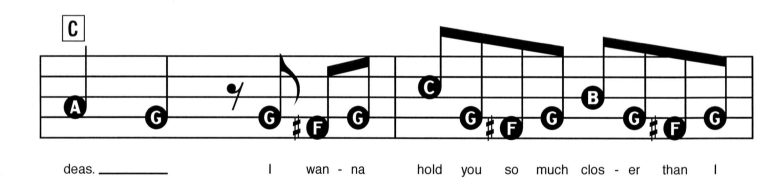

deas. _____ I wan - na hold you so much clos - er than I

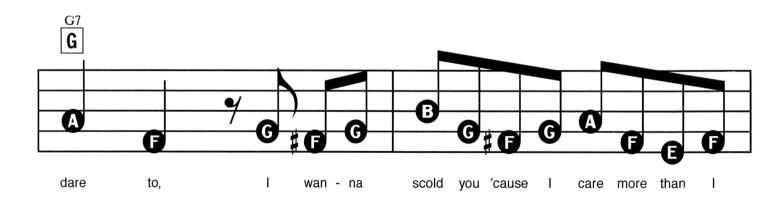

dare to, I wan - na scold you 'cause I care more than I

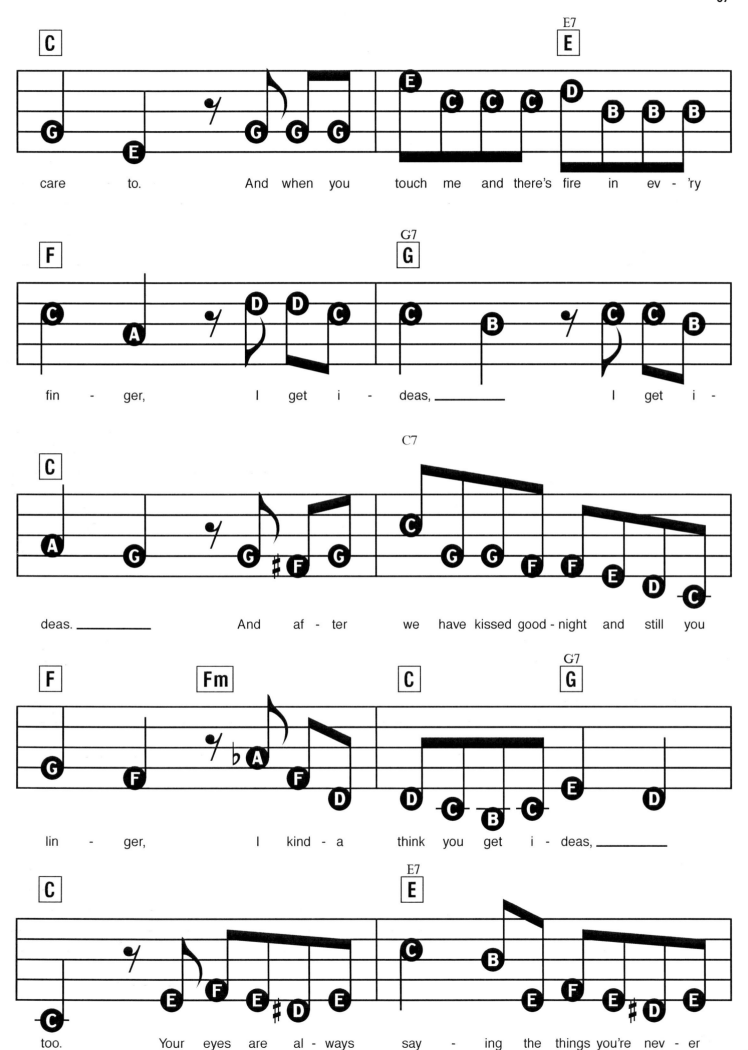

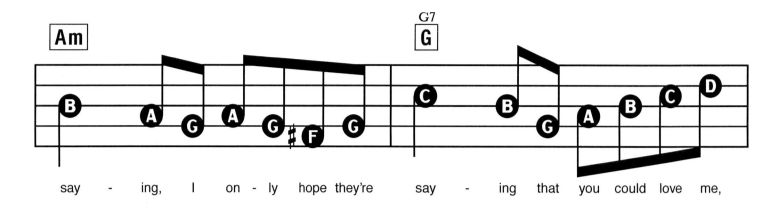

say - ing, I on - ly hope they're say - ing that you could love me,

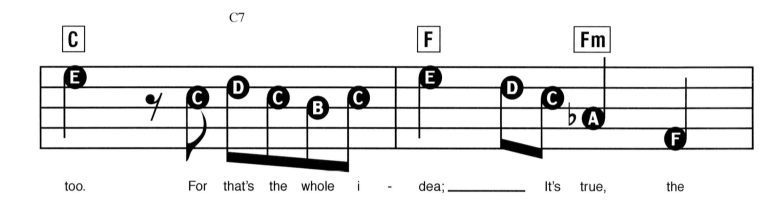

too. For that's the whole i - dea;_____ It's true, the

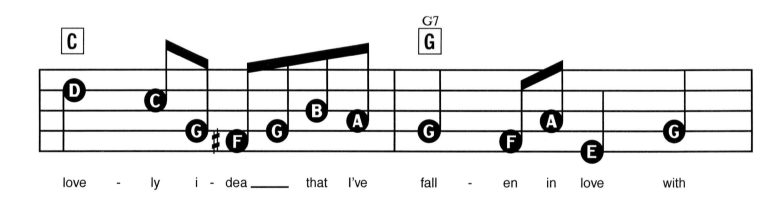

love - ly i - dea_____ that I've fall - en in love with

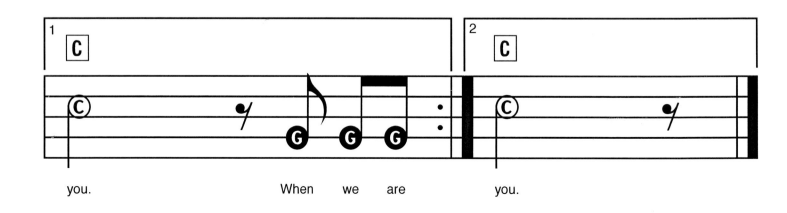

you. When we are you.

I'm Walking Behind You
(Look Over Your Shoulder)

Registration 7
Rhythm: Ballad or Fox Trot

Words and Music by
Billy Reid

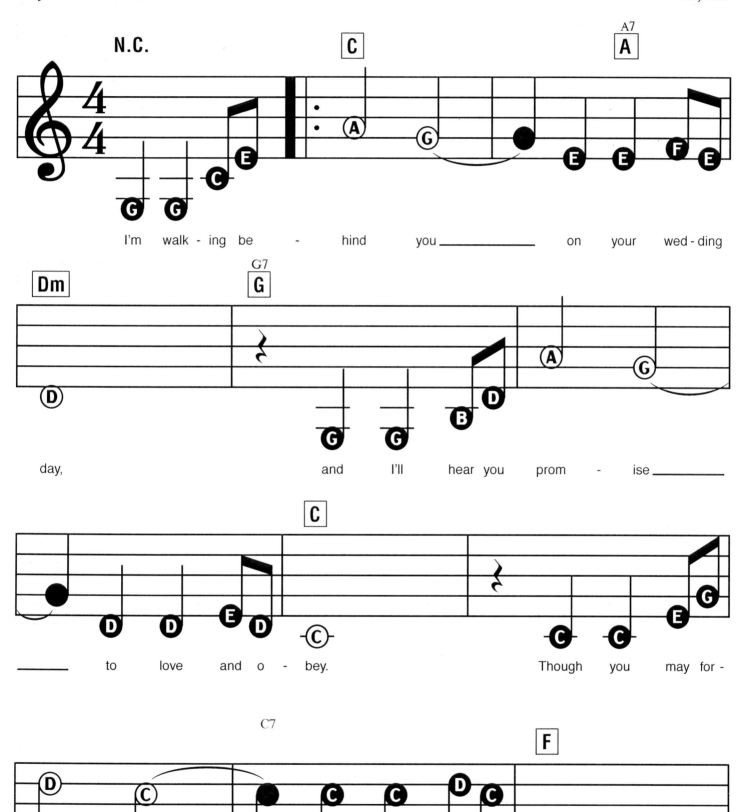

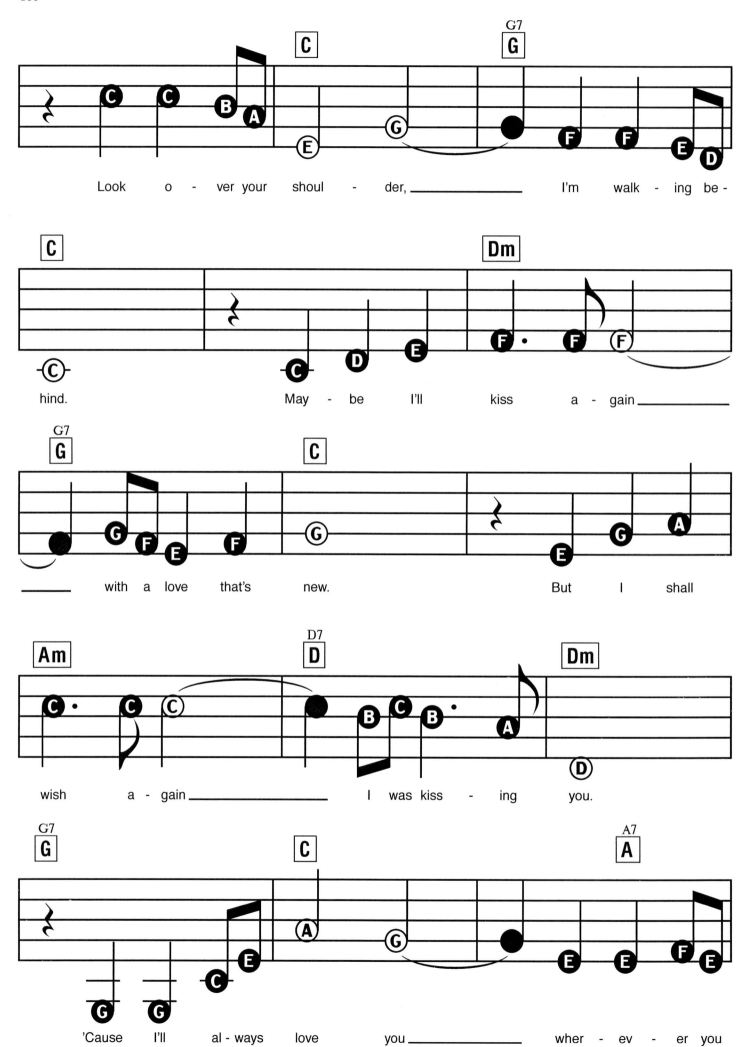

I've Got the World on a String

Registration 1
Rhythm: Swing

Lyric by Ted Koehler
Music by Harold Arlen

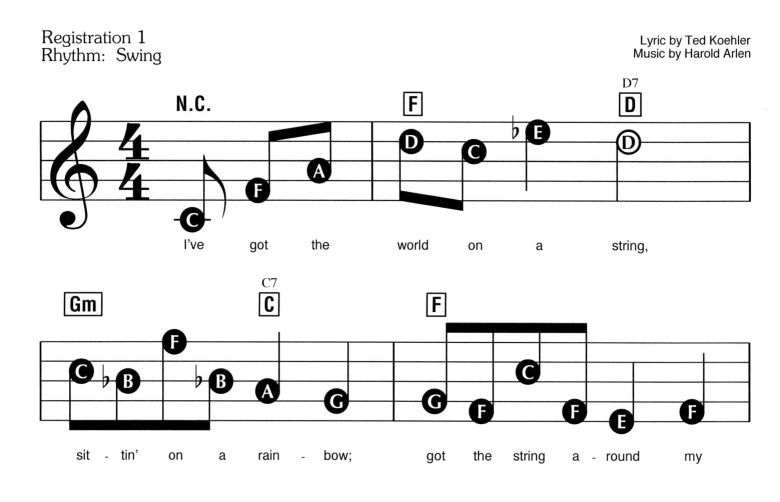

I've got the world on a string, sit-tin' on a rain-bow; got the string a-round my

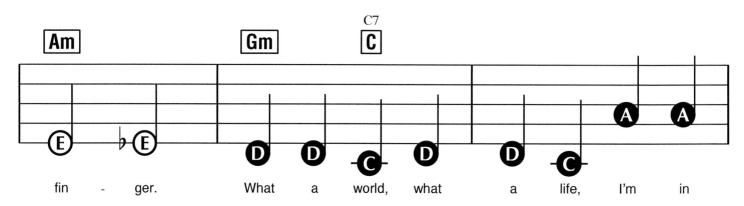

fin - ger. What a world, what a life, I'm in

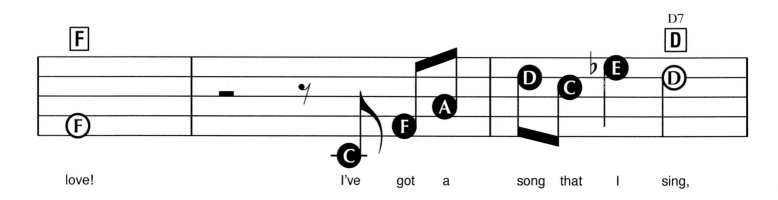

love! I've got a song that I sing,

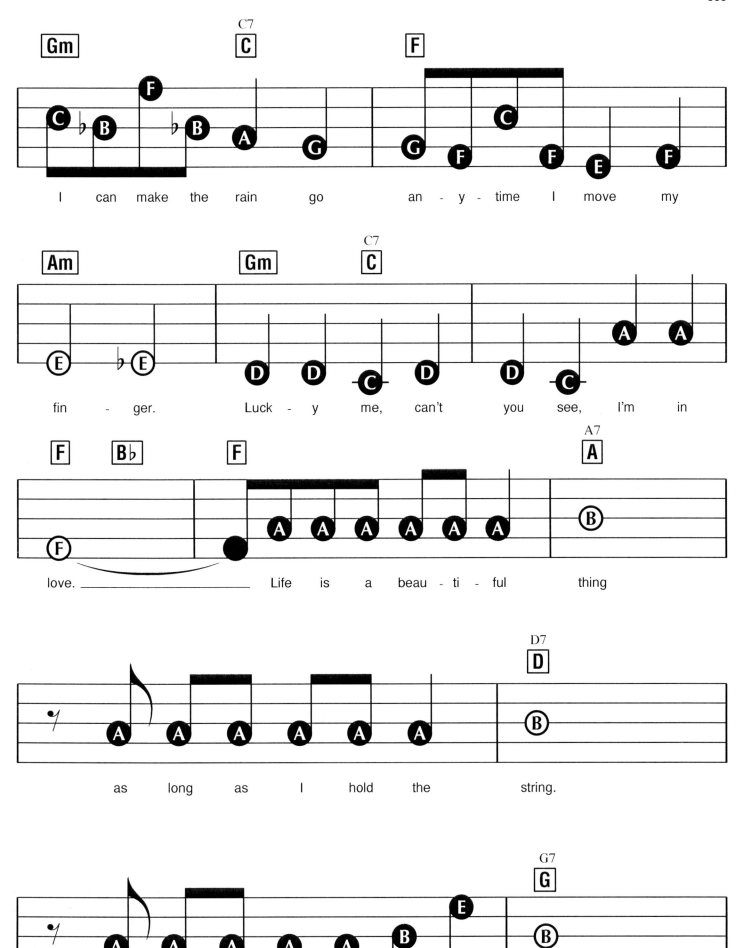

103

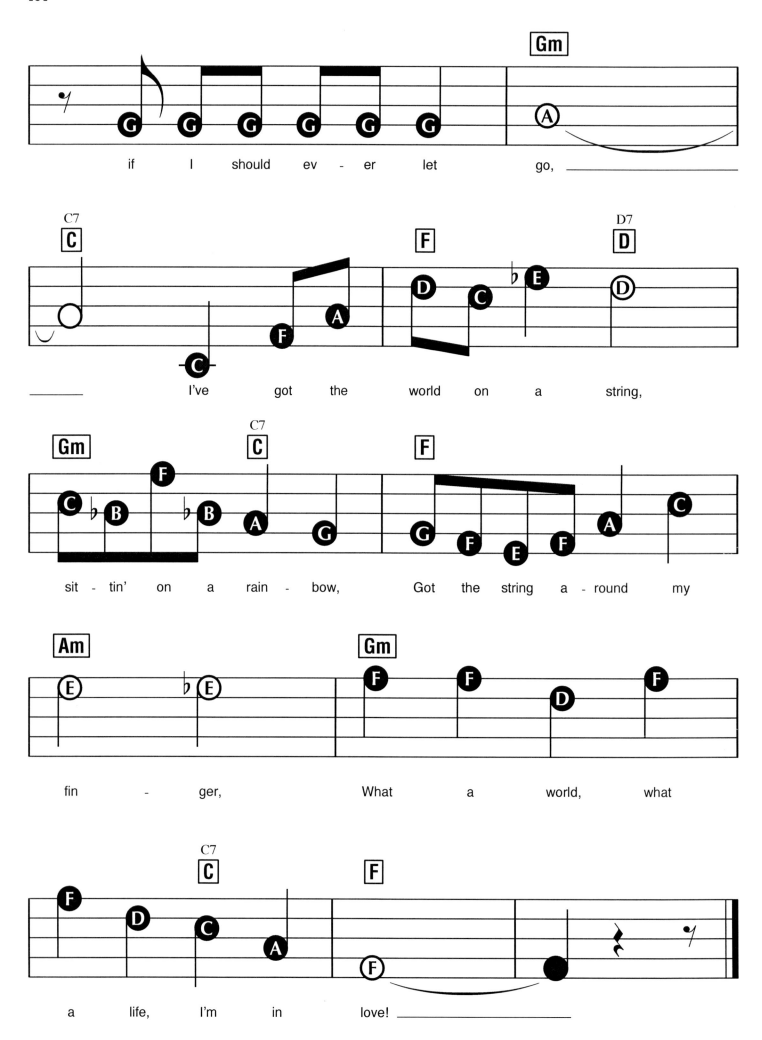

The Impossible Dream
(The Quest)
from MAN OF LA MANCHA

Registration 3
Rhythm: Waltz

Lyric by Joe Darion
Music by Mitch Leigh

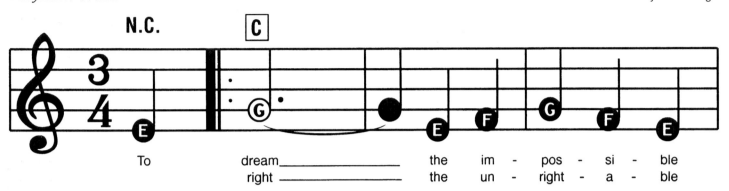

To
dream_____ the im - pos - si - ble
right _____ the un - right - a - ble

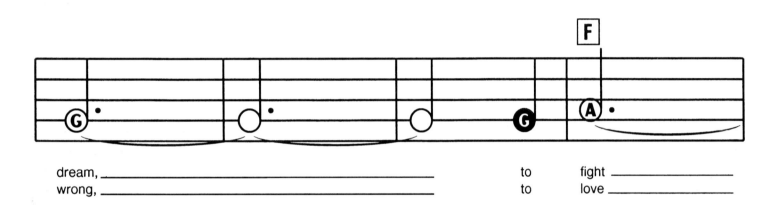

dream,_____ to fight _____
wrong,_____ to love _____

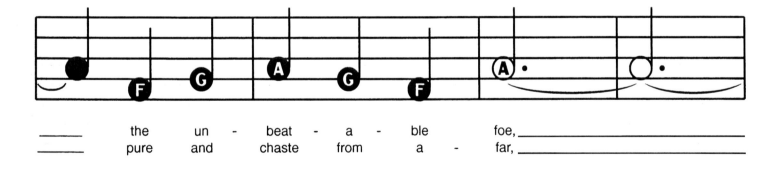

_____ the un - beat - a - ble foe,_____
pure and chaste from a - far,_____

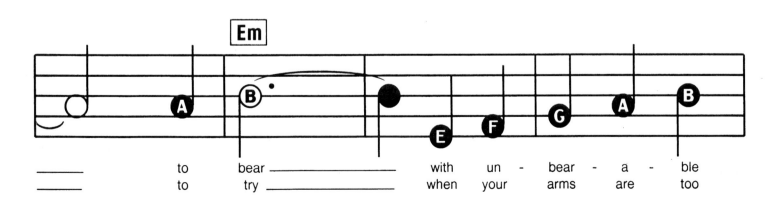

_____ to bear _____ with un - bear - a - ble
_____ to try _____ when your arms are too

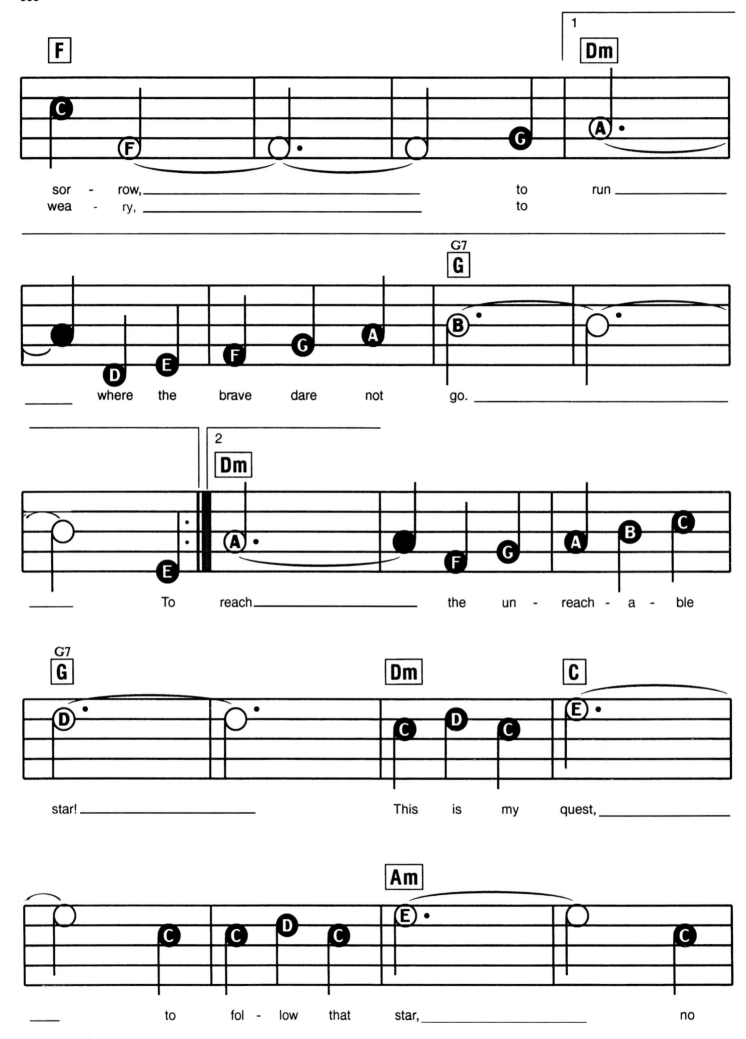

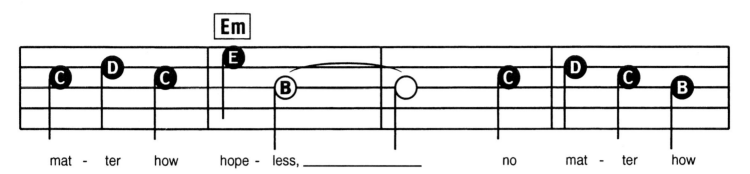

mat - ter how hope - less, _____ no mat - ter how

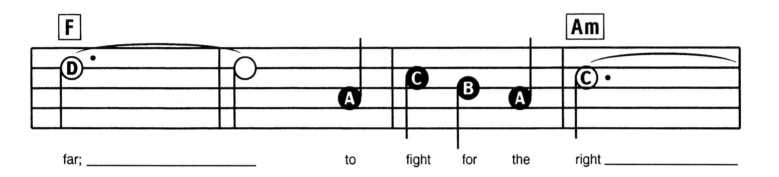

far; _____ to fight for the right _____

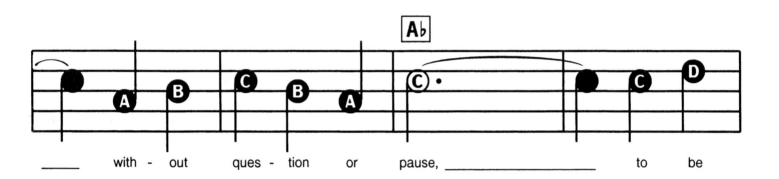

___ with - out ques - tion or pause, _____ to be

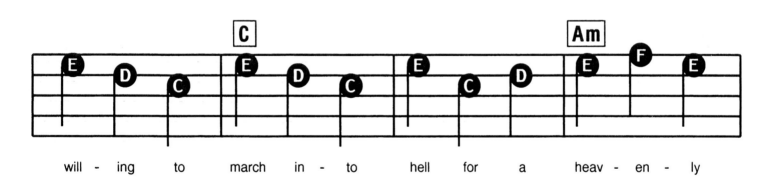

will - ing to march in - to hell for a heav - en - ly

cause! _____ And I know, _____

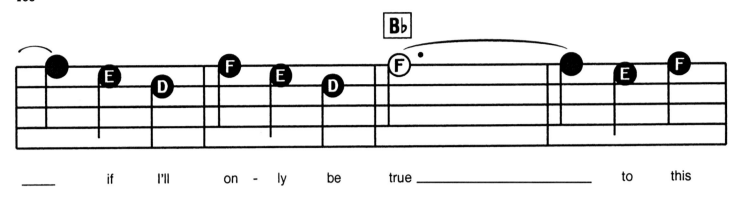

_____ if I'll on - ly be true _____ to this

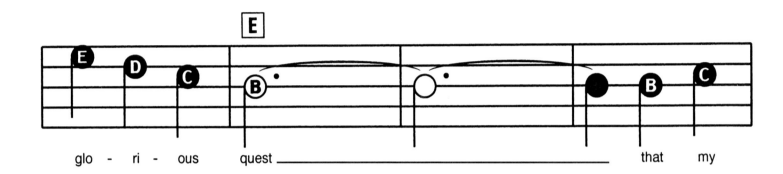

glo - ri - ous quest _____ that my

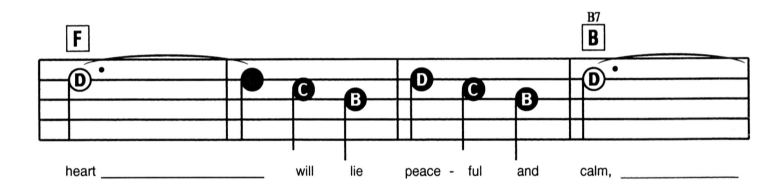

heart _____ will lie peace - ful and calm, _____

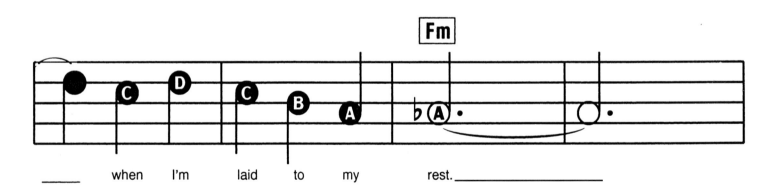

_____ when I'm laid to my rest._____

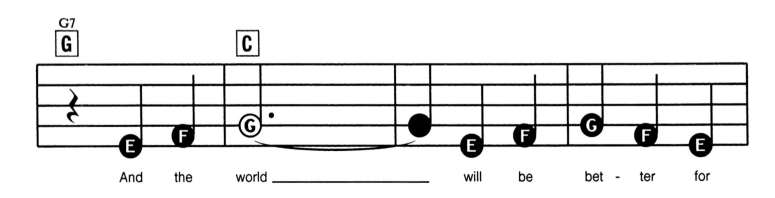

And the world _____ will be bet - ter for

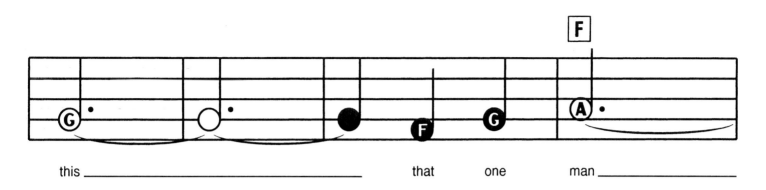

this _____ that one man _____

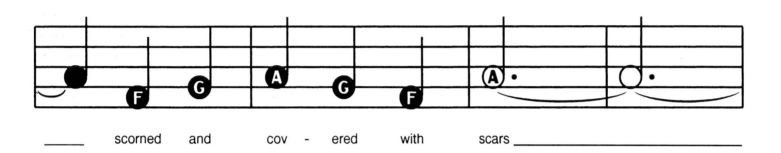

_____ scorned and cov - ered with scars _____

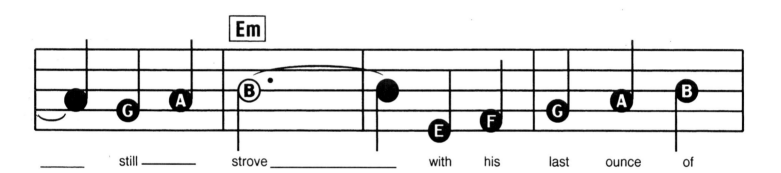

_____ still _____ strove _____ with his last ounce of

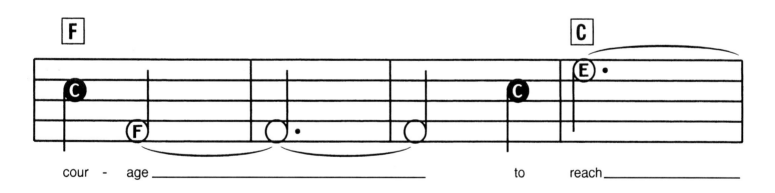

cour - age _____ to reach _____

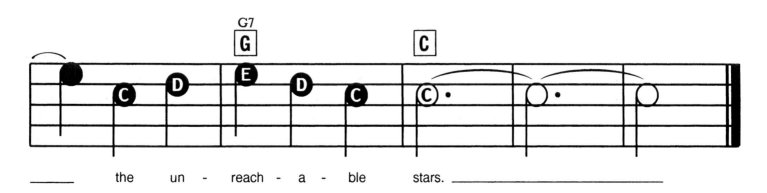

_____ the un - reach - a - ble stars. _____

I've Got You Under My Skin

from BORN TO DANCE

Registration 5
Rhythm: Ballad or Fox Trot

Words and Music by
Cole Porter

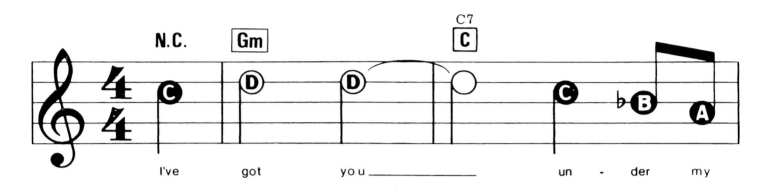

I've got you _____ un - der my

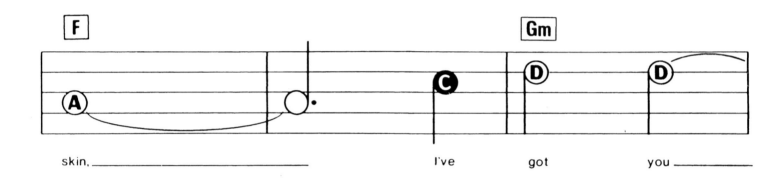

skin, _____ I've got you _____

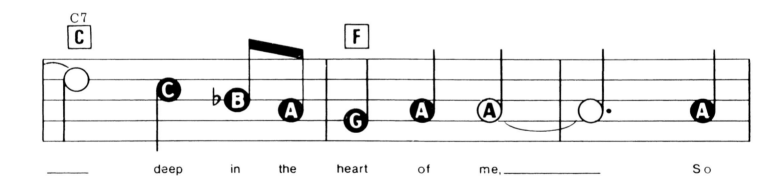

_____ deep in the heart of me, _____ So

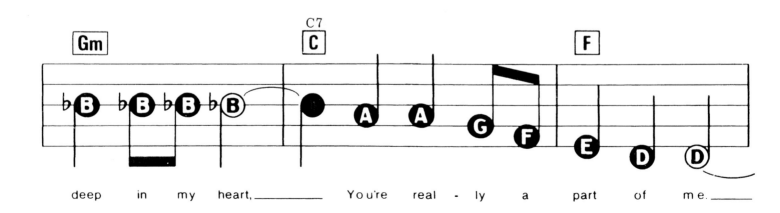

deep in my heart, _____ You're real - ly a part of me. _____

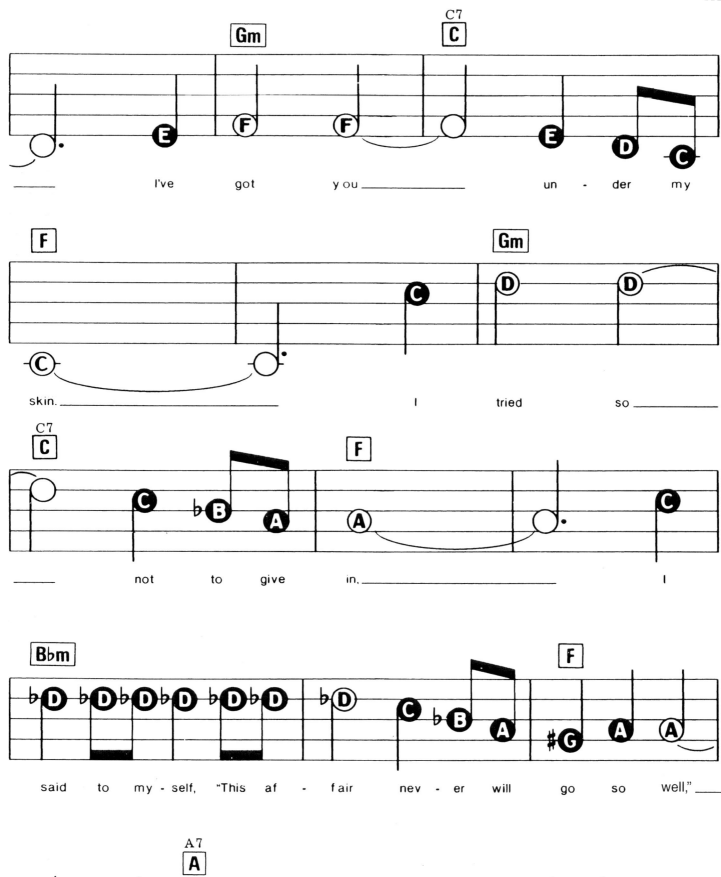

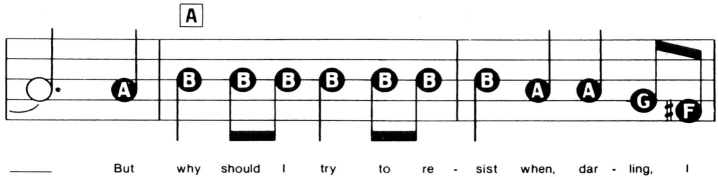

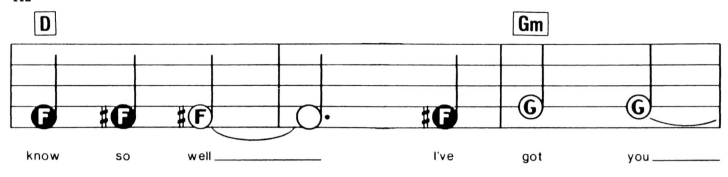

know   so   well _____   I've   got   you ___

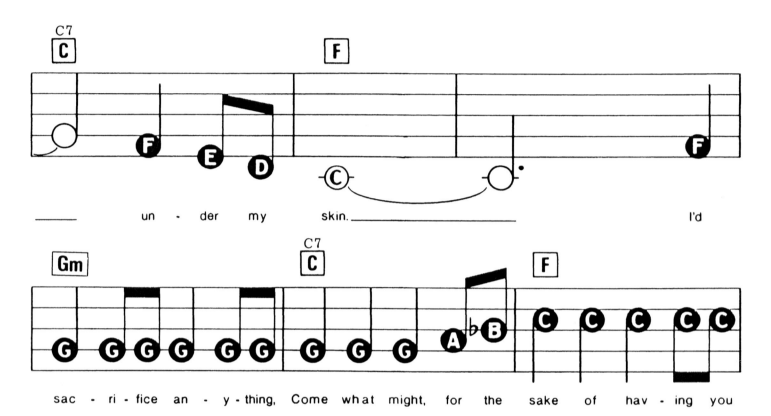

_____   un - der   my   skin. _____   I'd

sac - ri - fice an - y - thing,   Come   what   might,   for   the   sake   of   hav - ing   you

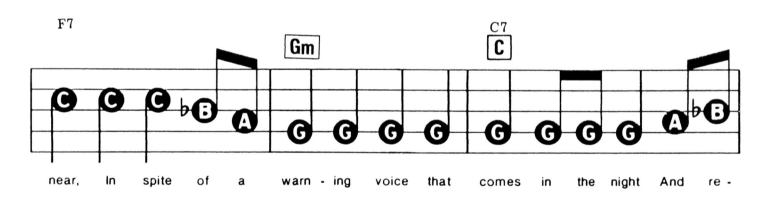

near,   In   spite   of   a   warn - ing   voice   that   comes   in   the   night   And   re -

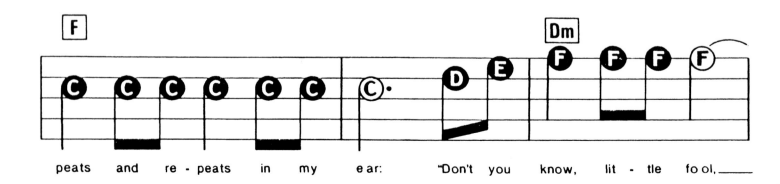

peats   and   re - peats   in   my   ear: "Don't   you   know,   lit - tle   fool, ___

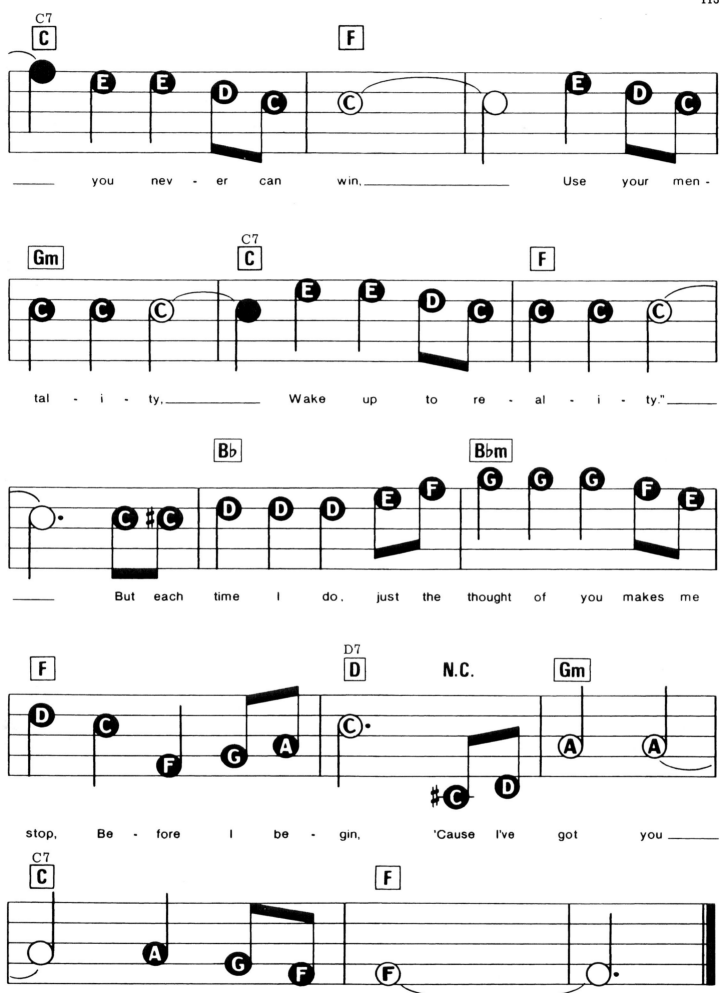

If

Registration 9
Rhythm: Waltz

Words by Robert Hargreaves and Stanley J. Damerell
Music by Tolchard Evans

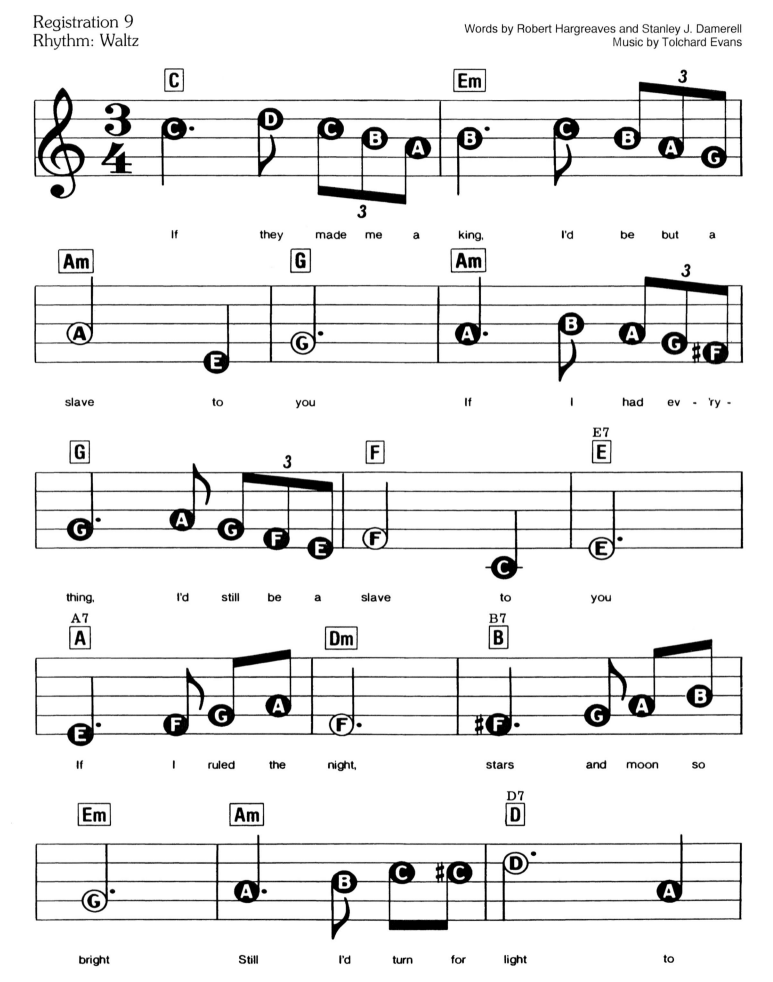

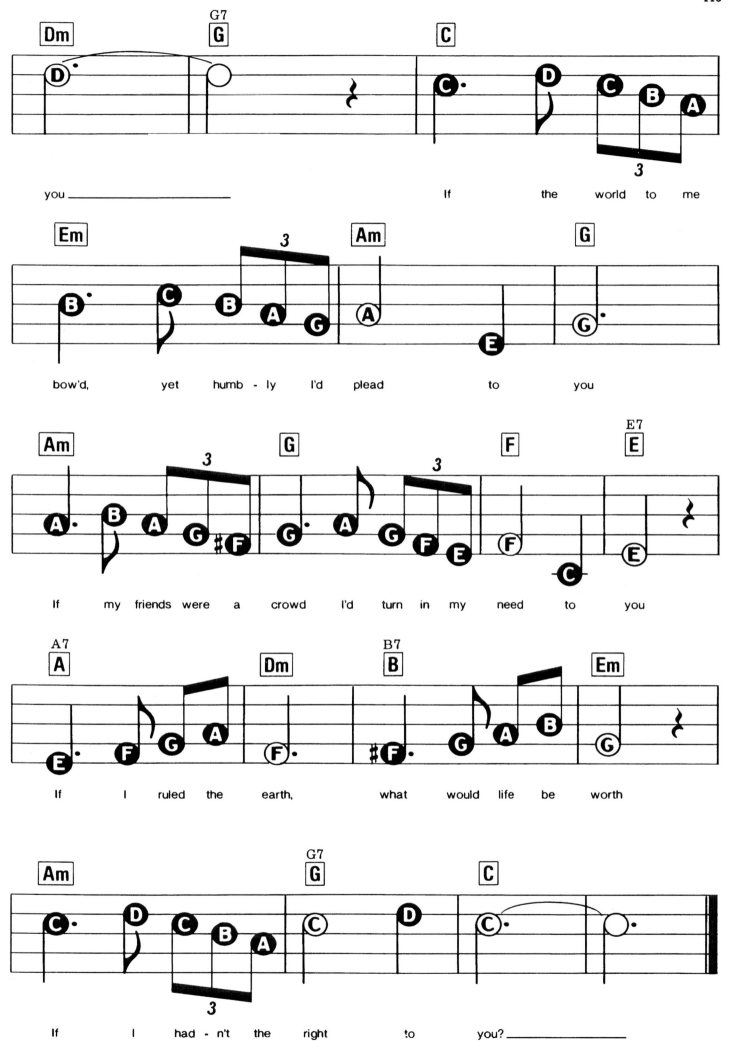

115

It's Just a Matter of Time

Registration 6
Rhythm: Country

Words and Music by Brook Benton,
Clyde Otis and Belford Hendricks

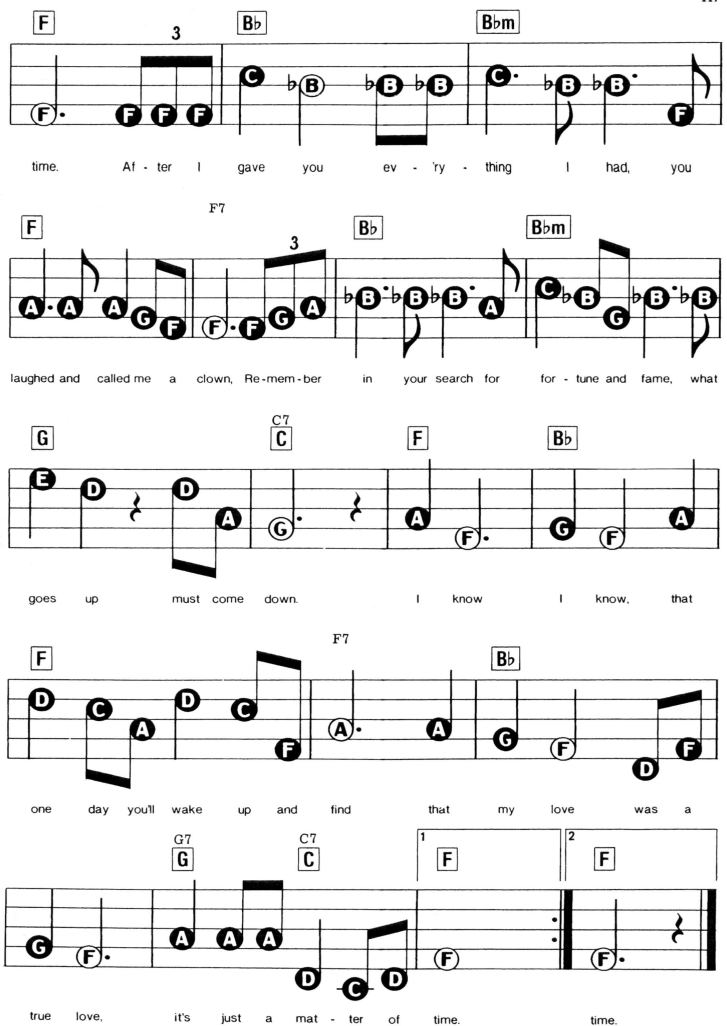

It's Not for Me to Say

Registration 3
Rhythm: Fox Trot

Words by Al Stillman
Music by Robert Allen

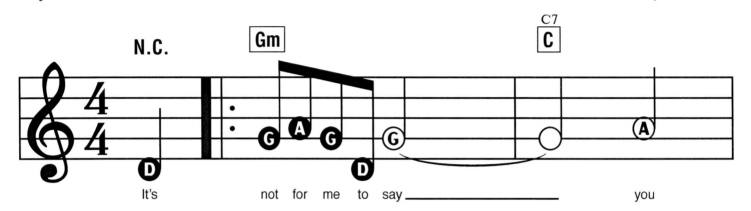

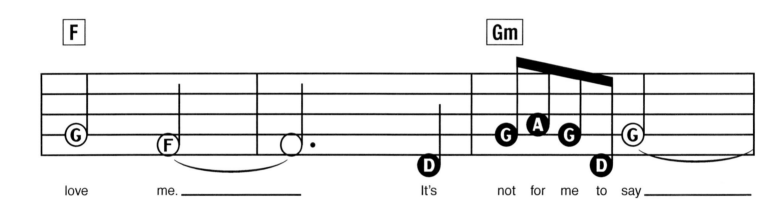

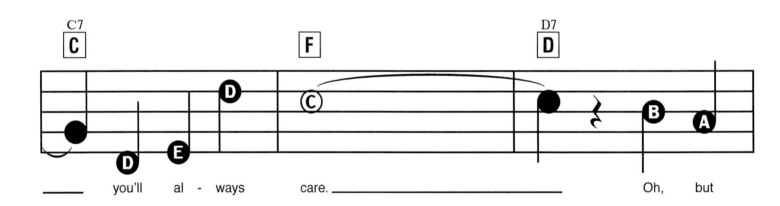

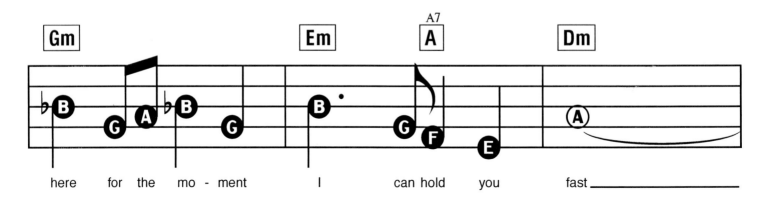

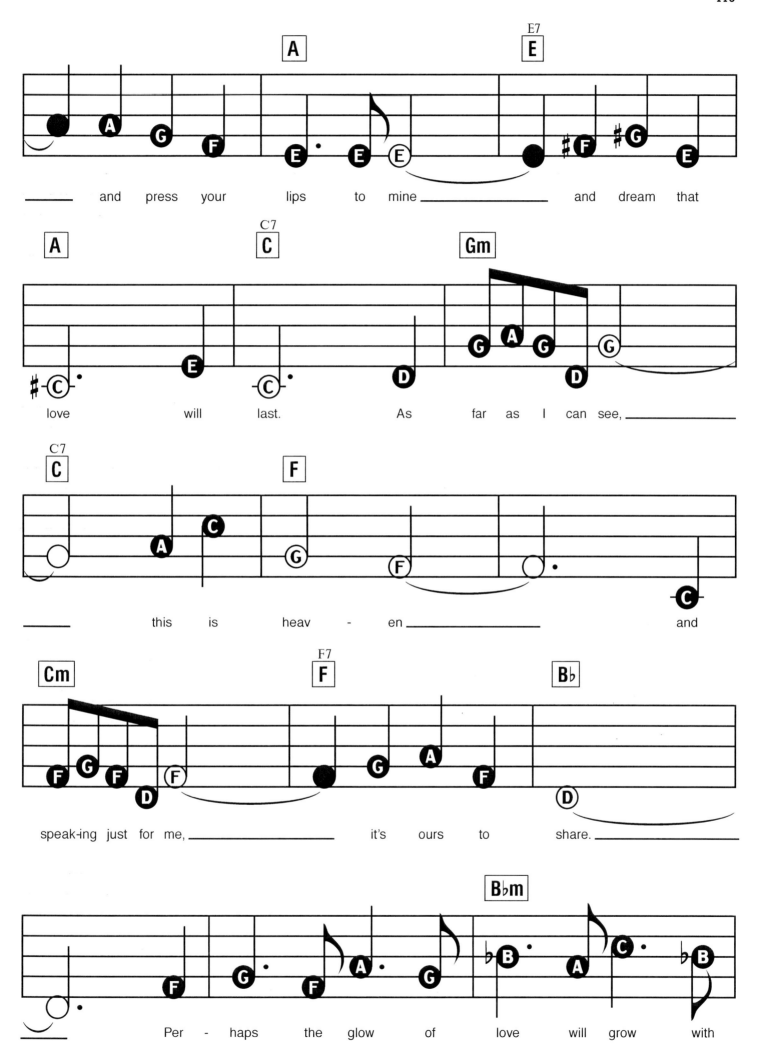

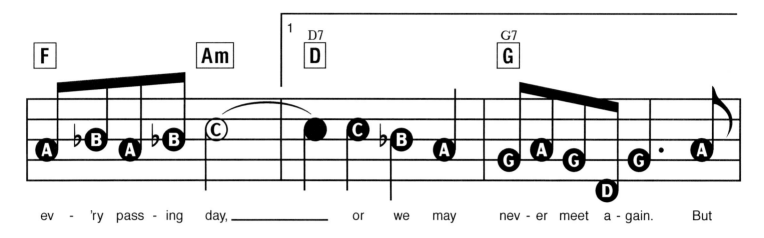

ev - 'ry pass - ing day, _____ or we may nev - er meet a - gain. But

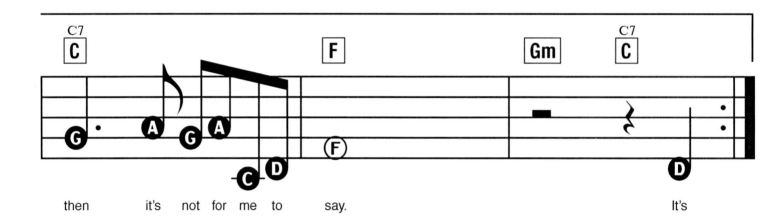

then it's not for me to say. It's

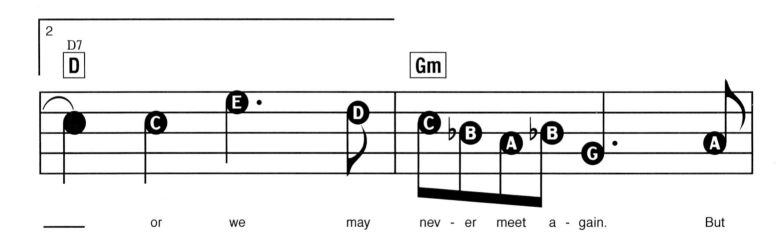

_____ or we may nev - er meet a - gain. But

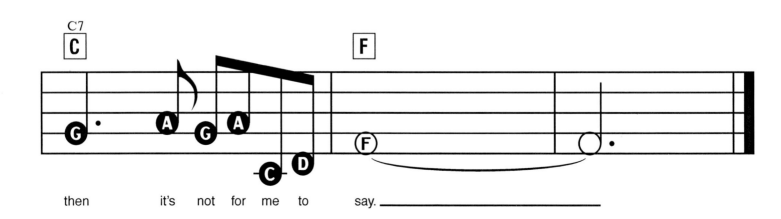

then it's not for me to say. _____

Learnin' the Blues

Registration 2
Rhythm: Swing

Words and Music by
Dolores "Vicki" Silvers

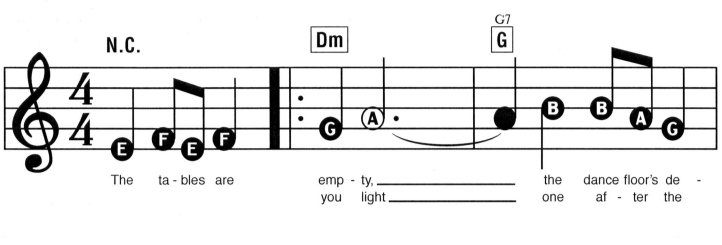

The ta - bles are emp - ty, _____ the dance floor's de -
you light _____ one af - ter the

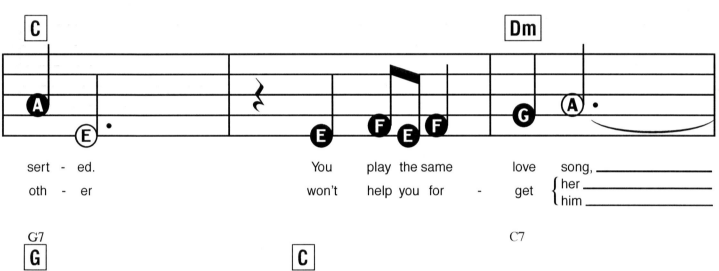

sert - ed. You play the same love song, _____
oth - er won't help you for - get { her _____
                                    { him _____

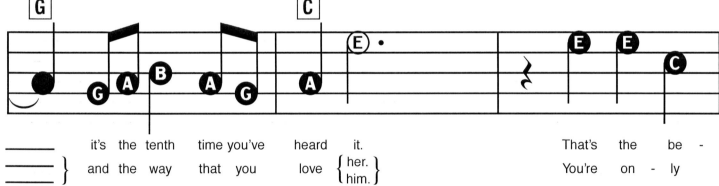

_____ it's the tenth time you've heard it. That's the be -
_____ } and the way that you love { her. You're on - ly
                                     { him.

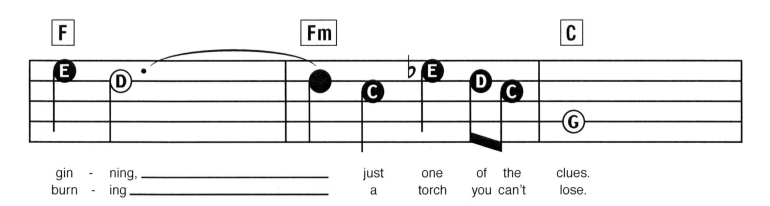

gin - ning, _____ just one of the clues.
burn - ing _____ a torch you can't lose.

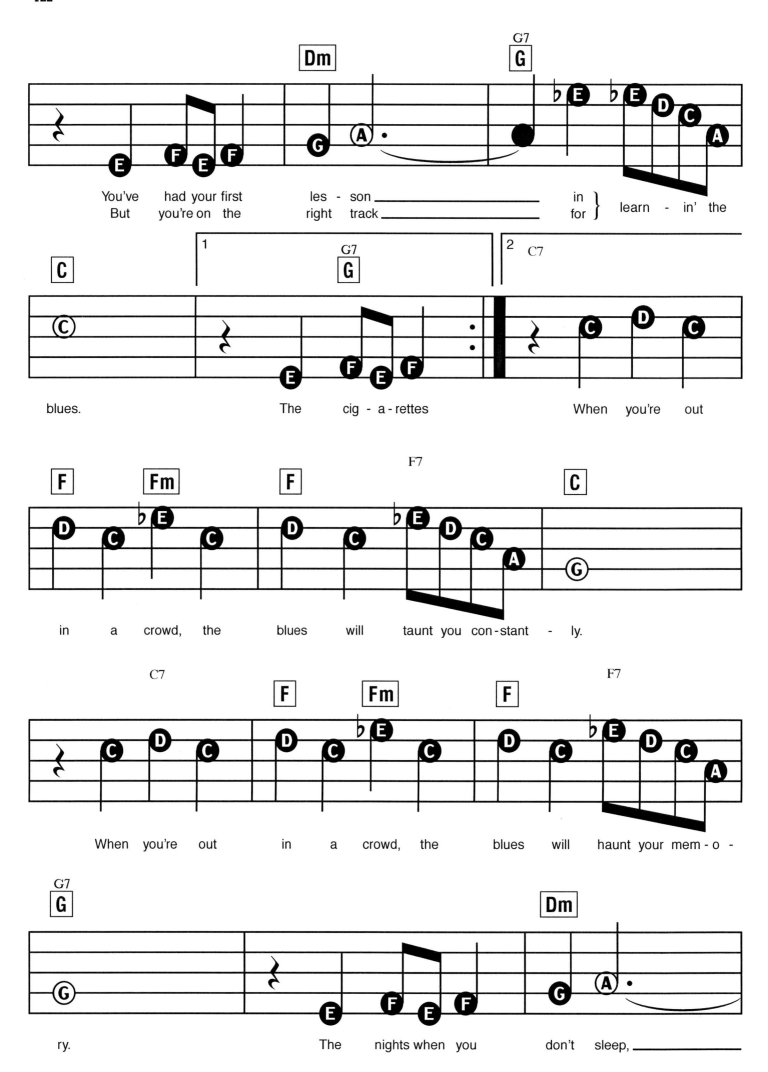

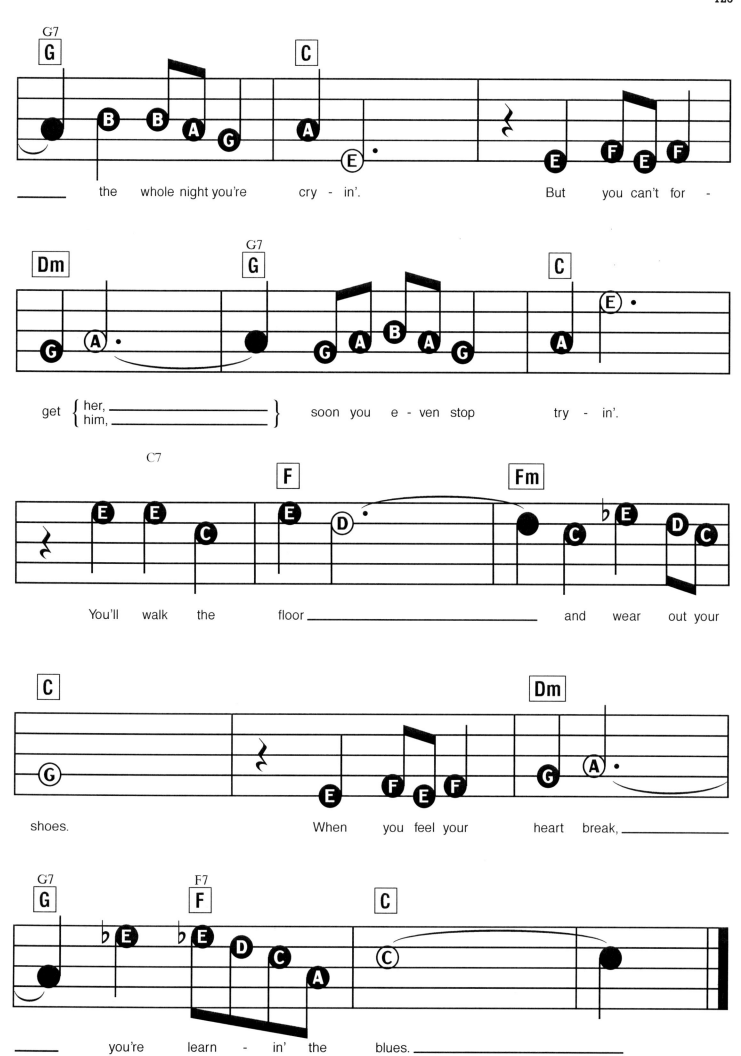

Just in Time
from BELLS ARE RINGING

Registration 2
Rhythm: Fox Trot or Swing

Words by Betty Comden and Adolph Green
Music by Jule Styne

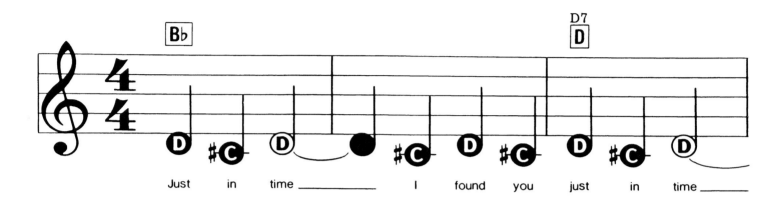

Just in time _____ I found you just in time _____

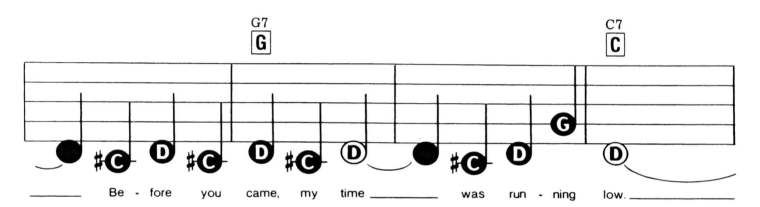

_____ Be - fore you came, my time _____ was run - ning low. _____

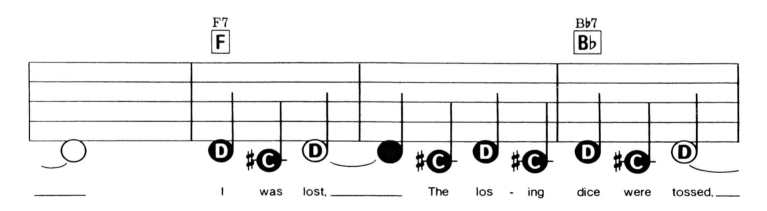

_____ I was lost, _____ The los - ing dice were tossed, _____

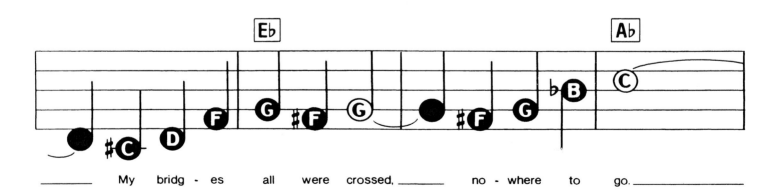

_____ My bridg - es all were crossed, _____ no - where to go. _____

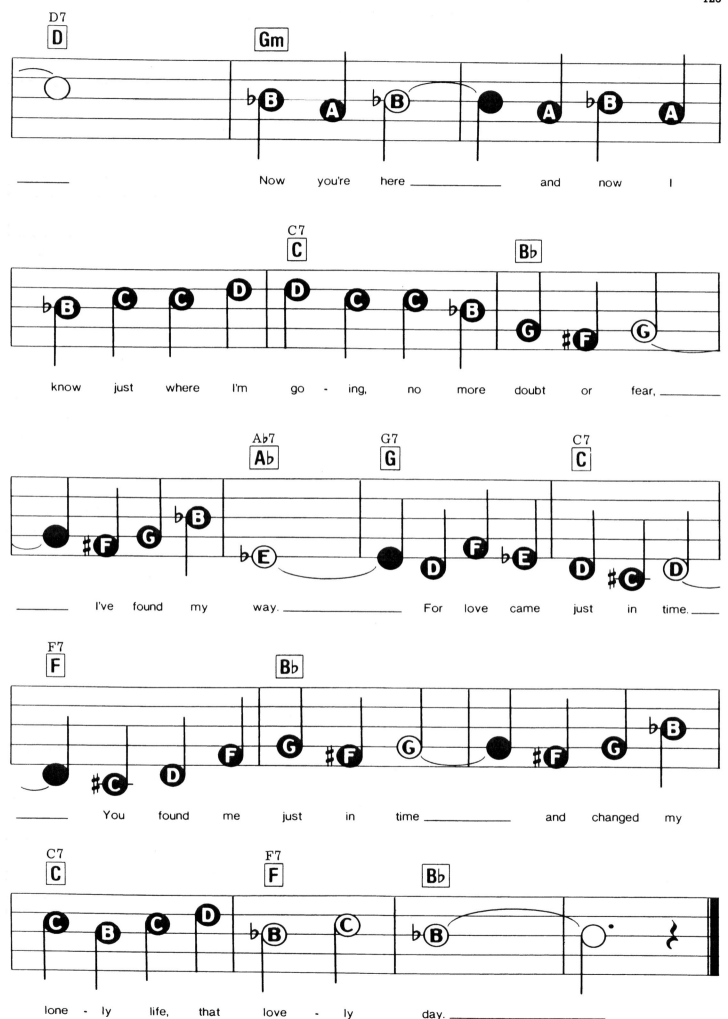

Just Walking in the Rain

Registration 7
Rhythm: Fox Trot

Words and Music by Johnny Bragg
and Robert S. Riley

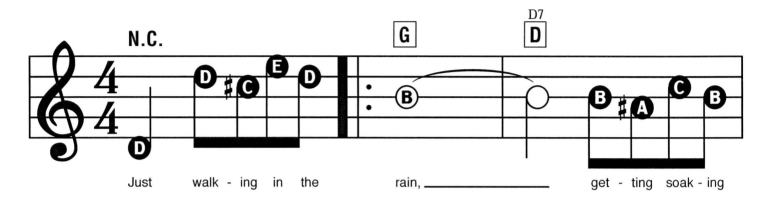

Just walk - ing in the rain, _____ get - ting soak - ing

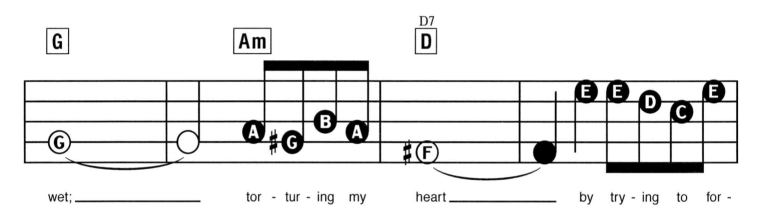

wet; _____ tor - tur - ing my heart _____ by try - ing to for -

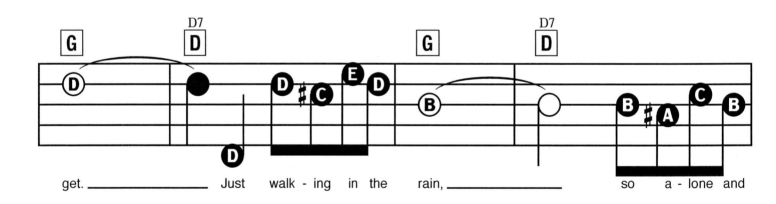

get. _____ Just walk - ing in the rain, _____ so a - lone and

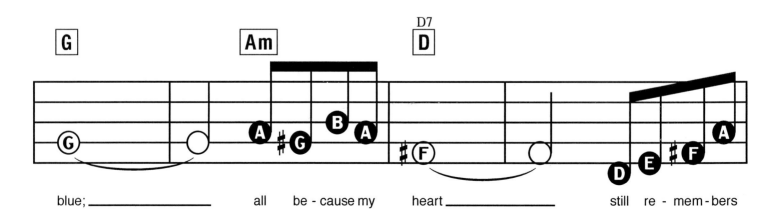

blue; _____ all be - cause my heart _____ still re - mem - bers

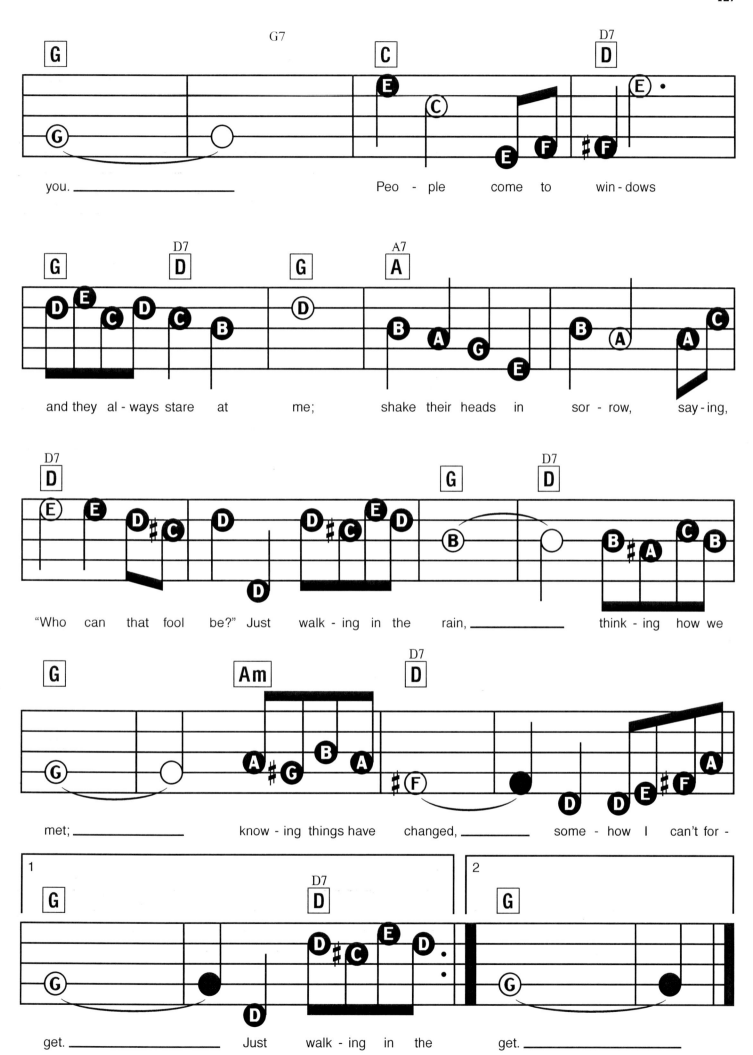

Lazy River
from THE BEST YEARS OF OUR LIVES

Registration 1
Rhythm: Fox Trot or Swing

Words and Music by Hoagy Carmichael
and Sidney Arodin

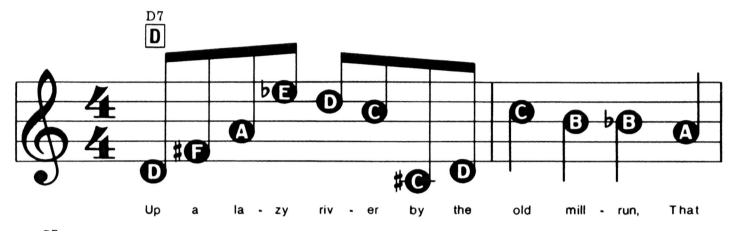

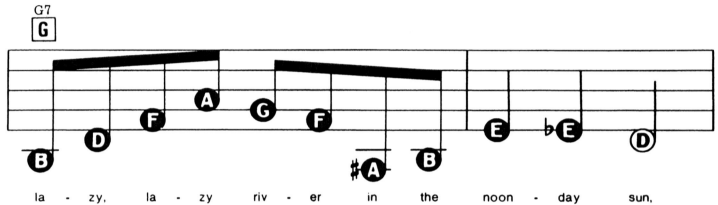

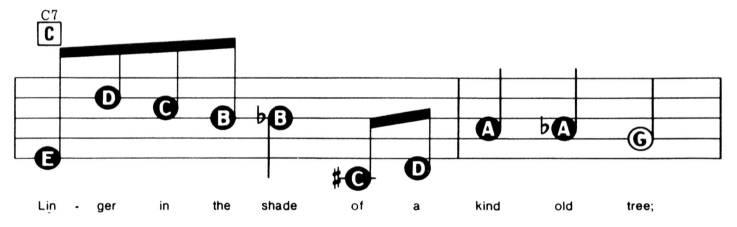

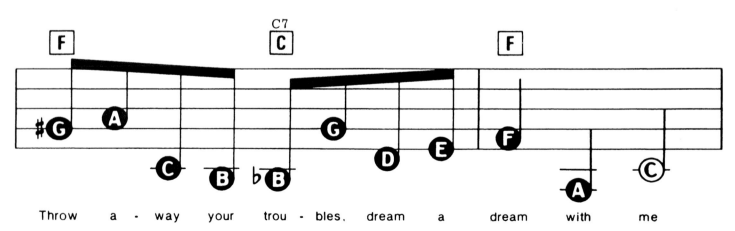

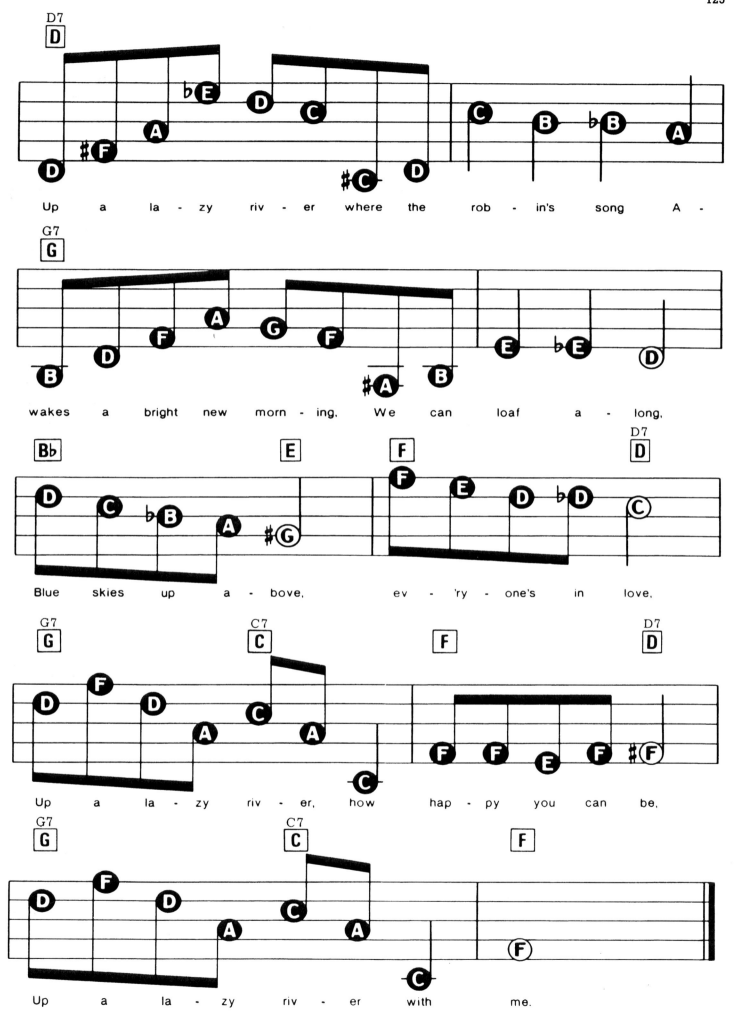

Lollipops and Roses

Registration 2
Rhythm: Waltz or Jazz Waltz

Words and Music by
Tony Velona

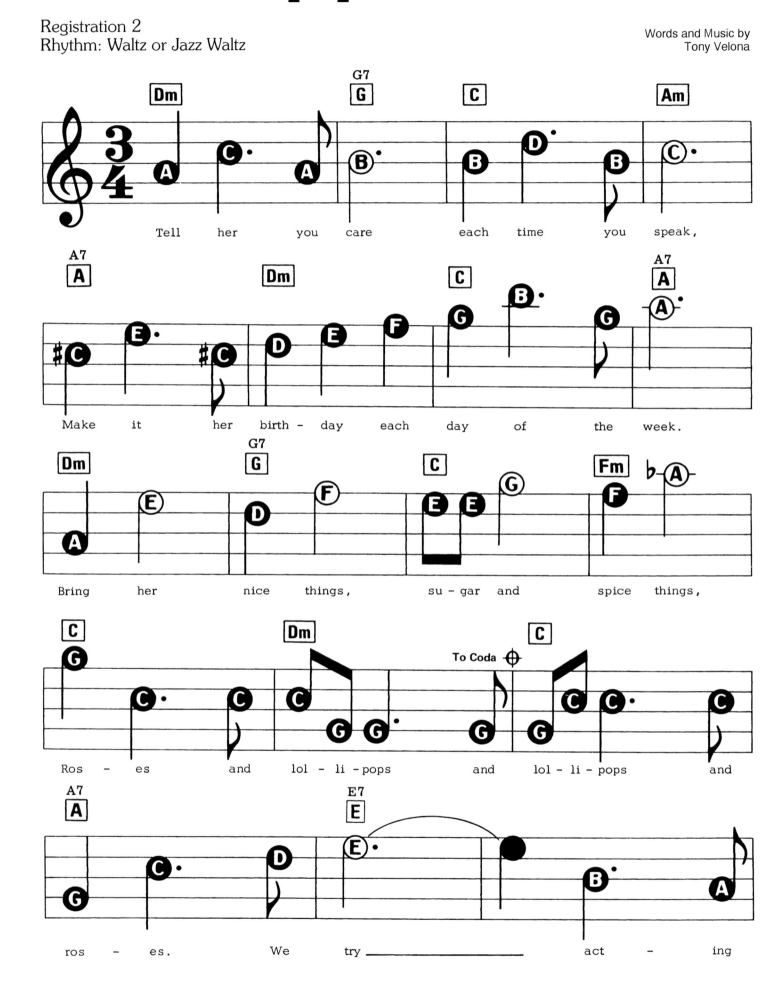

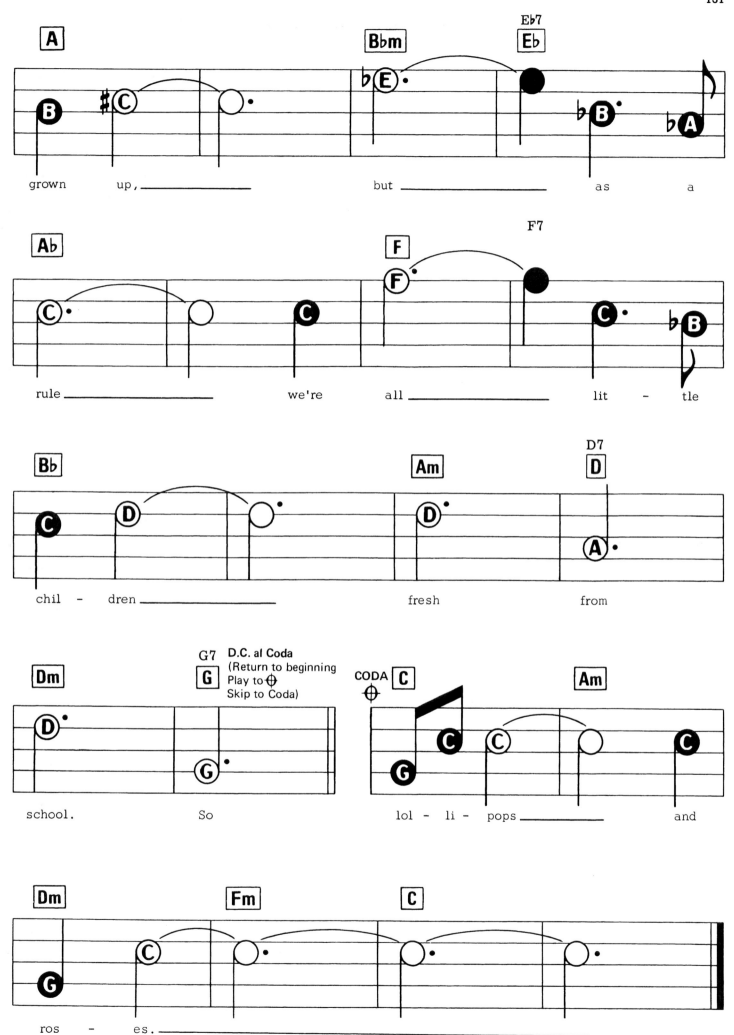

Love Letters in the Sand

Registration 1
Rhythm: Swing

Words by Nick Kenny and Charles Kenny
Music by J. Fred Coots

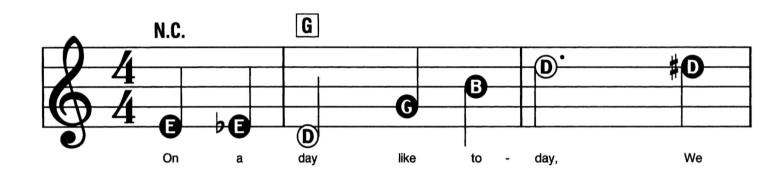

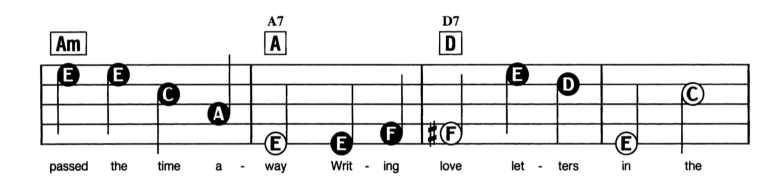

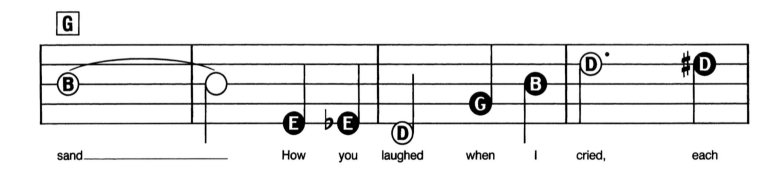

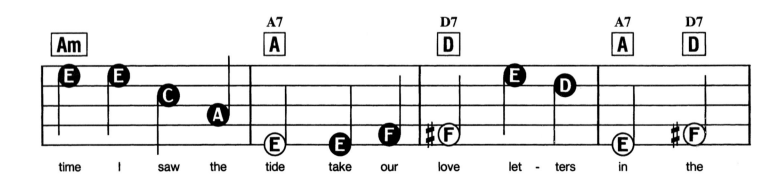

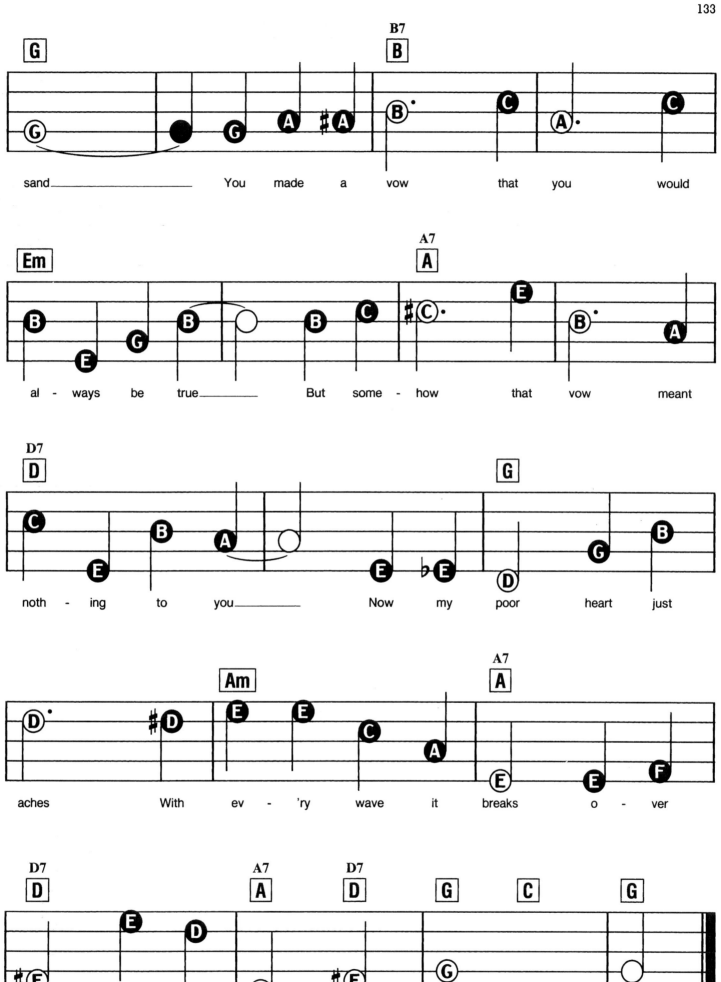

Mr. Lonely

Registration 2
Rhythm: Ballad or Fox Trot

Words and Music by Bobby Vinton
and Gene Allan

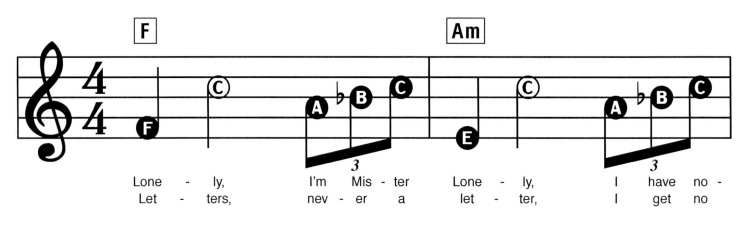

Lone - ly,   I'm Mis - ter   Lone - ly,   I have no
Let - ters,   nev - er a   let - ter,   I get no

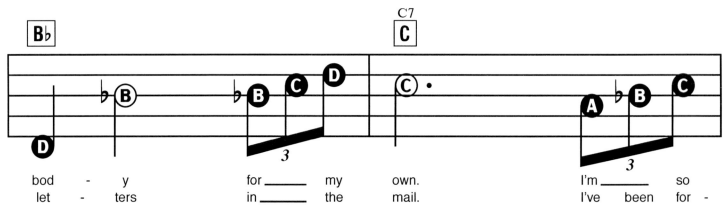

bod - y   for ____ my   own.   I'm ____ so
let - ters   in ____ the   mail.   I've been for -

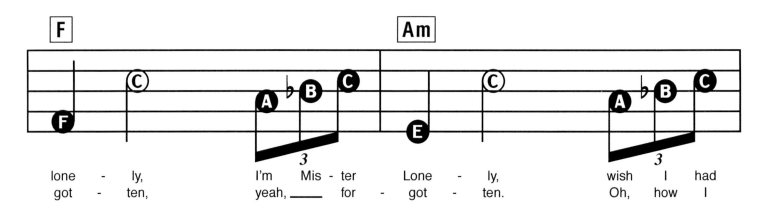

lone - ly,   I'm Mis - ter   Lone - ly,   wish I had
got - ten,   yeah, ____ for - got - ten.   Oh, how I

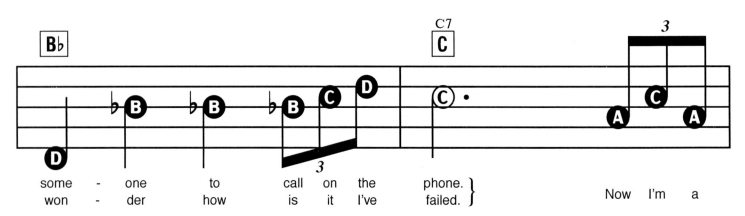

some - one   to   call   on the   phone.   Now I'm a
won - der   how   is   it I've   failed.

135

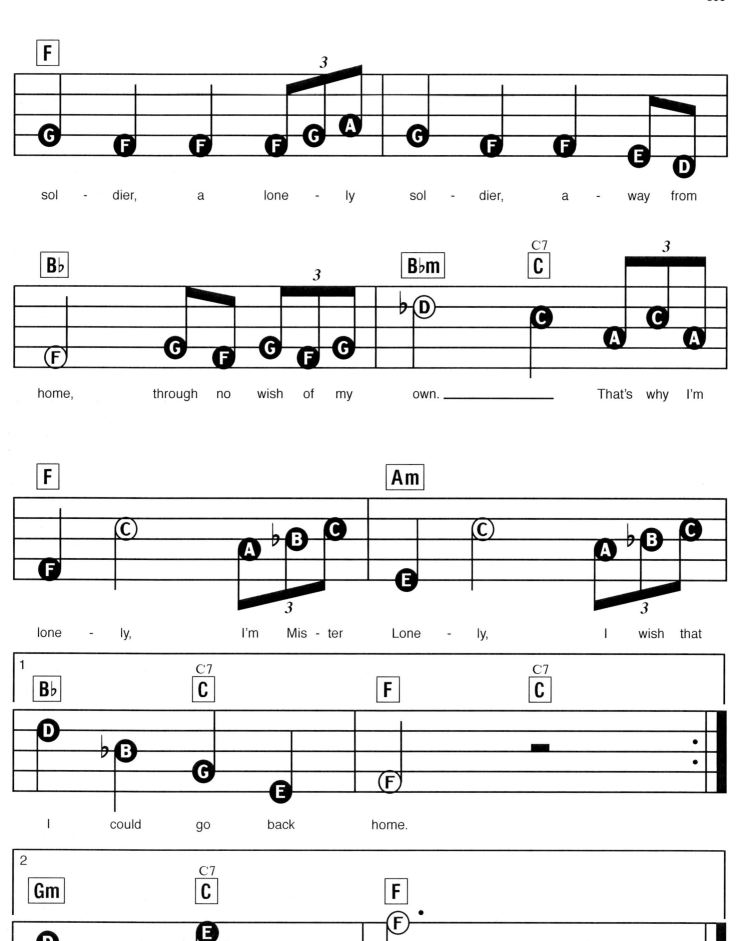

Misty

Registration 8
Rhythm: Swing or Jazz

Words by Johnny Burke
Music by Erroll Garner

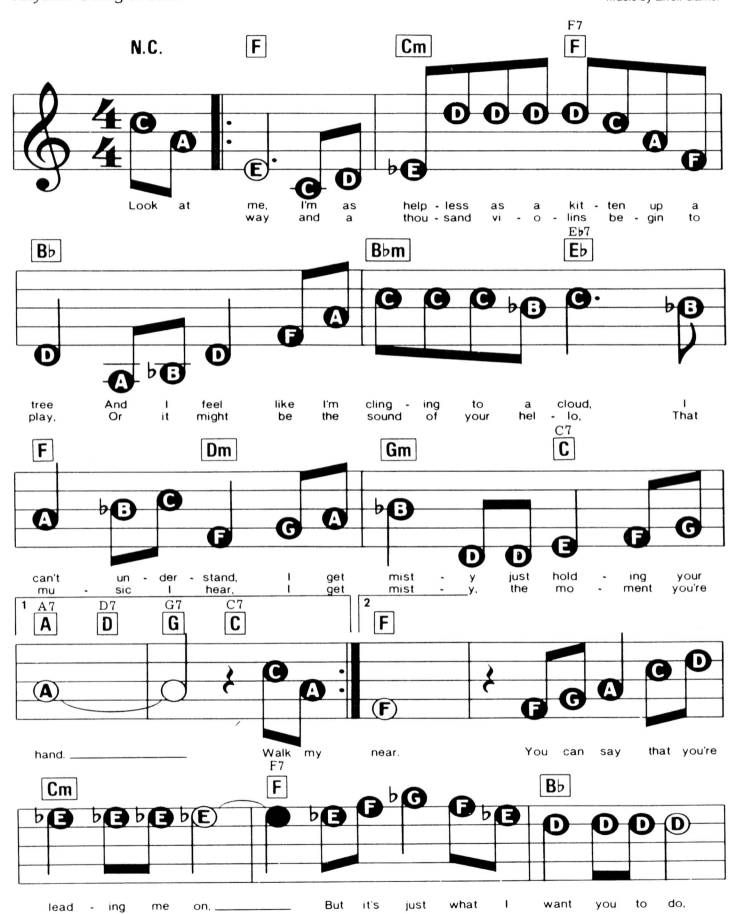

137

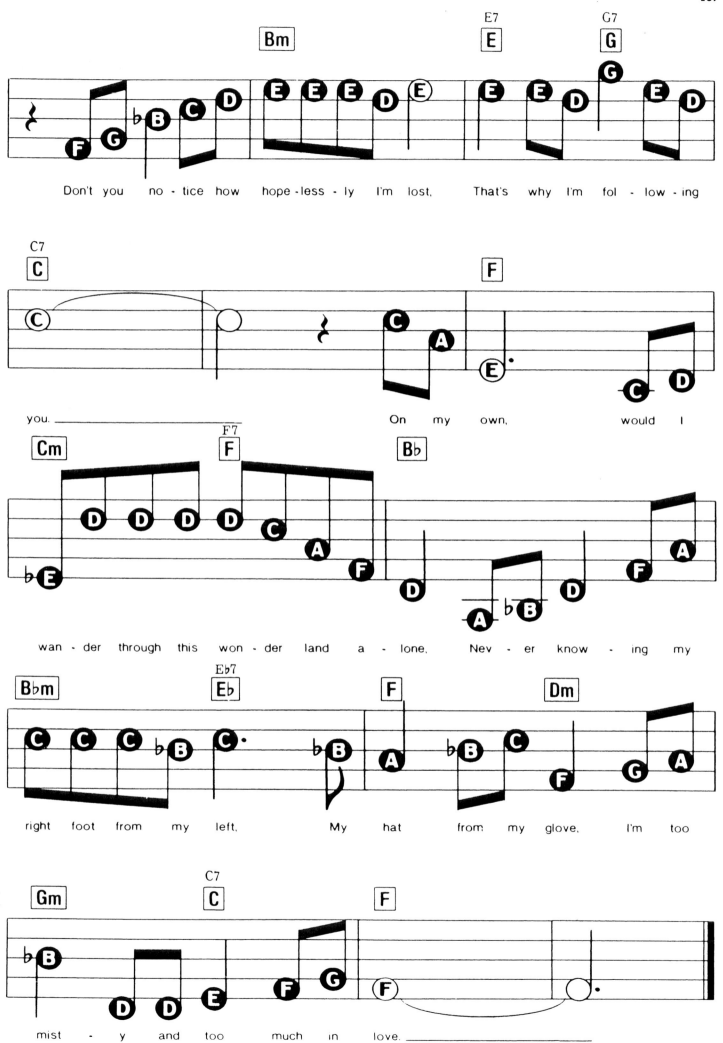

Mona Lisa
from the Paramount Picture CAPTAIN CAREY, U.S.A.

Registration 9
Rhythm: Swing or Ballad

Words and Music by Jay Livingston
and Ray Evans

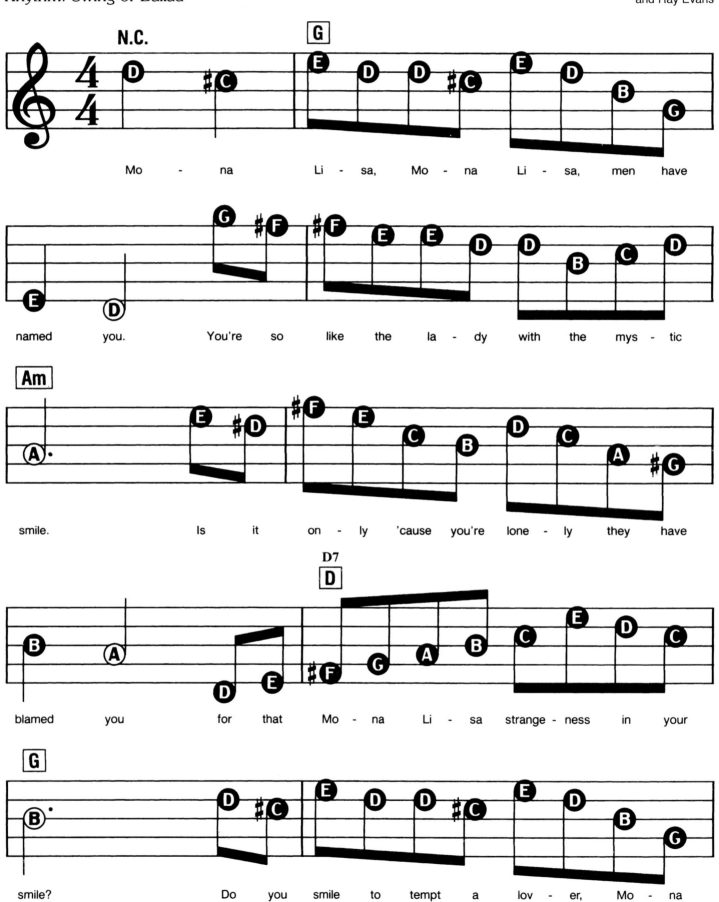

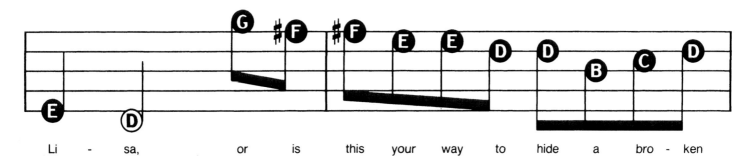

Li - sa, or is this your way to hide a bro - ken

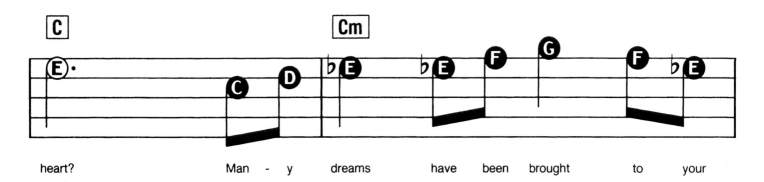

heart? Man - y dreams have been brought to your

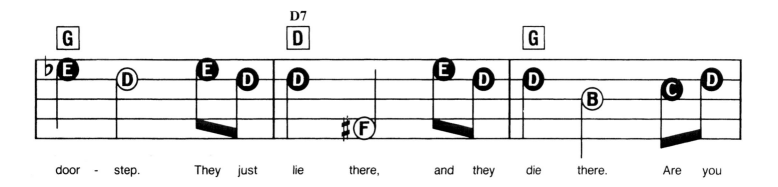

door - step. They just lie there, and they die there. Are you

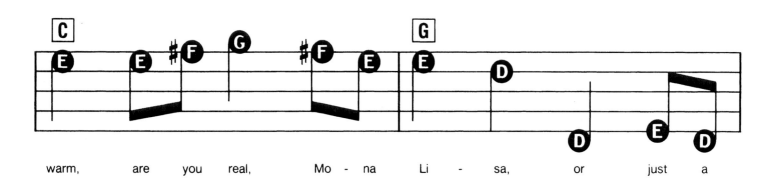

warm, are you real, Mo - na Li - sa, or just a

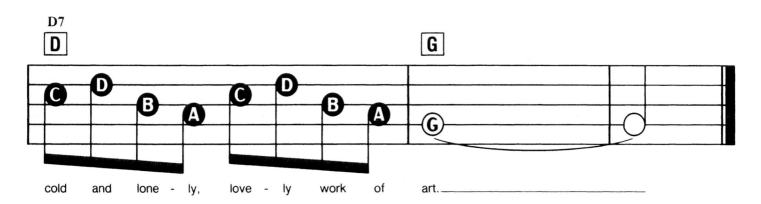

cold and lone - ly, love - ly work of art.

Moonlight Gambler

Registration 4
Rhythm: Country Swing or Fox Trot

Words by Bob Hilliard
Music by Philip Springer

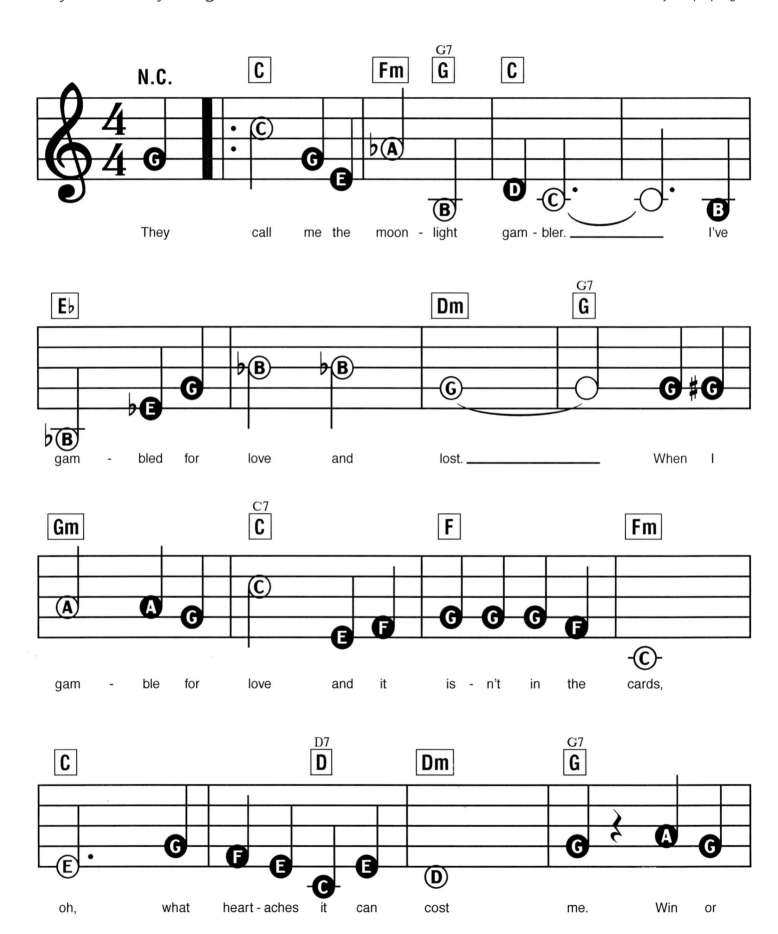

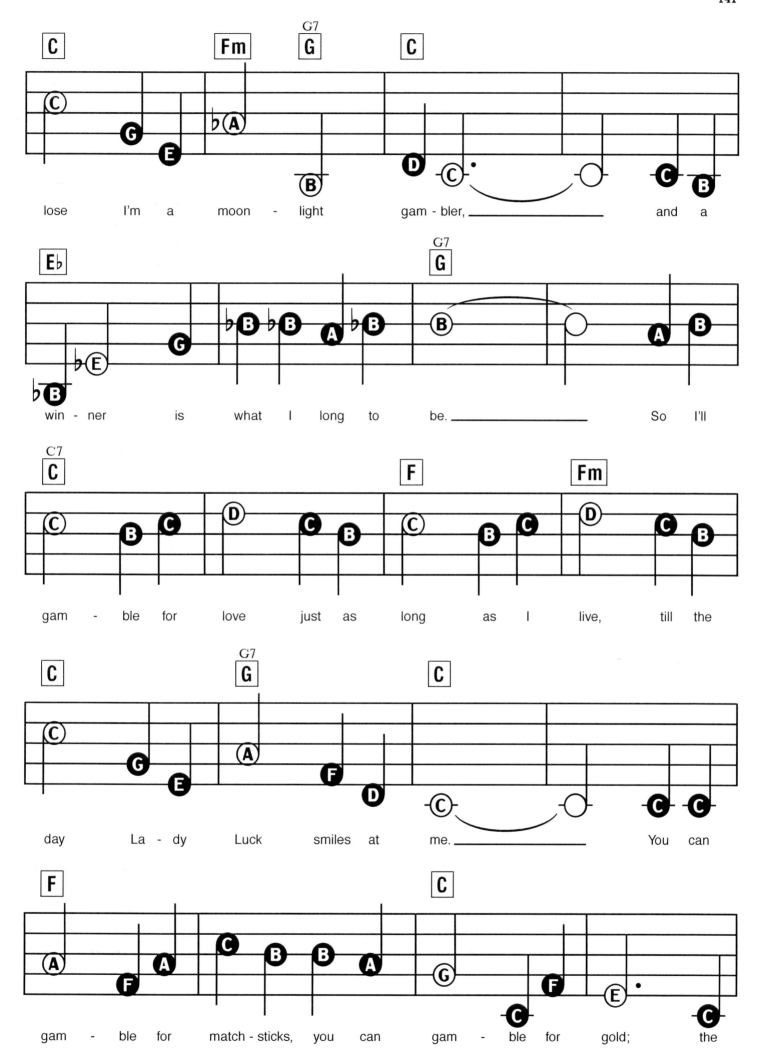

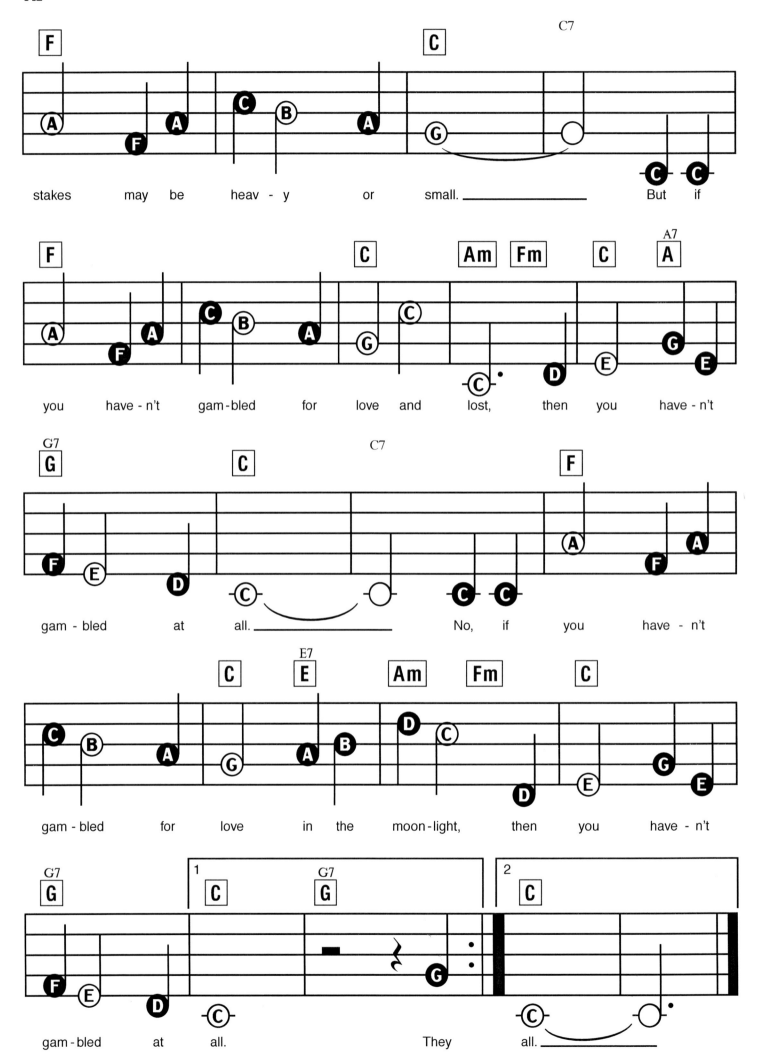

My Foolish Heart

from MY FOOLISH HEART

Registration 9
Rhythm: 8-Beat or Ballad

Words by Ned Washington
Music by Victor Young

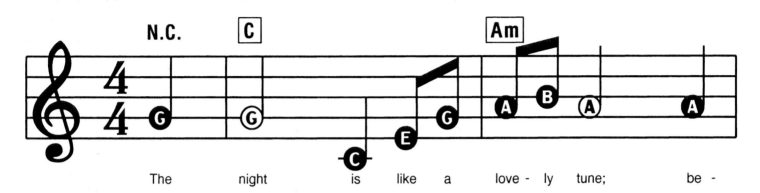

The night is like a love - ly tune; be -

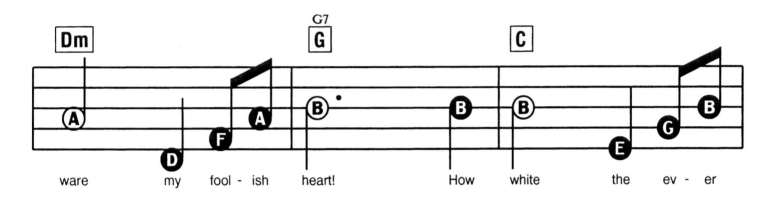

ware my fool - ish heart! How white the ev - er

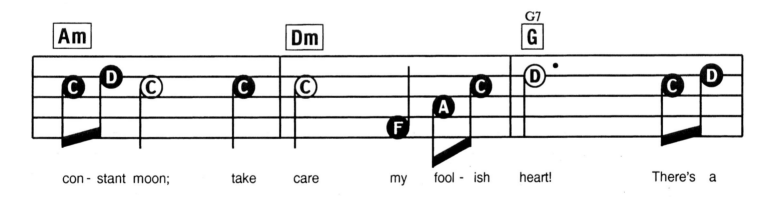

con - stant moon; take care my fool - ish heart! There's a

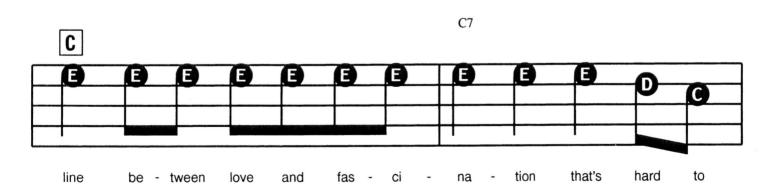

line be - tween love and fas - ci - na - tion that's hard to

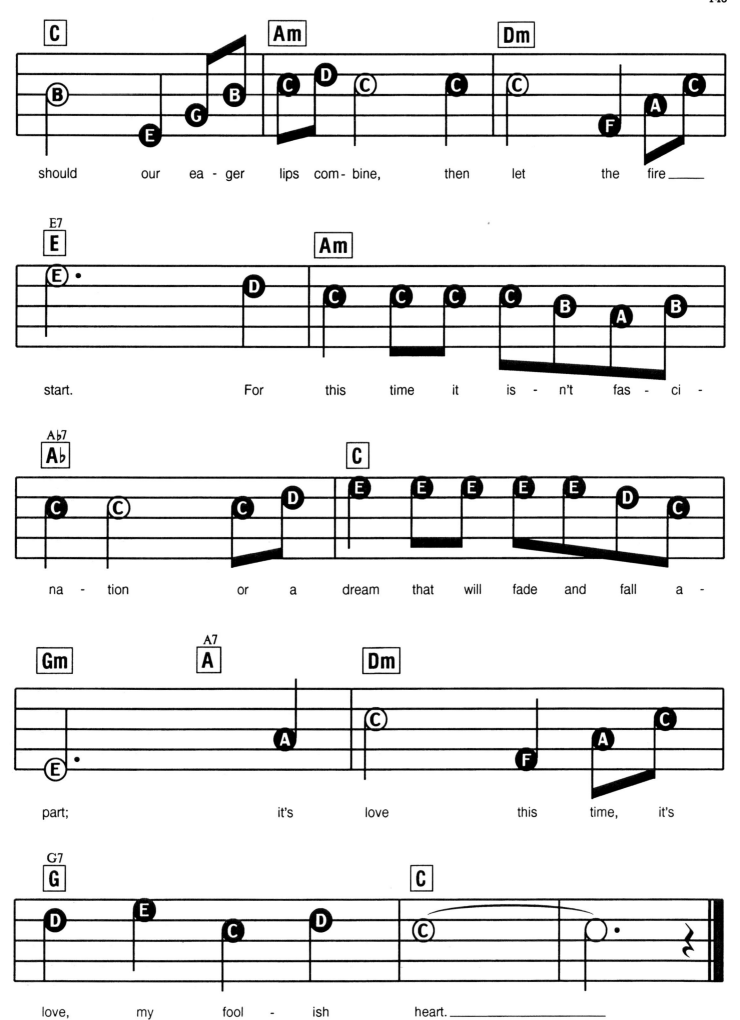

My Kind of Girl

Registration 9
Rhythm: Swing

Words and Music by
Leslie Bricusse

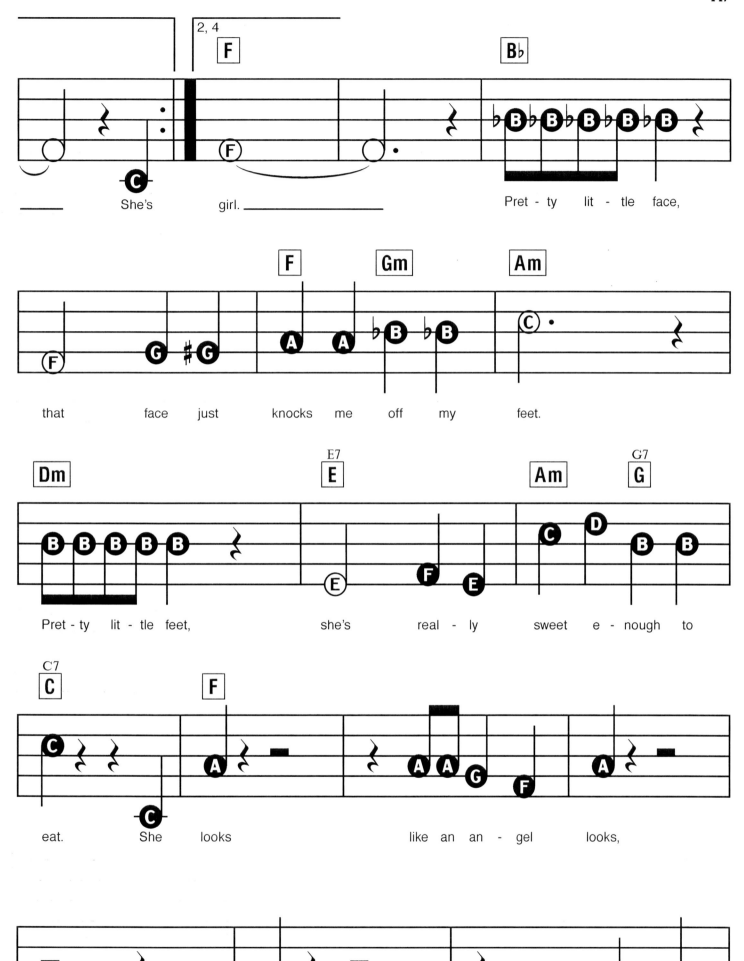

148

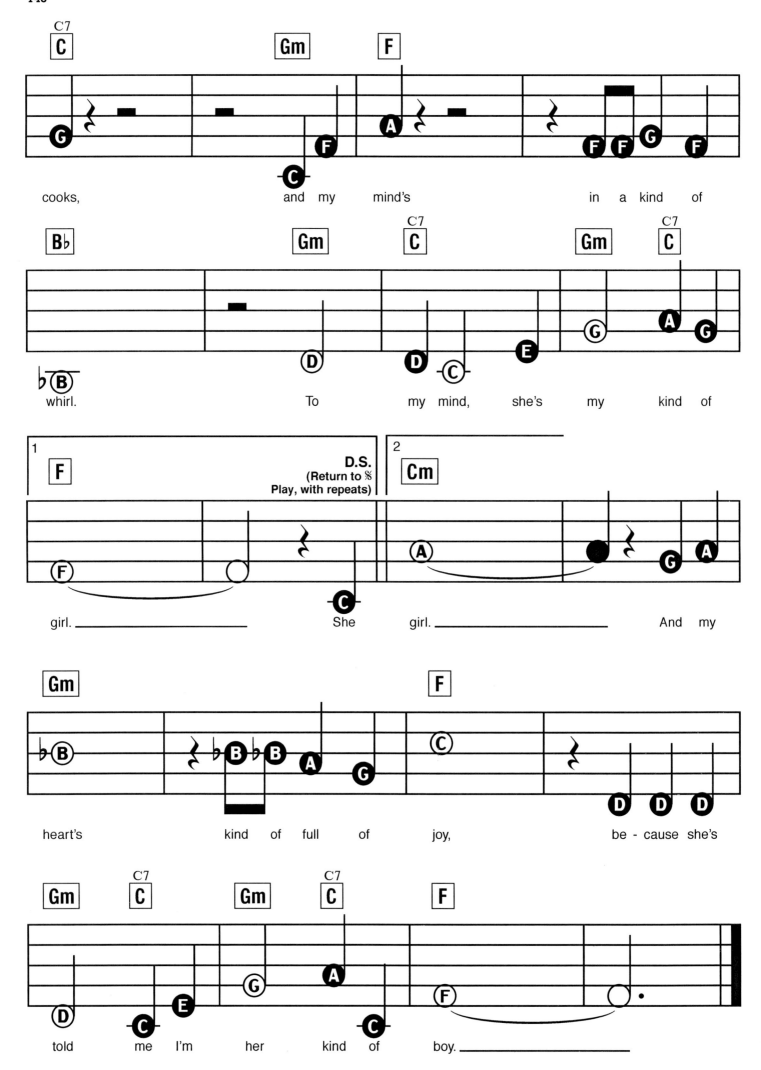

Nature Boy

Registration 3
Rhythm: Waltz

Words and Music by
Eden Ahbez

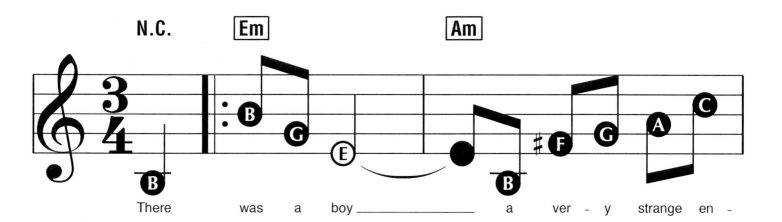

There was a boy _____ a ver - y strange en -

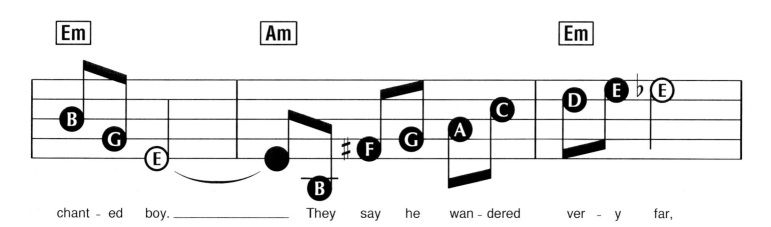

chant - ed boy. _____ They say he wan - dered ver - y far,

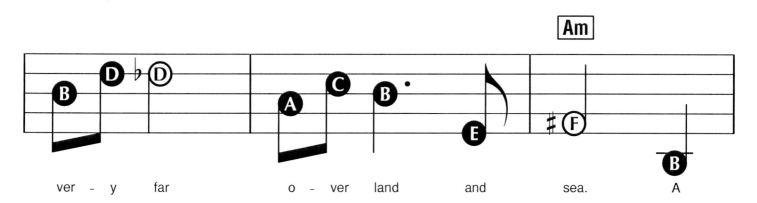

ver - y far o - ver land and sea. A

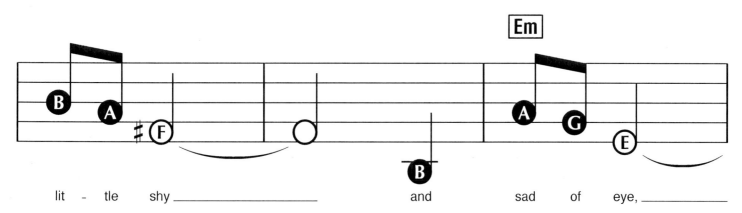

lit - tle shy _____ and sad of eye, _____

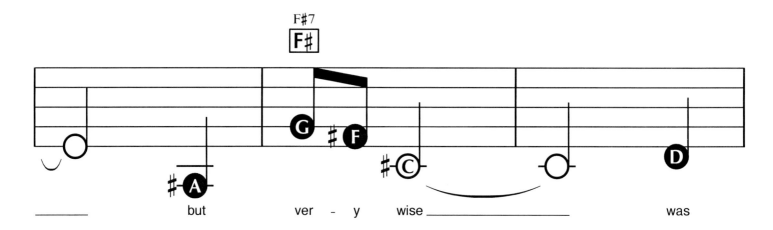

but ver - y wise _____ was

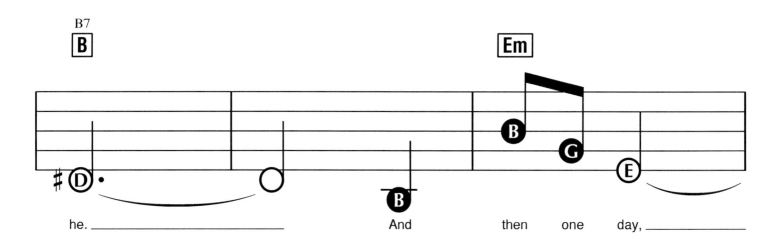

he. _____ And then one day, _____

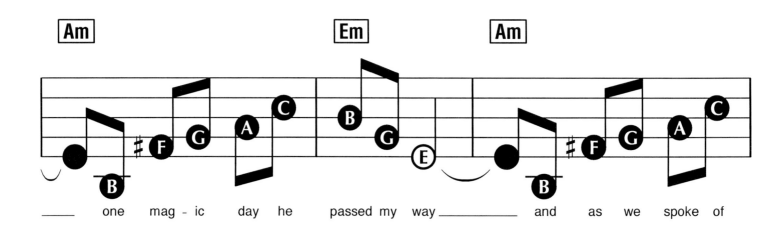

____ one mag - ic day he passed my way _____ and as we spoke of

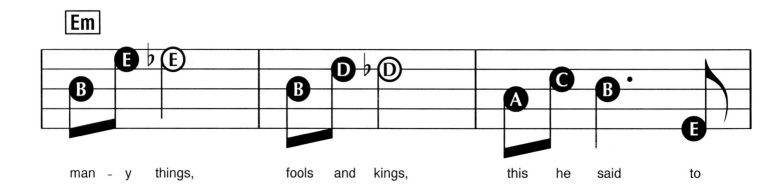

man - y things, fools and kings, this he said to

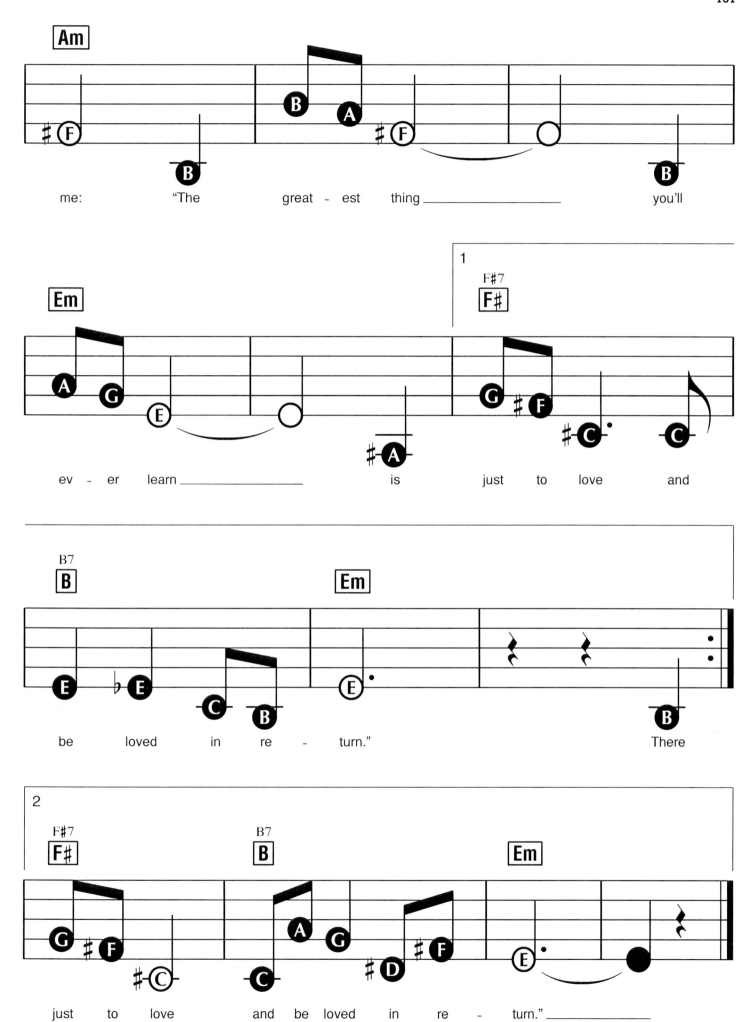

My One and Only Love

Registration 2
Rhythm: Ballad or Fox Trot

Words by Robert Mellin
Music by Guy Wood

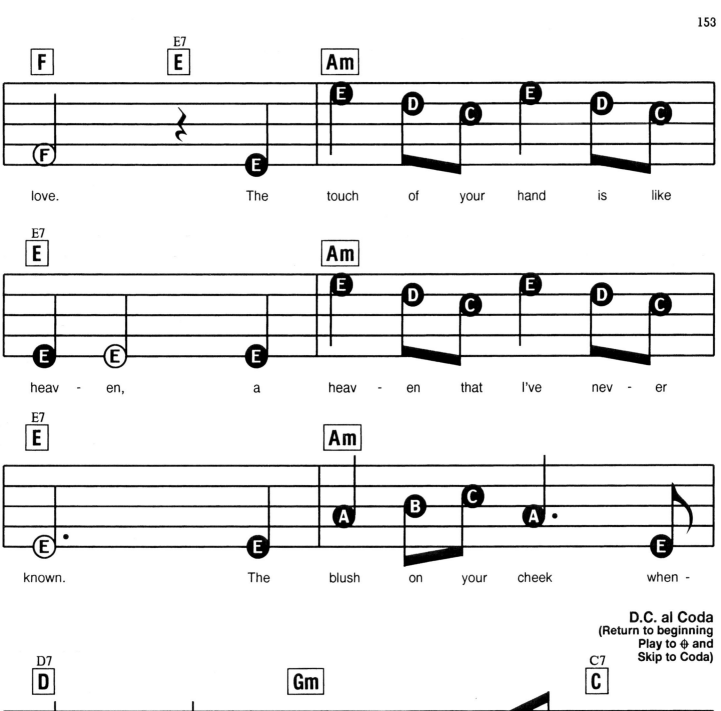

love. The touch of your hand is like

heav - en, a heav - en that I've nev - er

known. The blush on your cheek when -

D.C. al Coda
(Return to beginning
Play to ⊕ and
Skip to Coda)

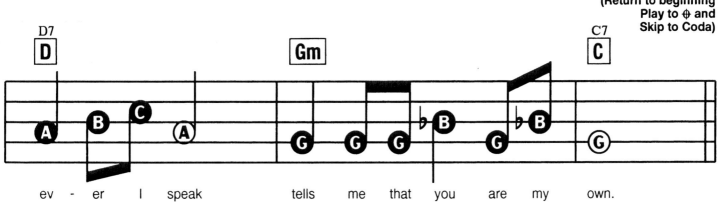

ev - er I speak tells me that you are my own.

CODA
⊕

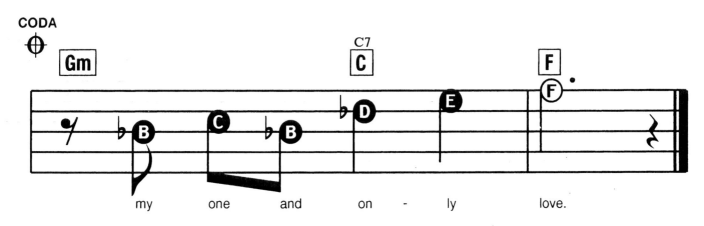

my one and on - ly love.

The Nearness of You
from the Paramount Picture ROMANCE IN THE DARK

Registration 9
Rhythm: Ballad or Fox Trot

Words by Ned Washington
Music by Hoagy Carmichael

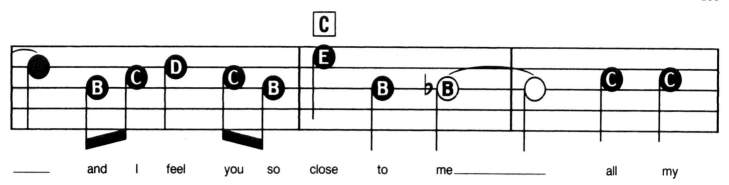

_____ and I feel you so close to me_____ all my

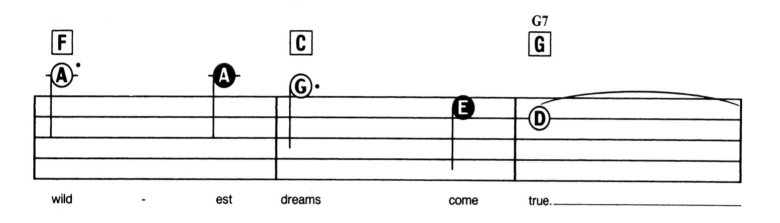

wild - est dreams come true._____

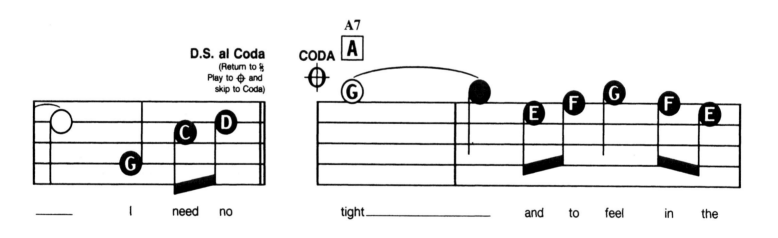

D.S. al Coda
(Return to %
Play to ⊕ and
skip to Coda)

CODA

_____ I need no   tight_____ and to feel in the

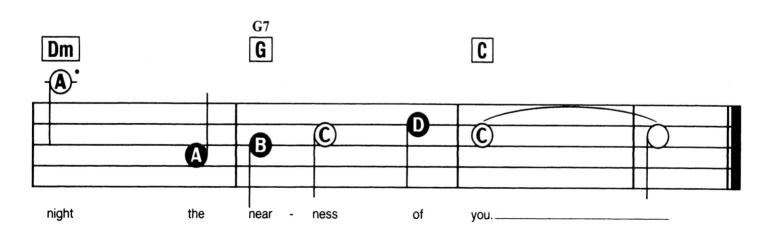

night the near - ness of you._____

Night Song
from GOLDEN BOY

Registration 7
Rhythm: Ballad or Fox Trot

Lyric by Lee Adams
Music by Charles Strouse

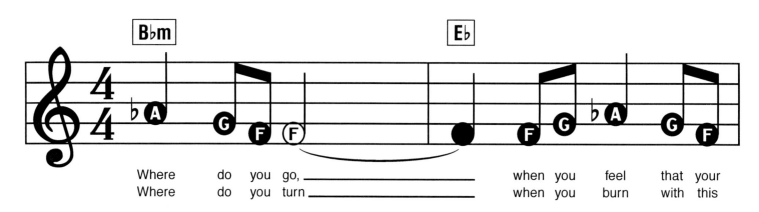

Where do you go, _____ when you feel that your
Where do you turn _____ when you burn with this

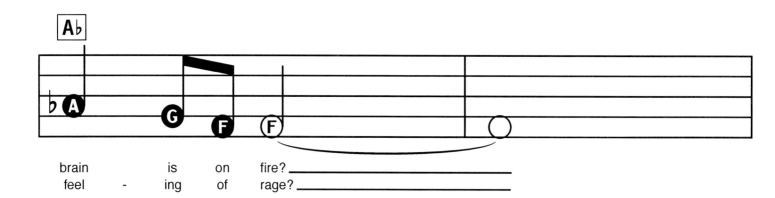

brain is on fire? _____
feel - ing of rage? _____

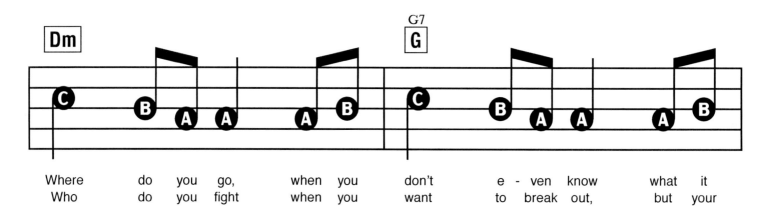

Where do you go, when you don't e - ven know what it
Who do you fight when you don't want to break out, but your

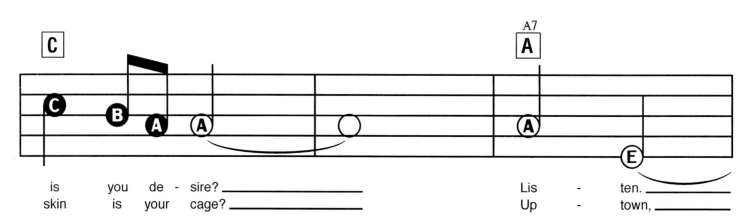

is you de - sire? _____ Lis - ten. _____
skin is your cage? _____ Up - town, _____

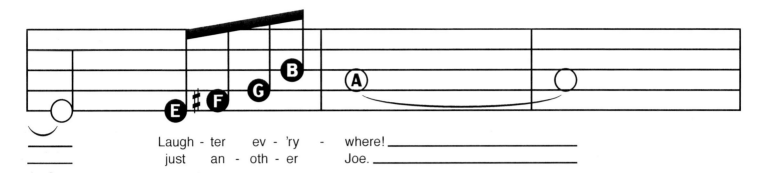

Laugh - ter ev - 'ry - where! _____
just an - oth - er Joe. _____

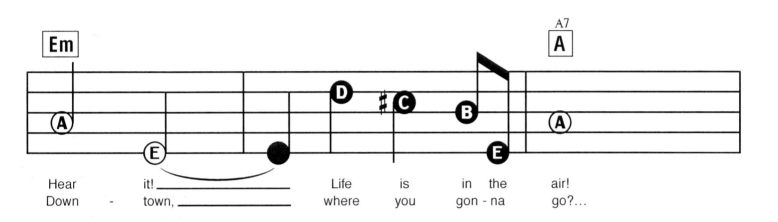

Em   A7
                          A

Hear   it! _____ Life   is   in the   air!
Down - town, _____ where you gon - na go?…

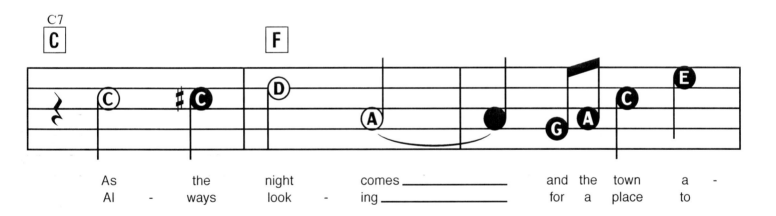

C7
C   **F**

As   the   night comes _____ and the town a -
Al - ways look - ing _____ for a   place to

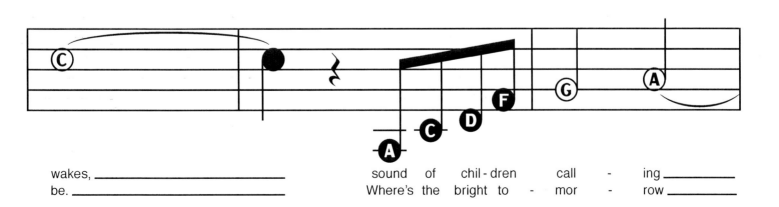

wakes, _____   sound of chil - dren call - ing _____
be. _____   Where's the bright to - mor - row _____

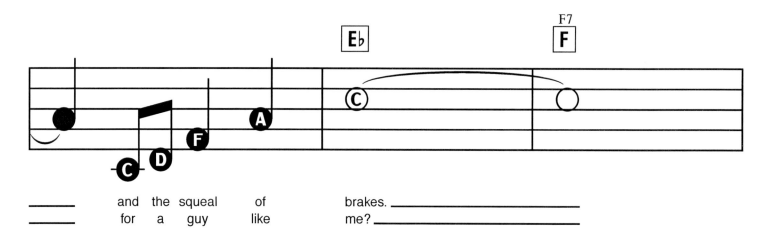

and the squeal of brakes. _____
for a guy like me? _____

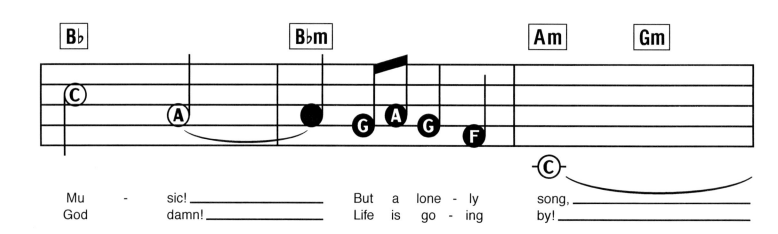

Mu - sic! _____ But a lone - ly song, _____
God damn! _____ Life is go - ing by! _____

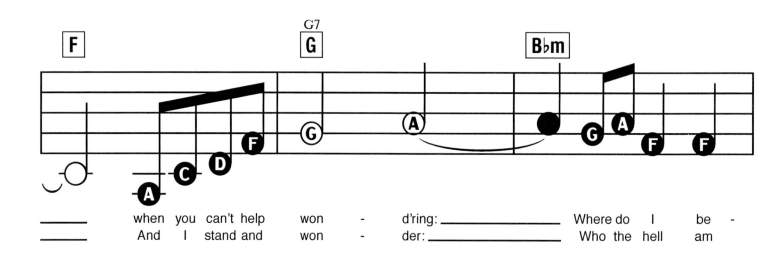

_____ when you can't help won - d'ring: _____ Where do I be -
_____ And I stand and won - der: _____ Who the hell am

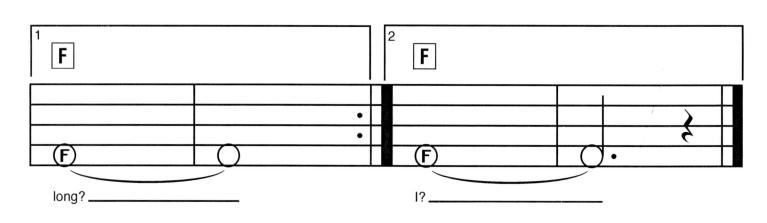

long? _____   I? _____

Oh! My Pa-Pa
(O Mein Papa)

Registration 7
Rhythm: Swing

English Words by John Turner and Geoffrey Parsons
Music and Original Lyric by Paul Burkhard

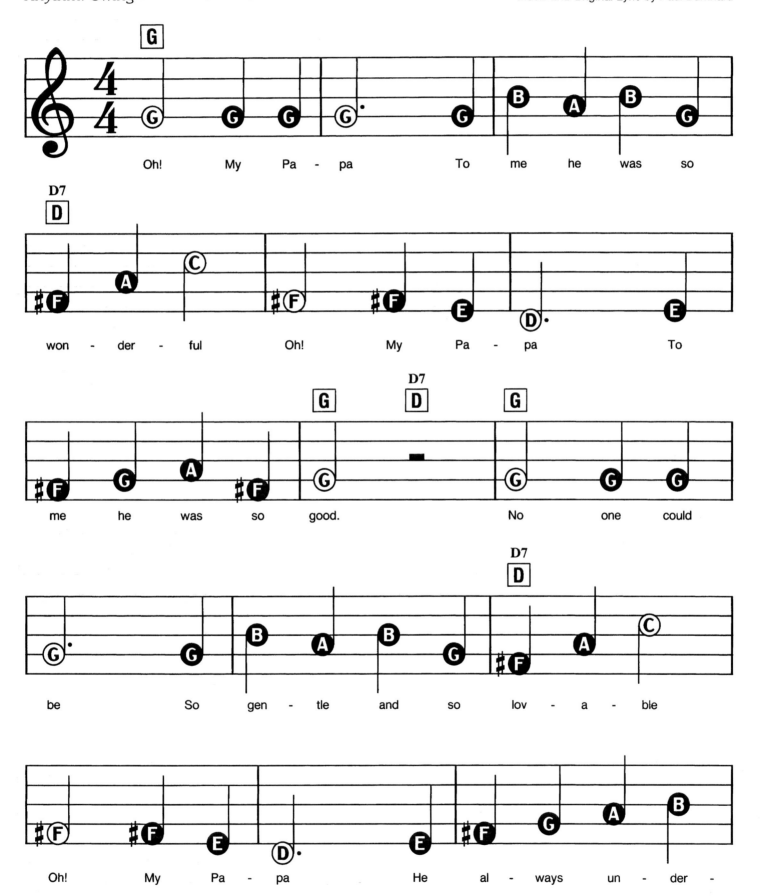

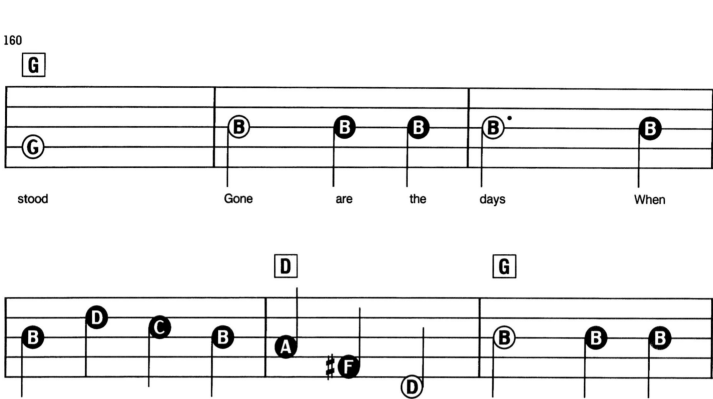

stood   Gone   are   the   days   When

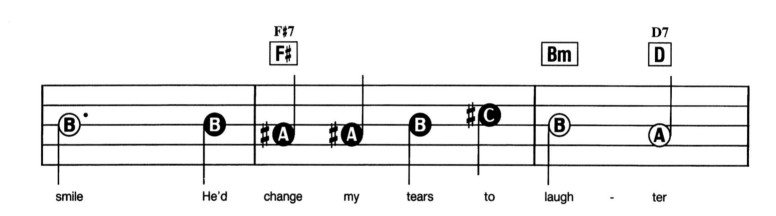

he   would   take   me   on   his   knee   And   with   a

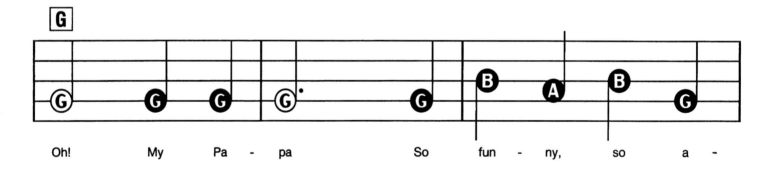

smile   He'd   change   my   tears   to   laugh - ter

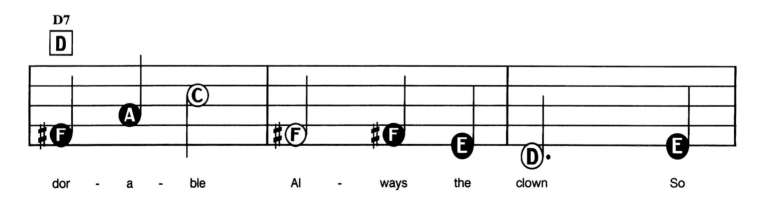

Oh!   My   Pa - pa   So   fun - ny,   so   a -

dor - a - ble   Al - ways   the   clown   So

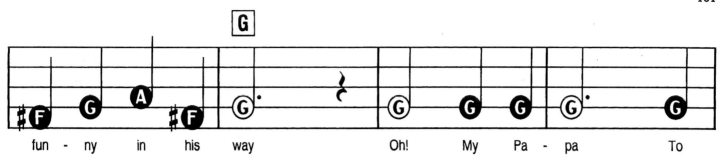

fun - ny in his way Oh! My Pa - pa To

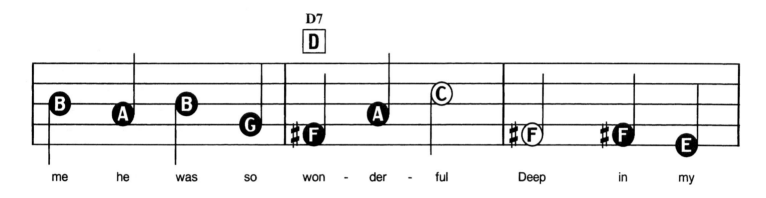

me he was so won - der - ful Deep in my

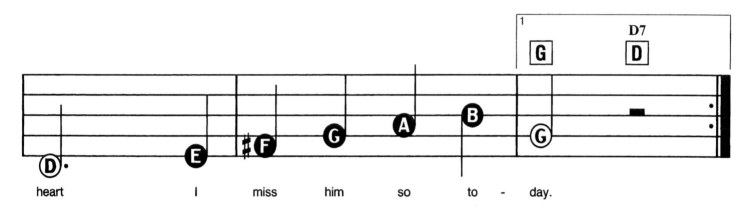

heart I miss him so to - day.

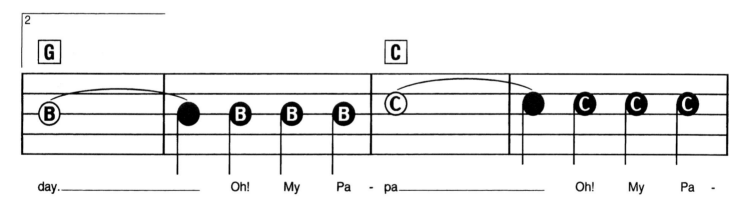

day._____ Oh! My Pa - pa_____ Oh! My Pa -

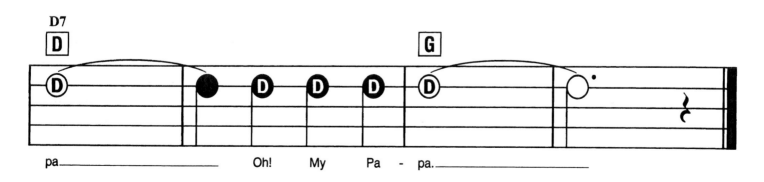

pa_____ Oh! My Pa - pa._____

Oh! What It Seemed to Be

Registration 1
Rhythm: Fox Trot

Words and Music by Bennie Benjamin,
George David Weiss and Frankie Carle

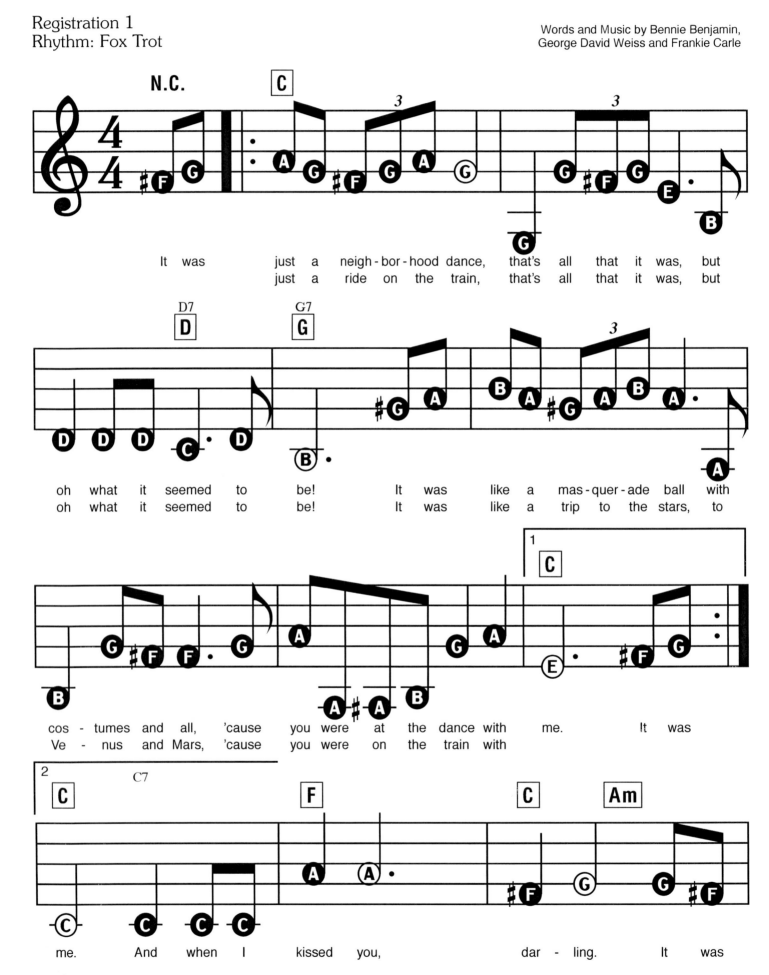

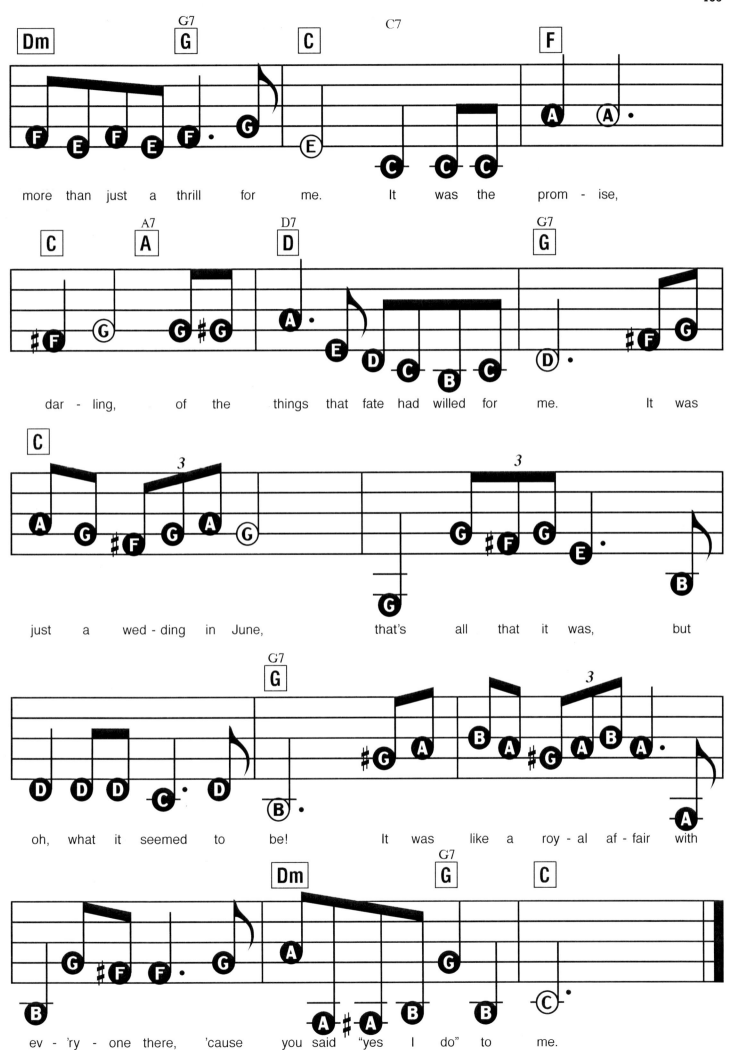

Ole Buttermilk Sky
from the Motion Picture CANYON PASSAGE

Registration 3
Rhythm: Swing or Fox Trot

Words and Music by Hoagy Carmichael
and Jack Brooks

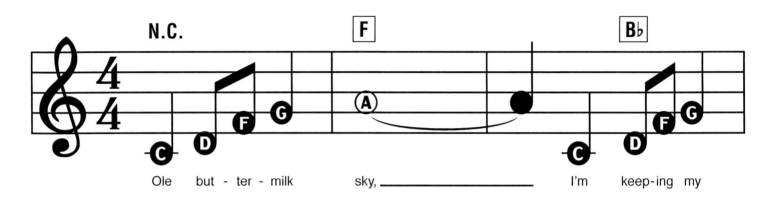

Ole but-ter-milk sky, _____ I'm keep-ing my

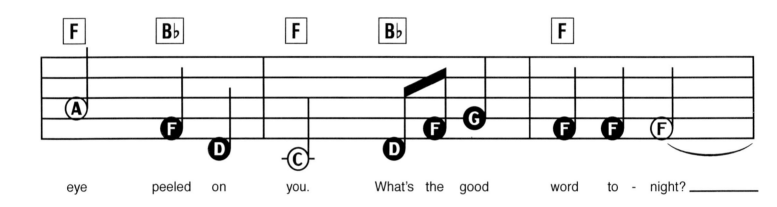

eye peeled on you. What's the good word to-night? _____

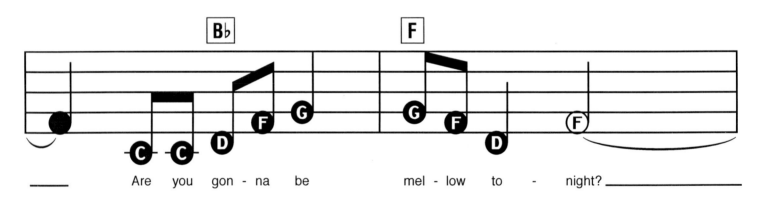

_____ Are you gon-na be mel-low to-night? _____

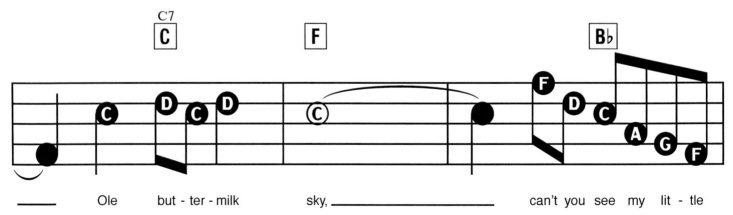

_____ Ole but-ter-milk sky, _____ can't you see my lit-tle

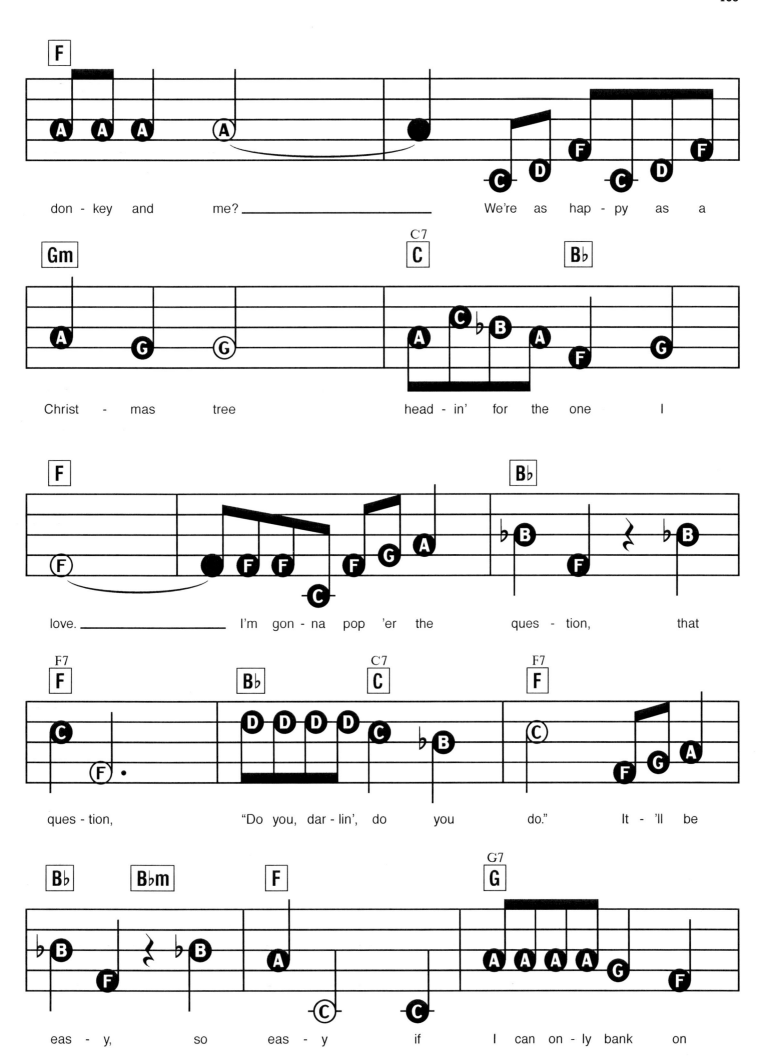

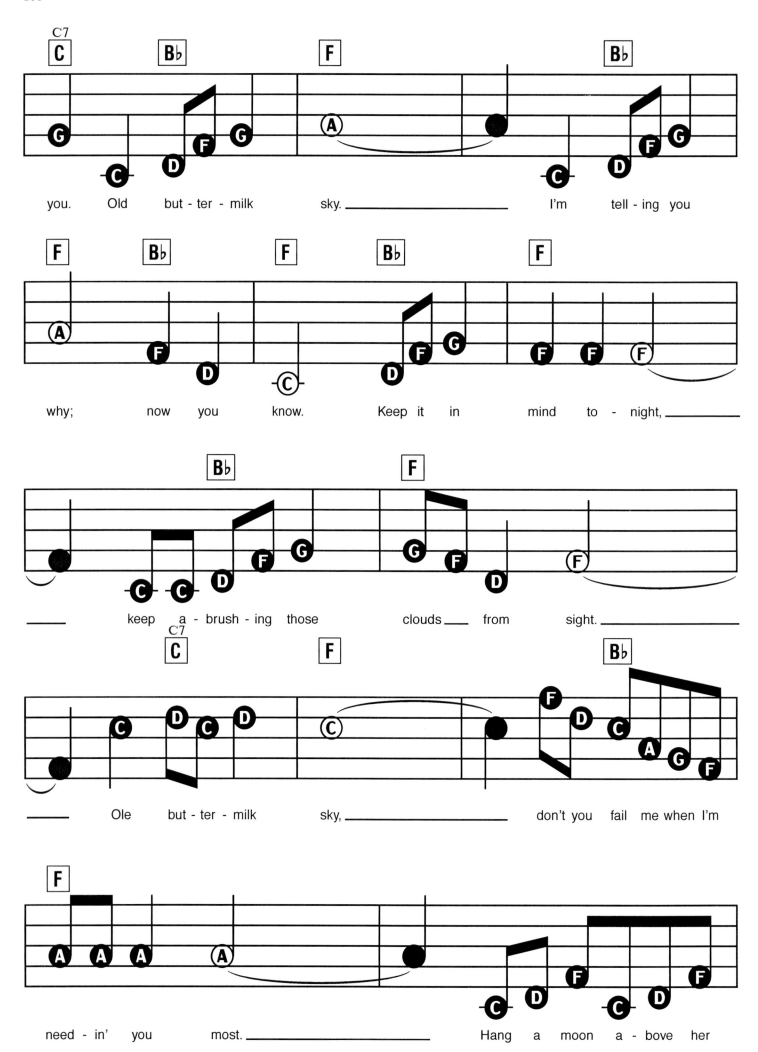

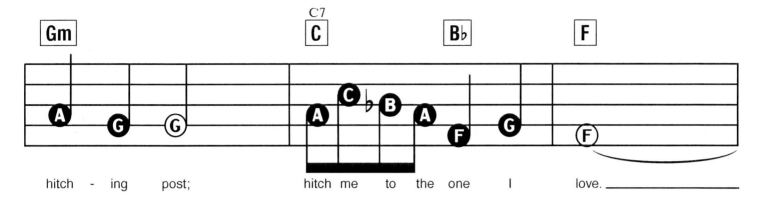

hitch - ing post; hitch me to the one I love. _____

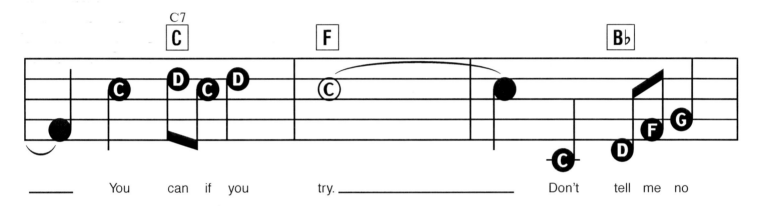

_____ You can if you try. _____ Don't tell me no

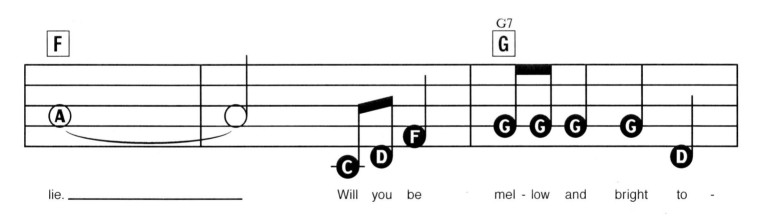

lie. _____ Will you be mel - low and bright to -

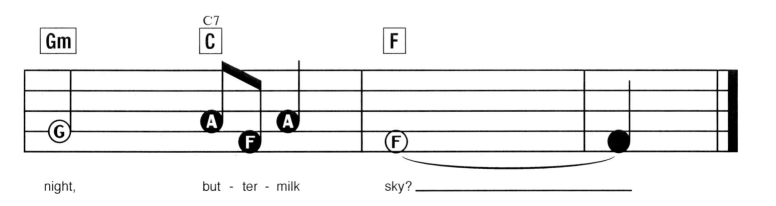

night, but - ter - milk sky? _____

On the Street Where You Live
from MY FAIR LADY

Registration 4
Rhythm: Beguine

Words by Alan Jay Lerner
Music by Frederick Loewe

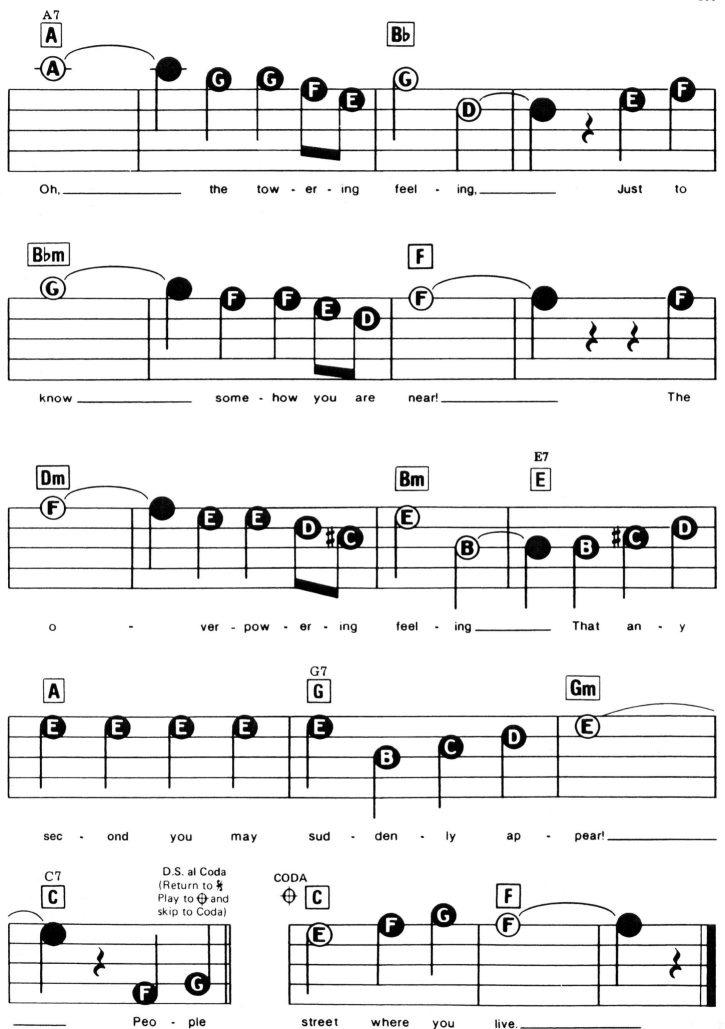

Pistol Packin' Mama

Registration 9
Rhythm: Polka, Country or Fox Trot

Words and Music by
Al Dexter

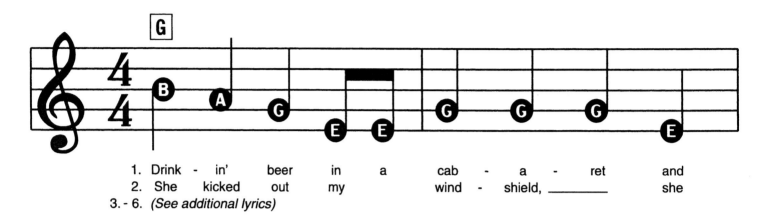

1. Drink - in' beer in a cab - a - ret and
2. She kicked out my wind - shield, _____ she
3. - 6. *(See additional lyrics)*

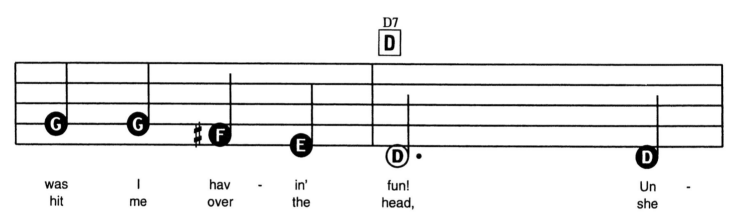

was   I   hav - in'   fun!   Un -
hit   me   over   the   head,   she

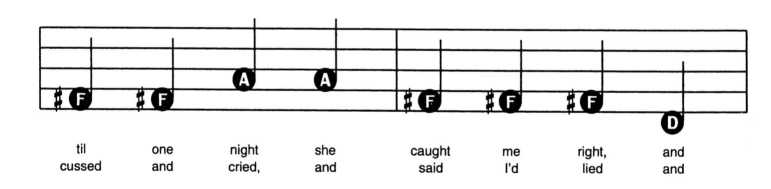

til   one   night   she   caught   me   right,   and
cussed   and   cried,   she   said   I'd   lied   and   and

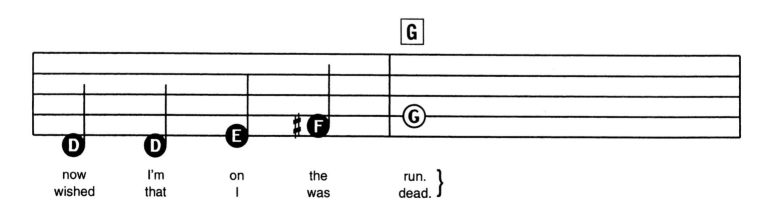

now   I'm   on   the   run.
wished   that   I   was   dead.

Chorus

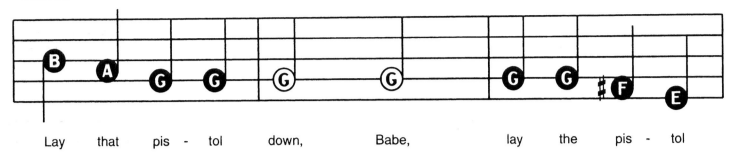

Lay that pis - tol down, Babe, lay the pis - tol

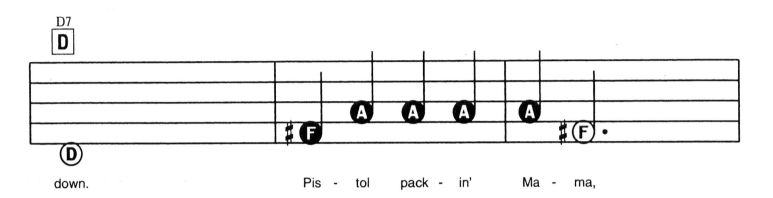

down. Pis - tol pack - in' Ma - ma,

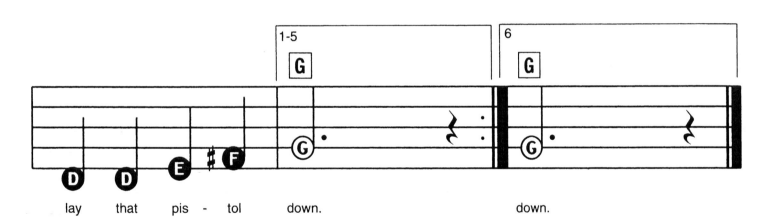

lay that pis - tol down. down.

Additional Lyrics

3. Drinkin' beer in a cabaret, and dancing with a blonde,
   Until one night she shot out the light. Bang! That blonde was gone.
   Chorus

4. See you ev'ry night, Babe, I'll woo you ev'ry day,
   I'll be your regular Daddy, if you'll put that gun away.
   Chorus

5. Drinkin' beer in a cabaret, and was I havin' fun!
   Until one night she caught me right, and now I'm on the run.
   Chorus

6. There was old Al Dexter, he always had his fun.
   But with some lead, she shot him dead; his honkin' days are done.
   Chorus

A Rainy Night in Georgia

Registration 5
Rhythm: Ballad or Fox Trot

Words and Music by
Tony Joe White

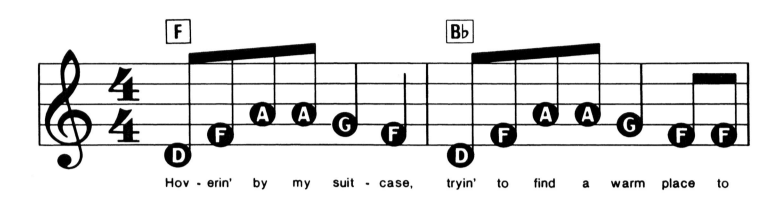

Hov - erin' by my suit - case, tryin' to find a warm place to

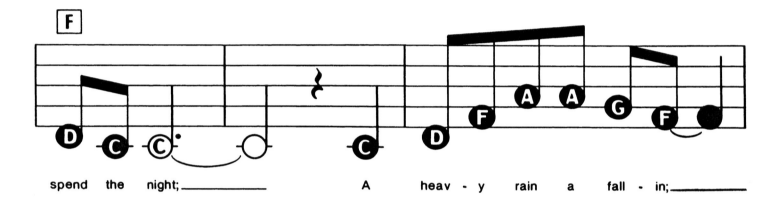

spend the night;_____ A heav - y rain a fall - in;_____

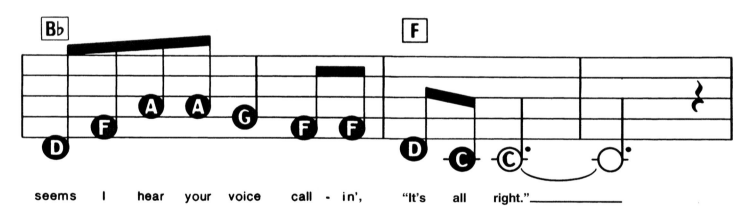

seems I hear your voice call - in', "It's all right."_____

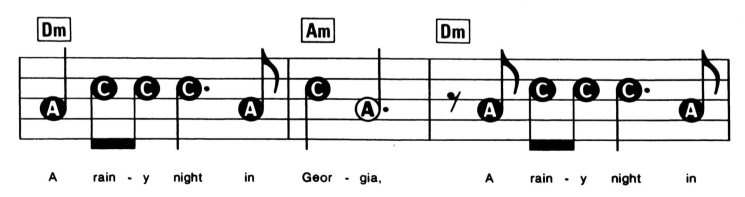

A rain - y night in Geor - gia, A rain - y night in

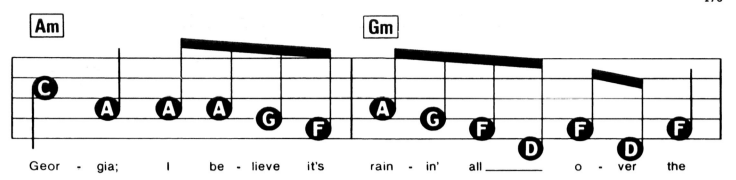

Geor - gia; I be - lieve it's rain - in' all _____ o - ver the

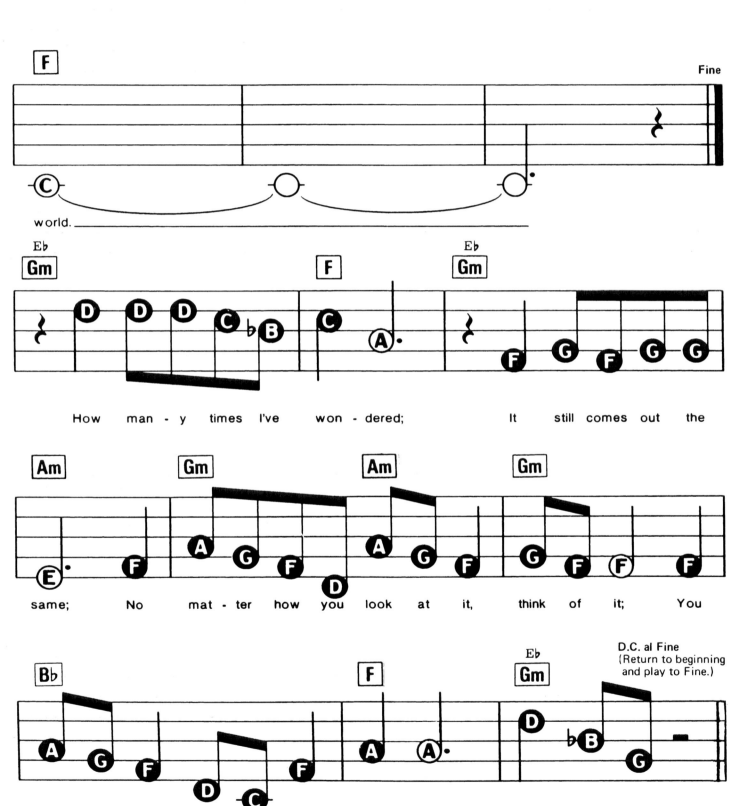

world. _____

How man - y times I've won - dered; It still comes out the

same; No mat - ter how you look at it, think of it; You

just got to do _____ your own thing. _____

Red Roses for a Blue Lady

Registration 1
Rhythm: Fox Trot

Words and Music by Sid Tepper
and Roy C. Bennett

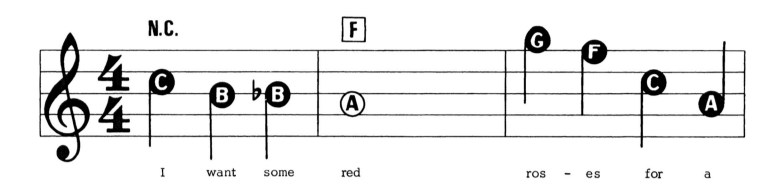

I want some red ros - es for a

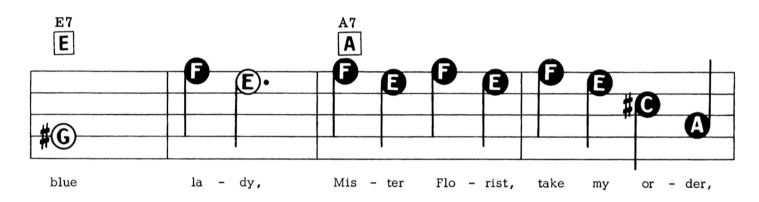

blue la - dy, Mis - ter Flo - rist, take my or - der,

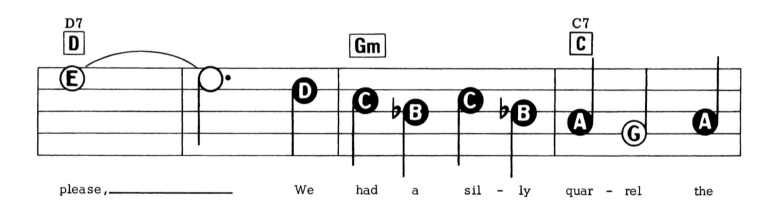

please,_____ We had a sil - ly quar - rel the

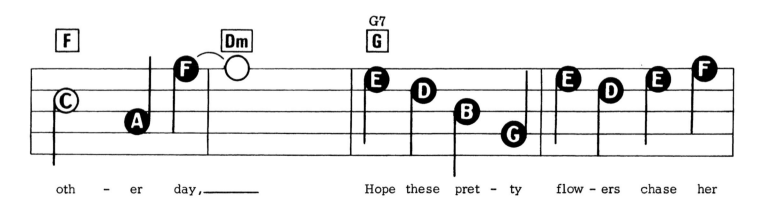

oth - er day,_____ Hope these pret - ty flow - ers chase her

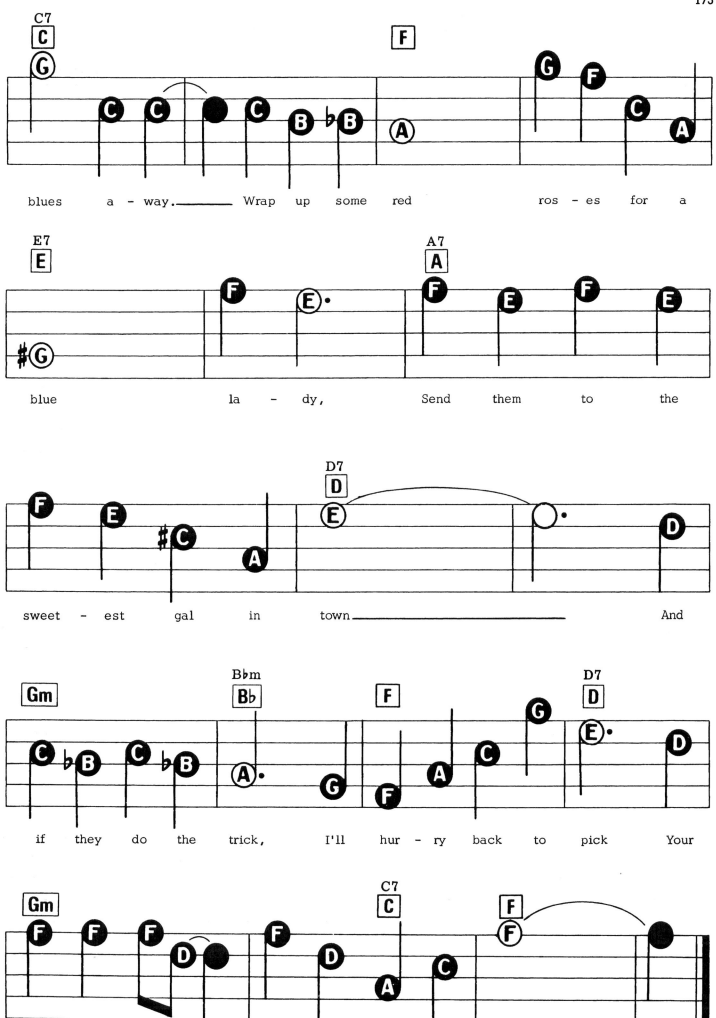

Return to Me

Registration 10
Rhythm: Rhumba or Latin

Words and Music by Danny Di Minno
and Carmen Lombardo

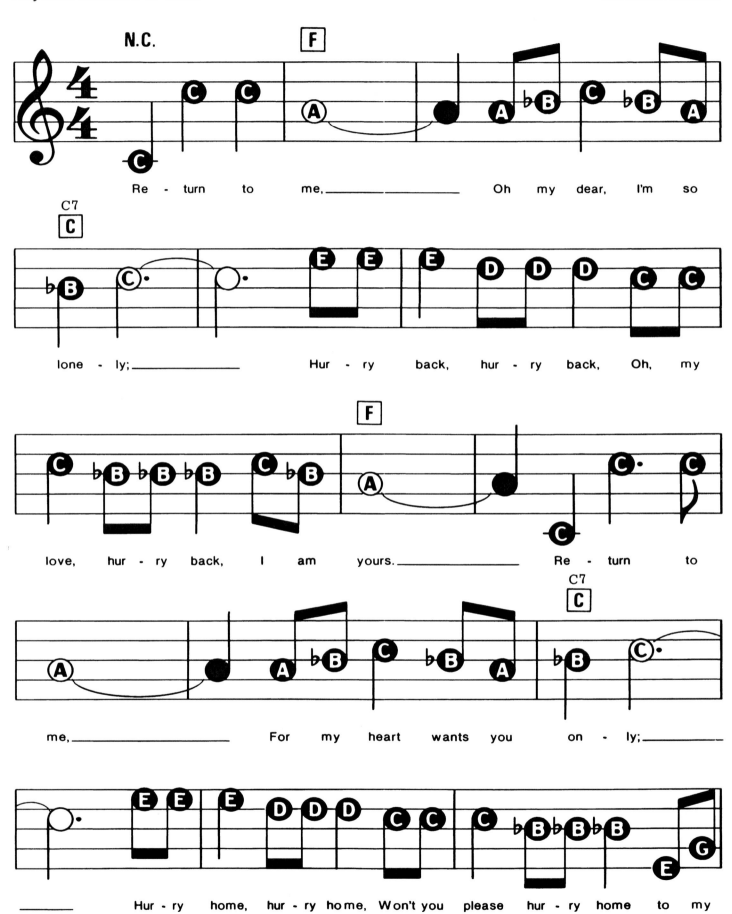

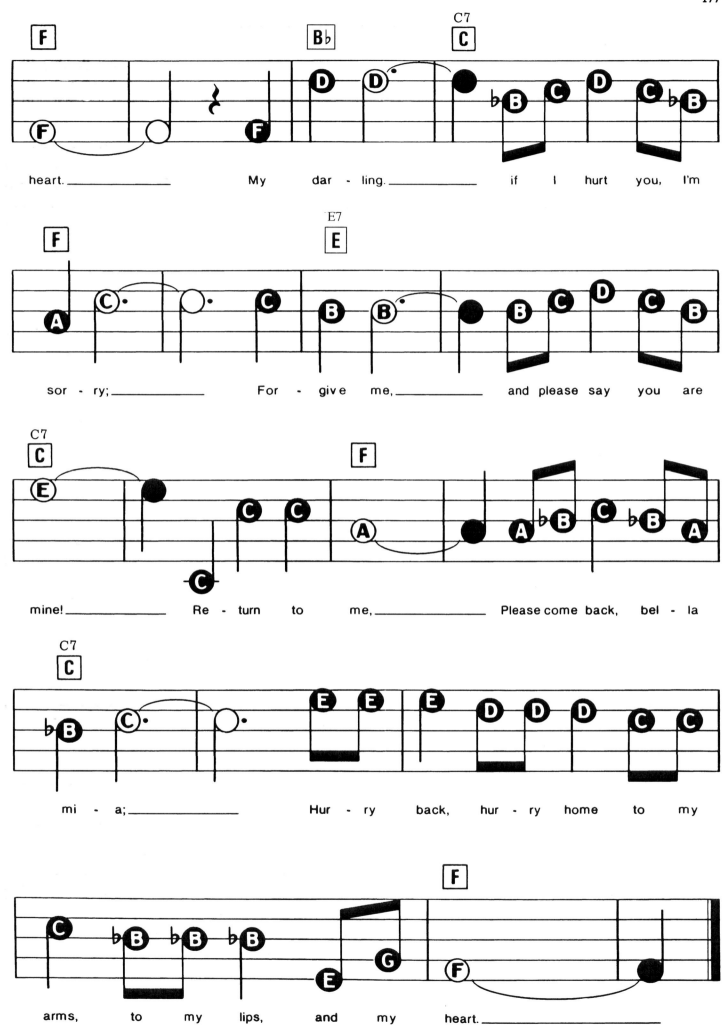

Rockin' Chair

Registration 1
Rhythm: Fox Trot

Words and Music by
Hoagy Carmichael

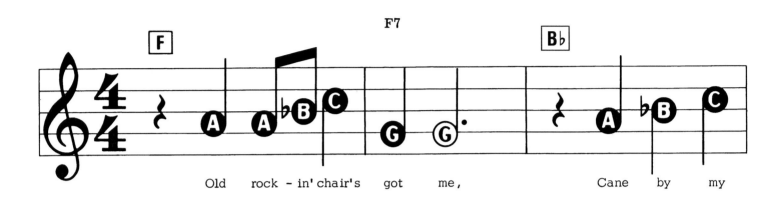

Old rock - in' chair's got me, Cane by my

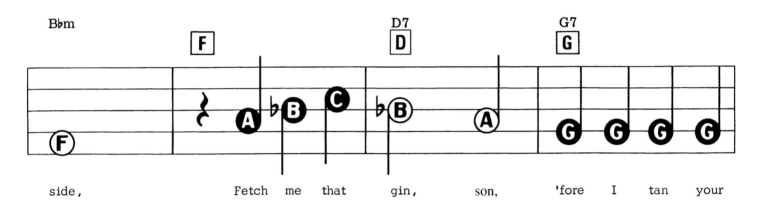

side, Fetch me that gin, son, 'fore I tan your

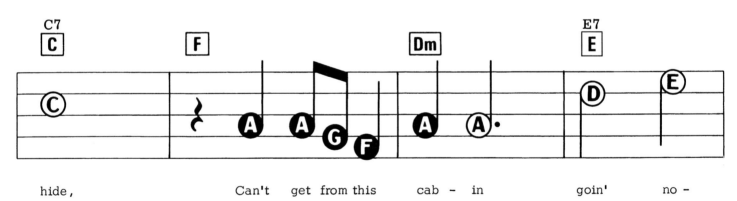

hide, Can't get from this cab - in goin' no-

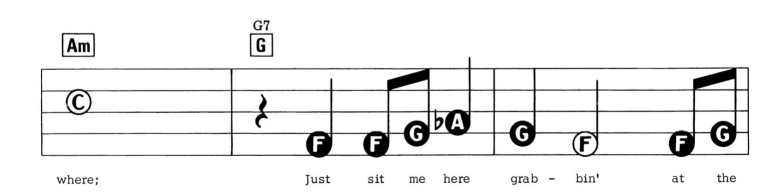

where; Just sit me here grab - bin' at the

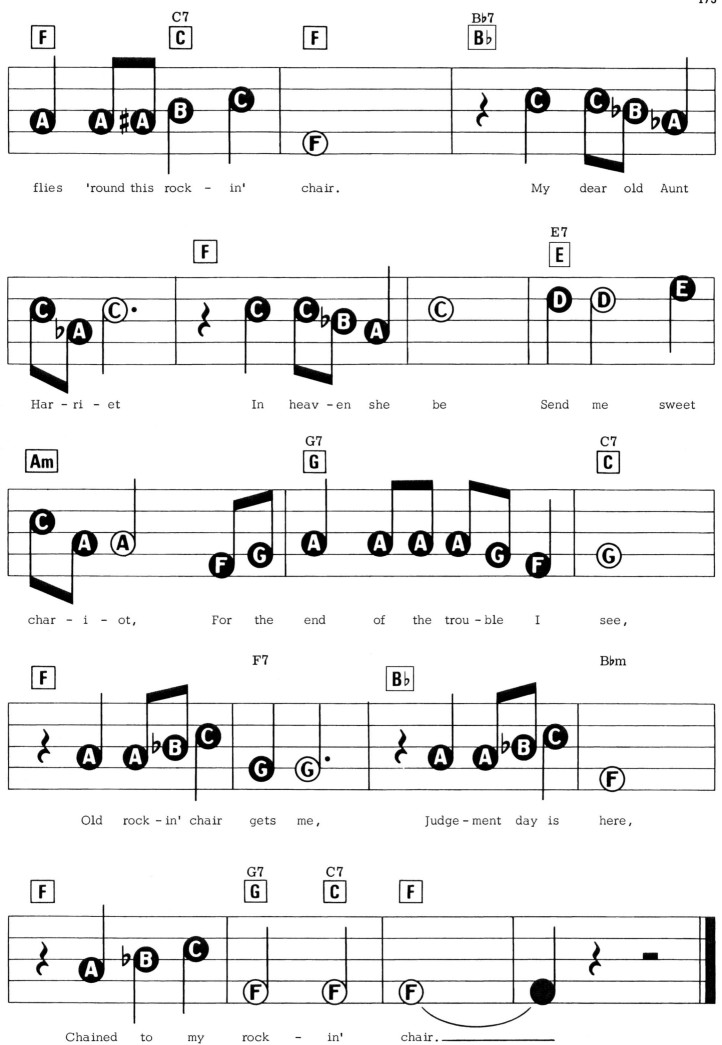

Seems Like Old Times

Registration 2
Rhythm: Fox Trot

Lyric and Music by John Jacob Loeb
and Carmen Lombardo

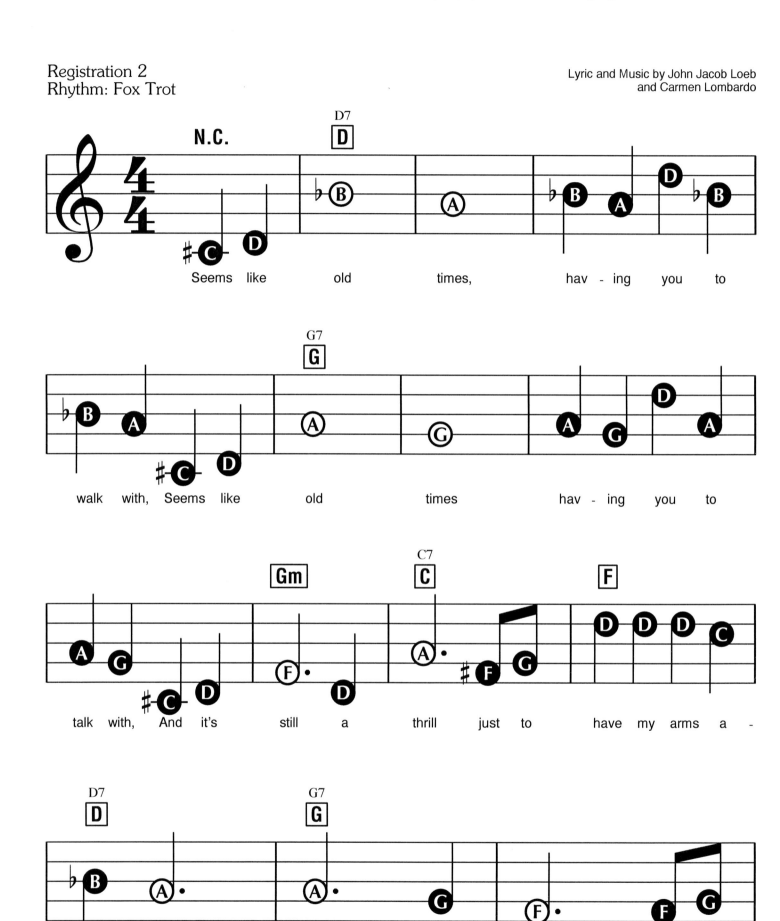

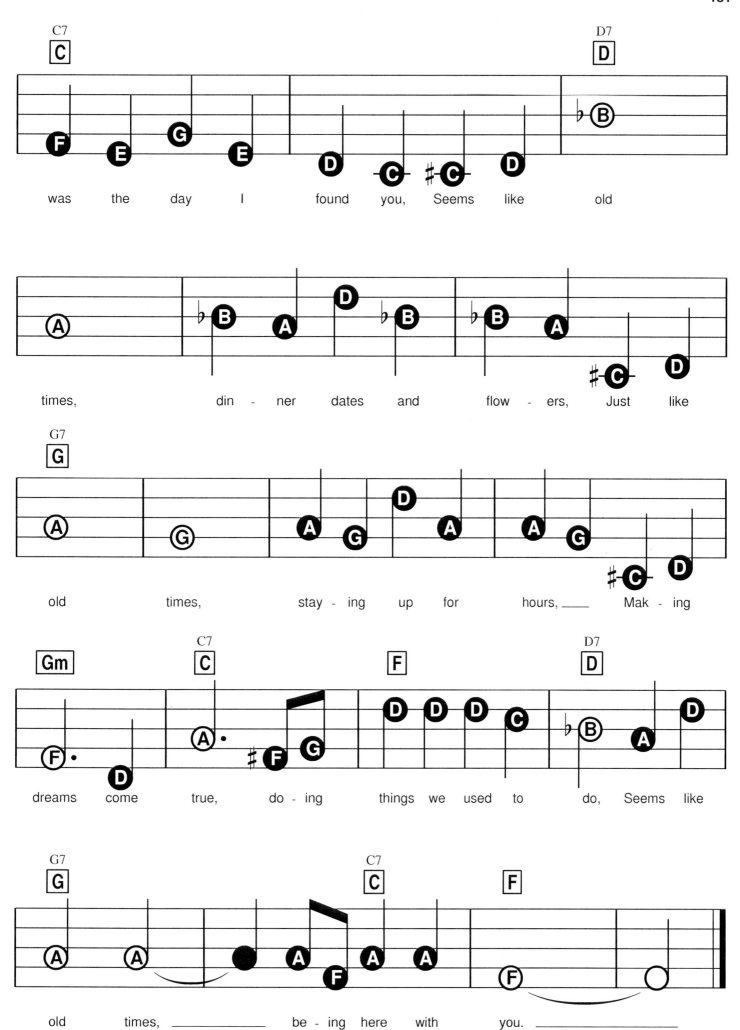

She Loves Me
from SHE LOVES ME

Registration 9
Rhythm: Rhumba

Words by Sheldon Harnick
Music by Jerry Bock

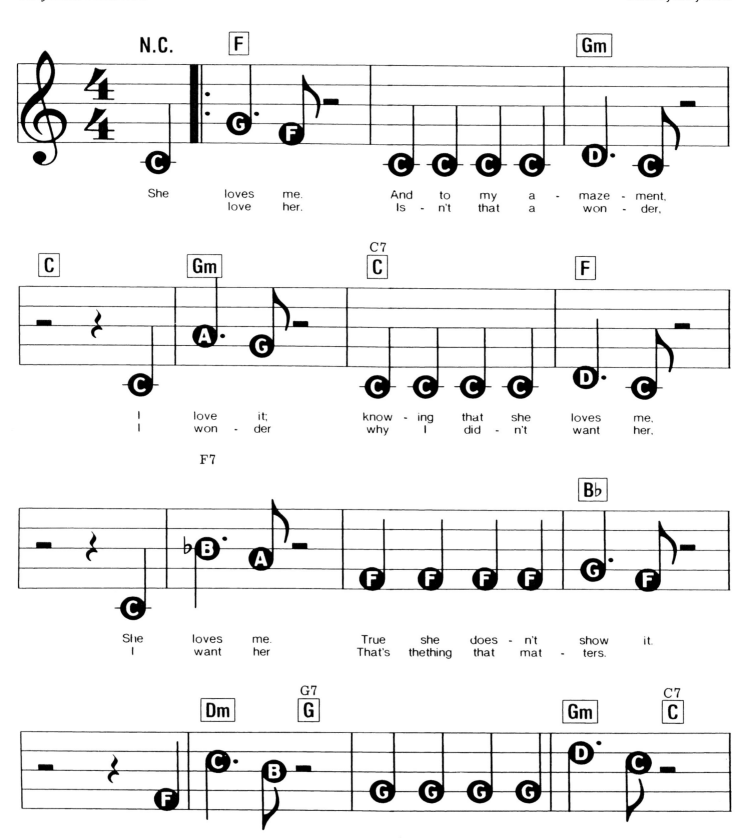

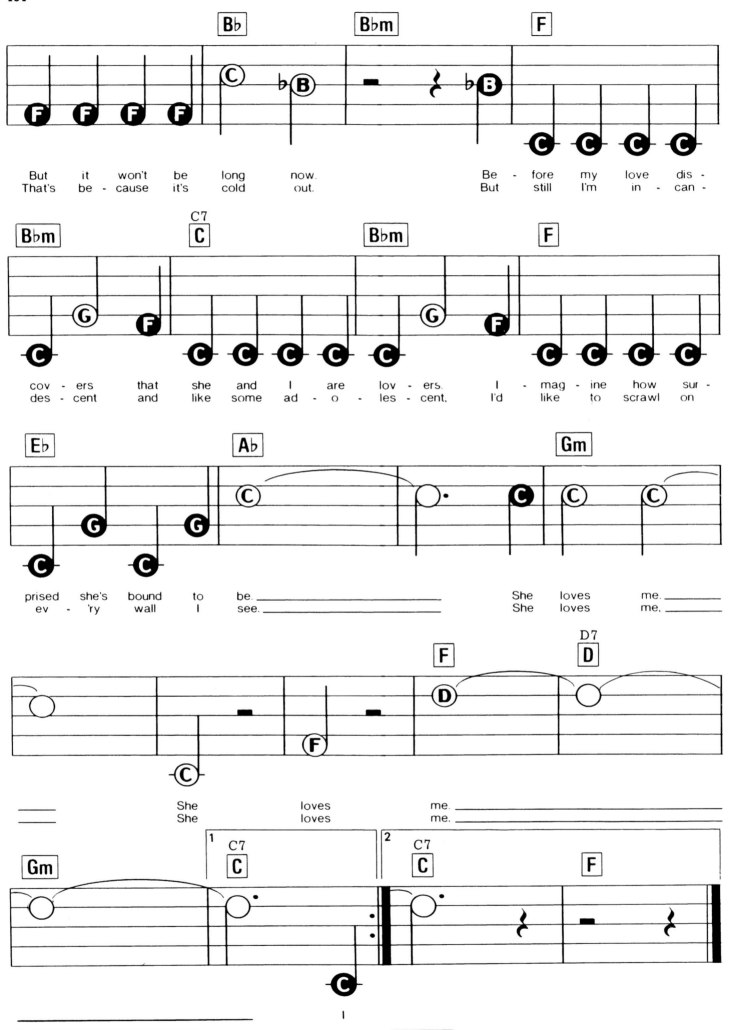

Stranger in Paradise
from KISMET

Words and Music by Robert Wright and
George Forrest
(Music Based on Themes of A. Borodin)

Registration 10
Rhythm: 8-Beat, Pops or Ballad

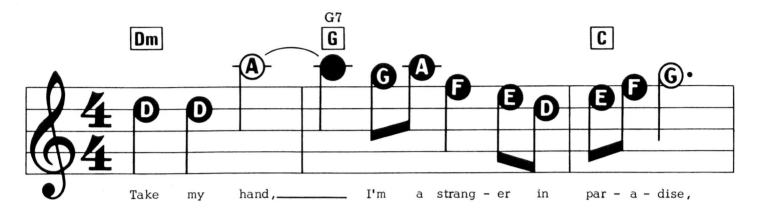

Take my hand,_____ I'm a strang - er in par - a - dise,

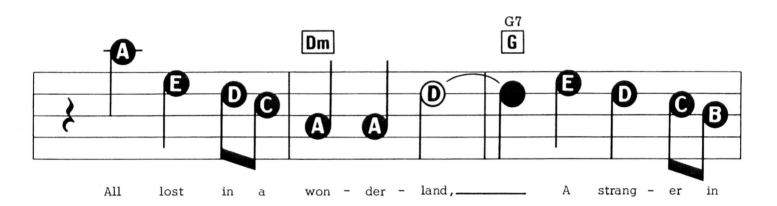

All lost in a won - der - land,_____ A strang - er in

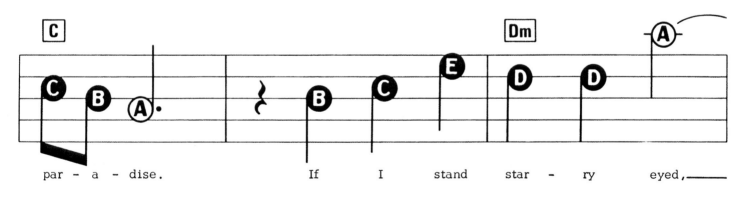

par - a - dise. If I stand star - ry eyed,_____

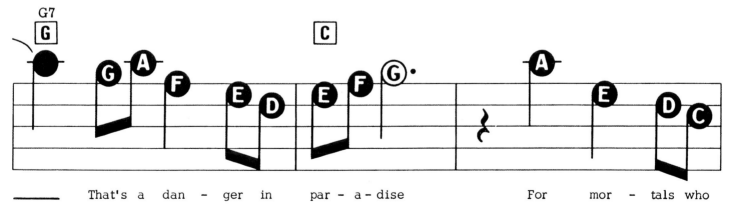

_____ That's a dan - ger in par - a - dise For mor - tals who

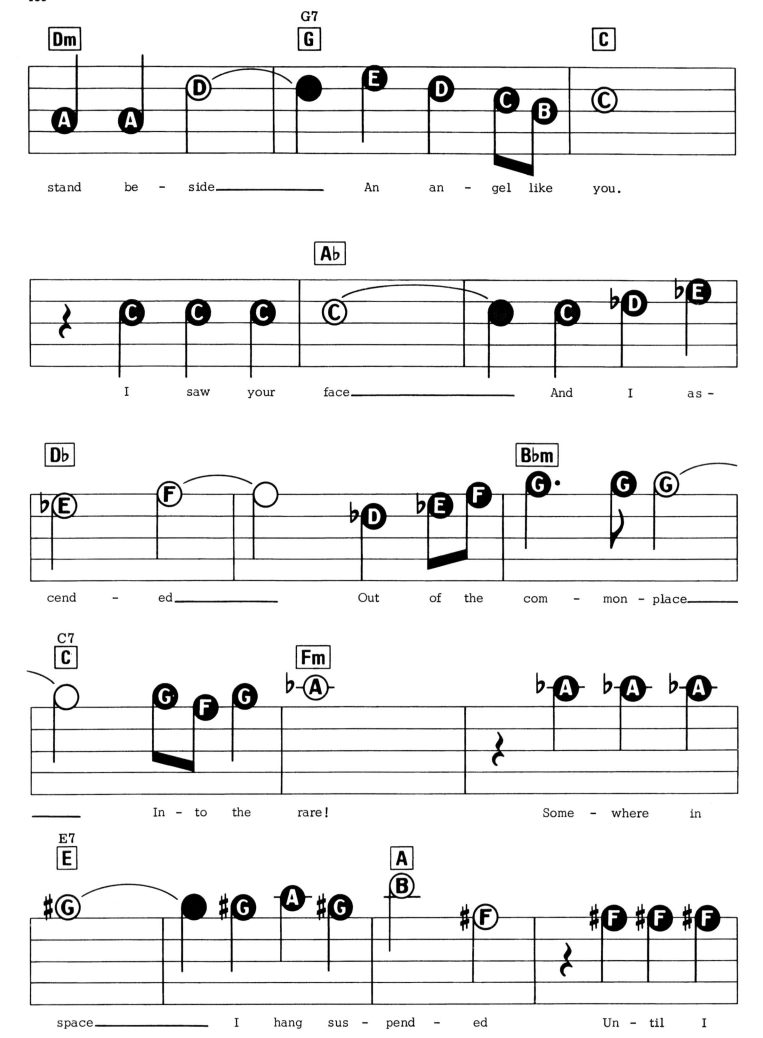

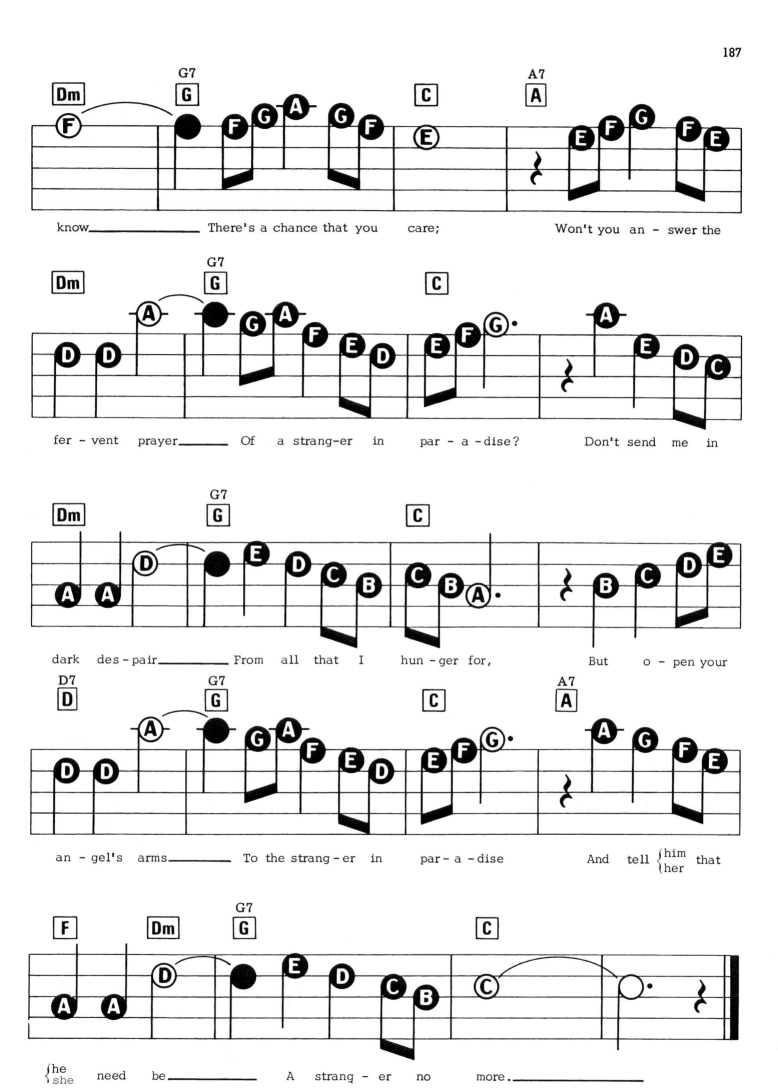

Teach Me Tonight

Registration 8
Rhythm: Fox Trot or Swing

Words by Sammy Cahn
Music by Gene DePaul

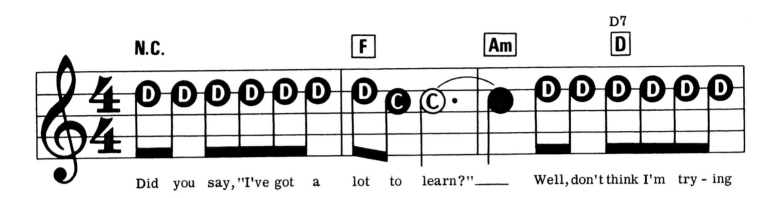

Did you say,"I've got a lot to learn?"____ Well,don't think I'm try-ing

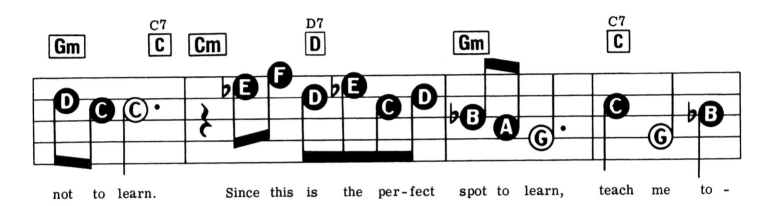

not to learn. Since this is the per-fect spot to learn, teach me to-

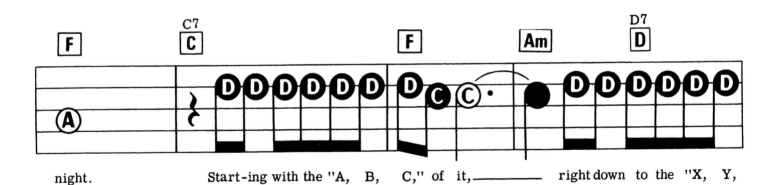

night. Start-ing with the "A, B, C," of it,_____ right down to the "X, Y,

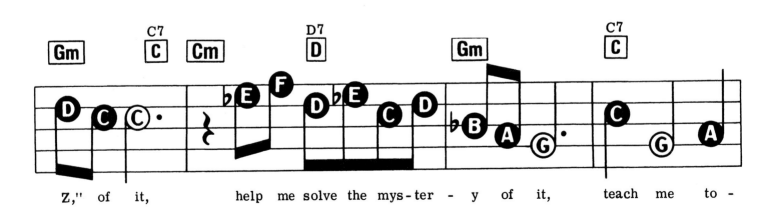

Z," of it, help me solve the mys-ter-y of it, teach me to-

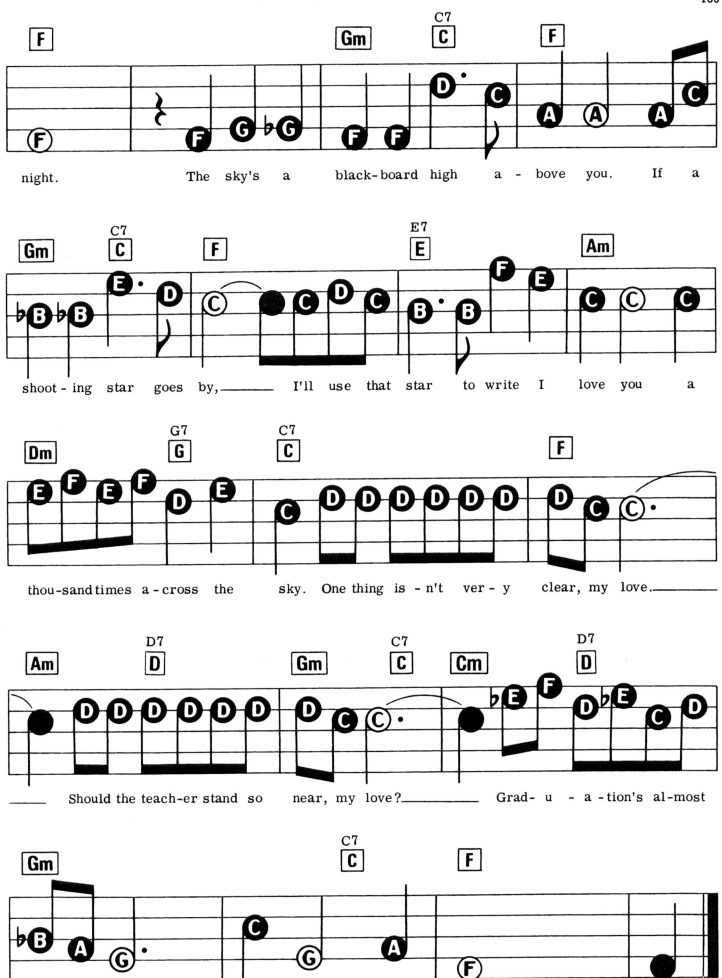

That's My Desire

Registration 2
Rhythm: Fox Trot or Ballad

Words by Carroll Loveday
Music by Helmy Kresa

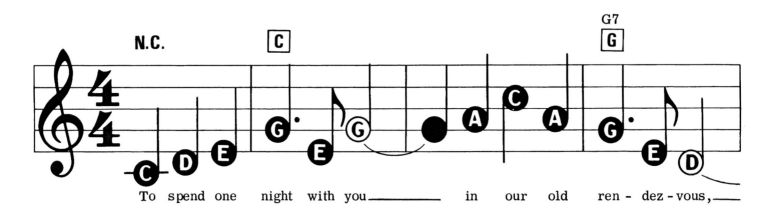

To spend one night with you_____ in our old ren - dez - vous,_____

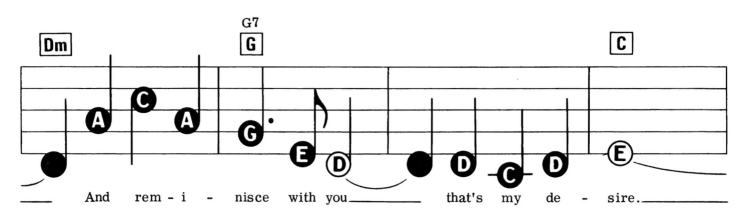

_____ And rem - i - nisce with you_____ that's my de - sire._____

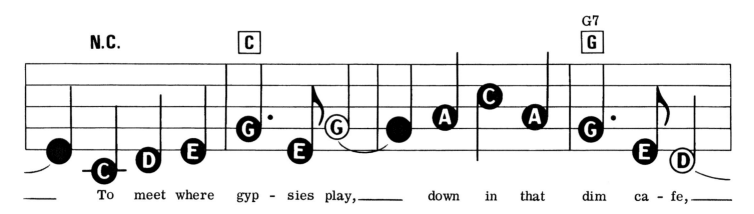

_____ To meet where gyp - sies play,_____ down in that dim ca - fe,_____

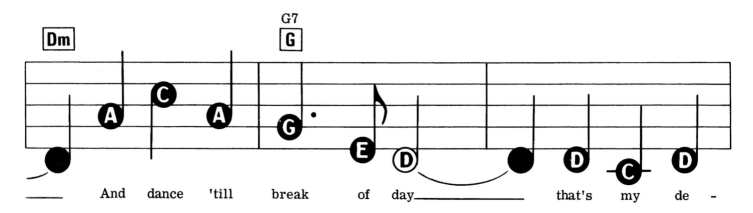

_____ And dance 'till break of day_____ that's my de -

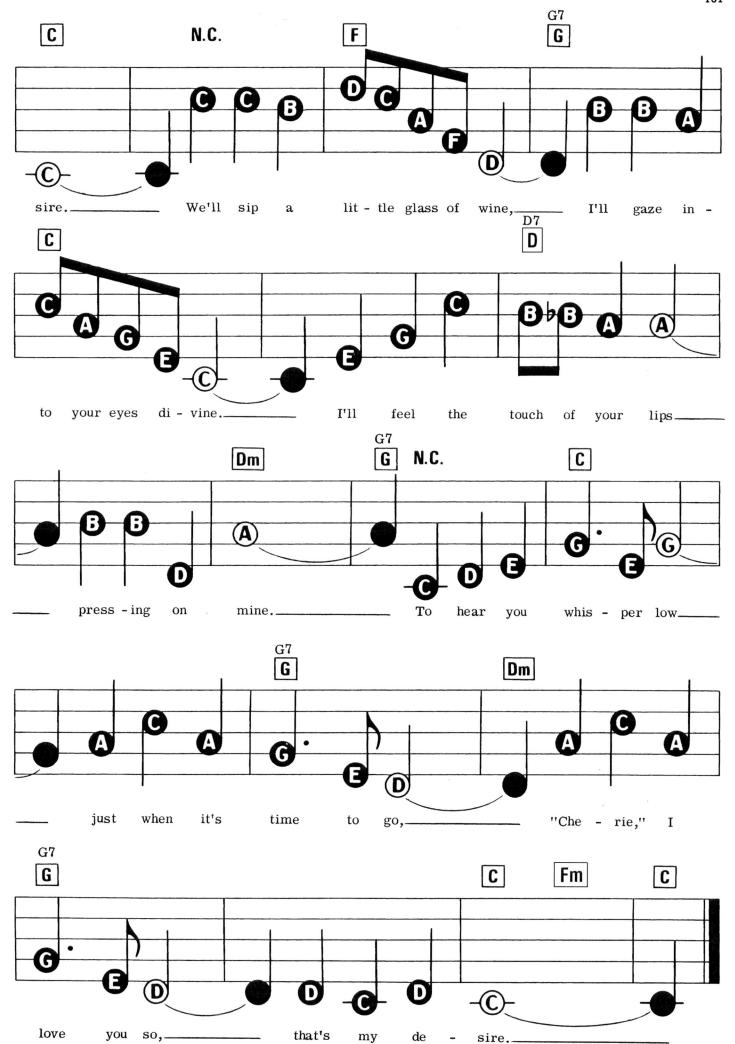

There! I've Said It Again

Registration 7
Rhythm: Fox Trot

Words and Music by Dave Mann
and Redd Evans

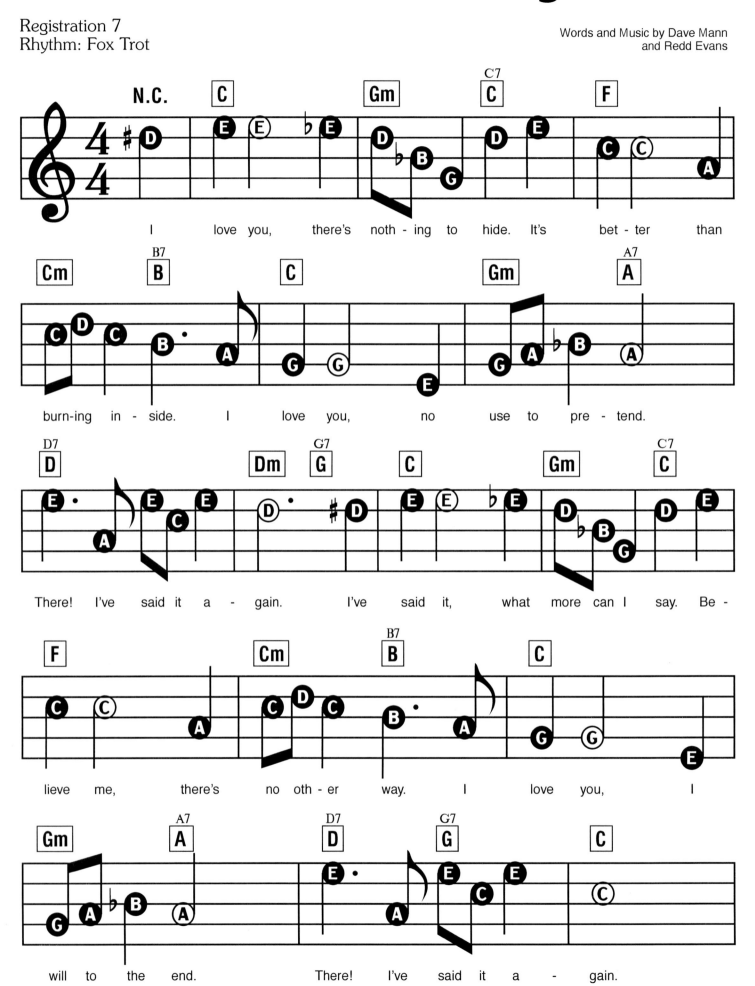

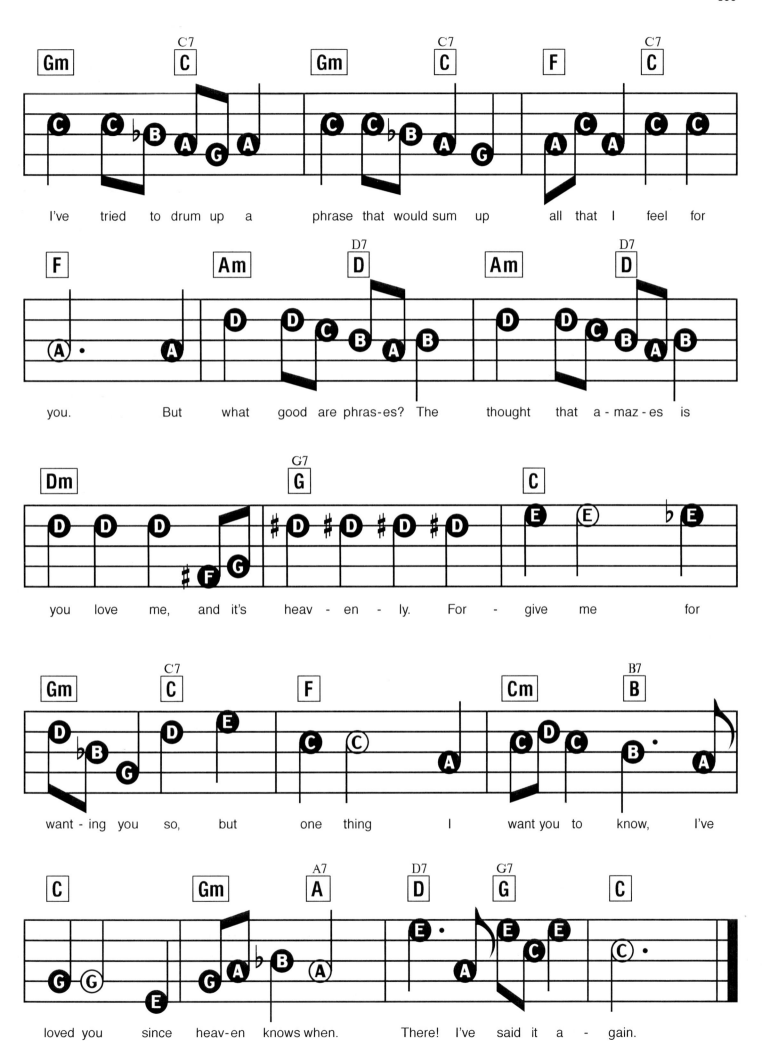

There Is No Greater Love

Registration 2
Rhythm: Swing

Words by Marty Symes
Music by Isham Jones

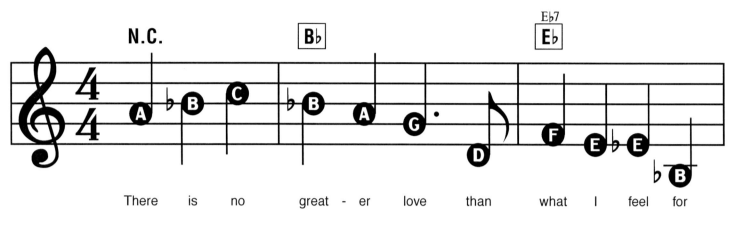

There is no great - er love than what I feel for

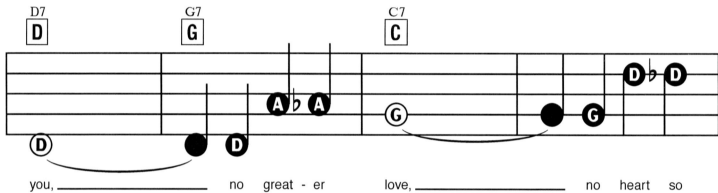

you, _____ no great - er love, _____ no heart so

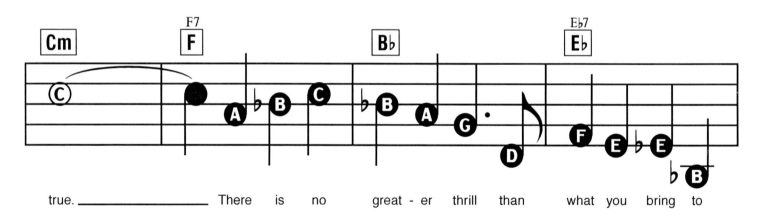

true. _____ There is no great - er thrill than what you bring to

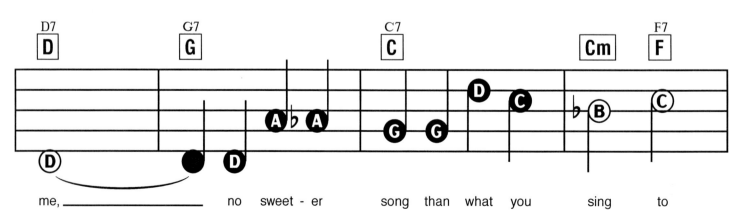

me, _____ no sweet - er song than what you sing to

195

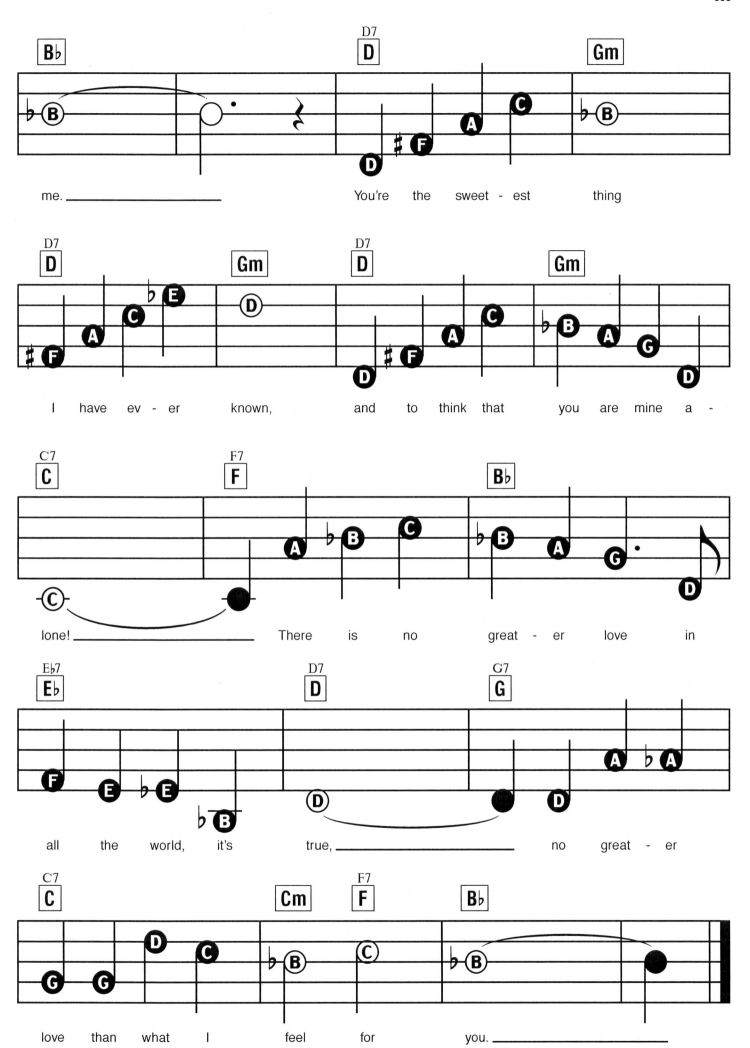

There's No Tomorrow

Registration 5
Rhythm: Bossa Nova or Latin

Written by Al Hoffman,
Leo Corday and Leon Carr

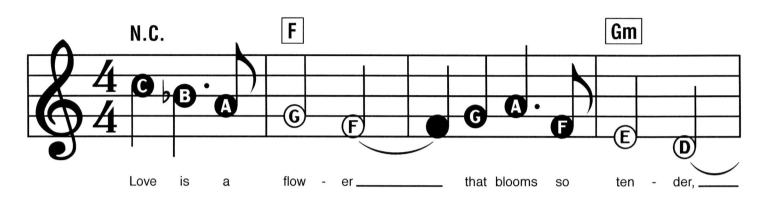

Love is a flow - er _____ that blooms so ten - der, _____

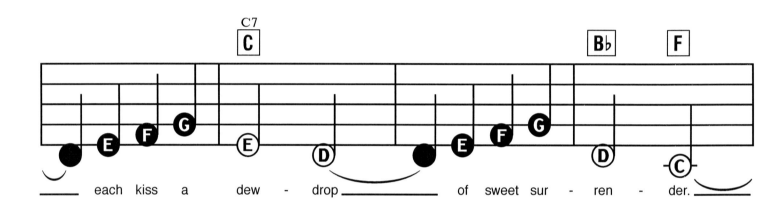

_____ each kiss a dew - drop _____ of sweet sur - ren - der. _____

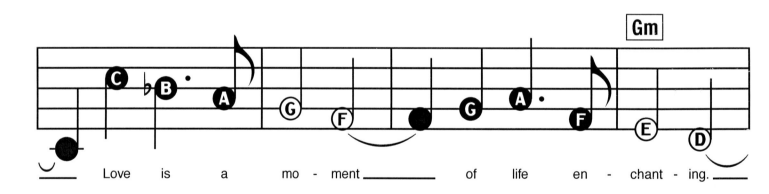

Love is a mo - ment _____ of life en - chant - ing. _____

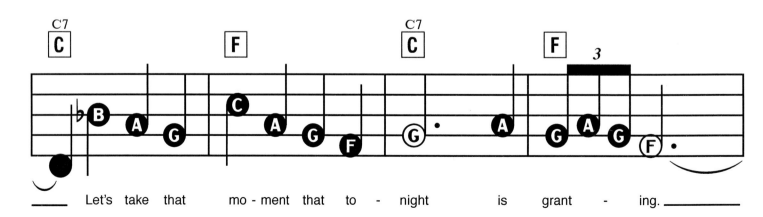

_____ Let's take that mo - ment that to - night is grant - ing. _____

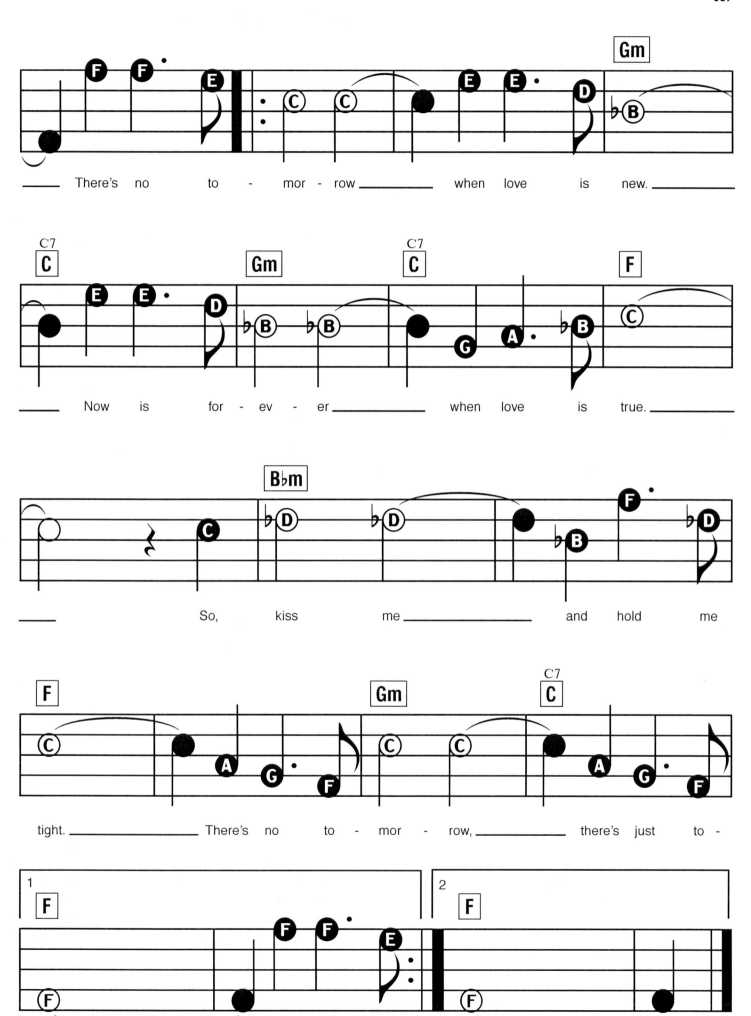

They Say It's Wonderful
from the Stage Production ANNIE GET YOUR GUN

Registration 10
Rhythm: Fox Trot or Ballad

Words and Music by
Irving Berlin

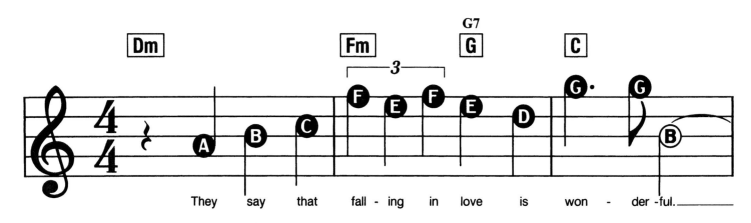

They say that fall - ing in love is won - der -ful.

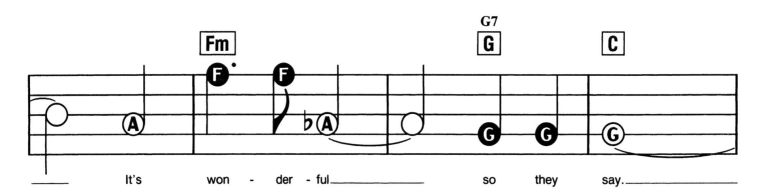

It's won - der -ful so they say.

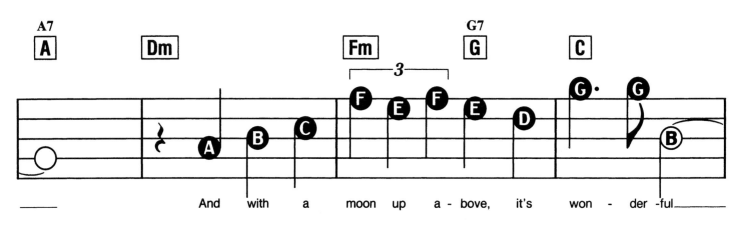

And with a moon up a - bove, it's won - der -ful

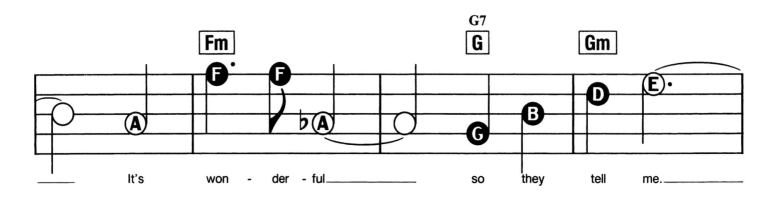

It's won - der -ful so they tell me.

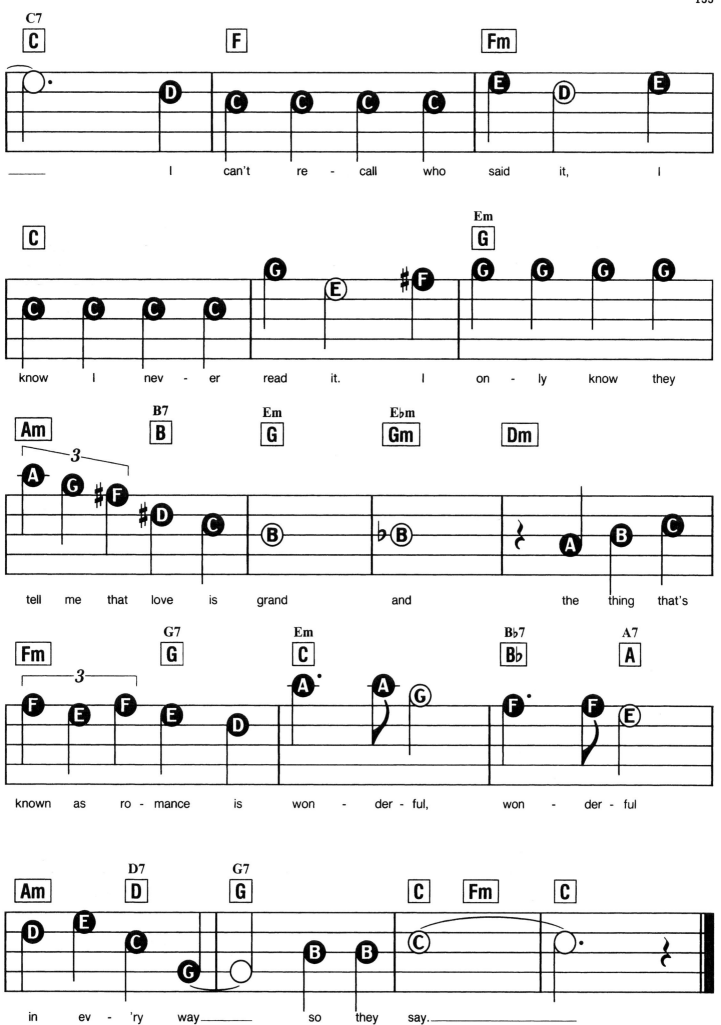

Till the End of Time

from TILL THE END OF TIME
(Based on Chopin's Polonaise)

Registration 5
Rhythm: Swing

Words and Music by Buddy Kaye
and Ted Mossman

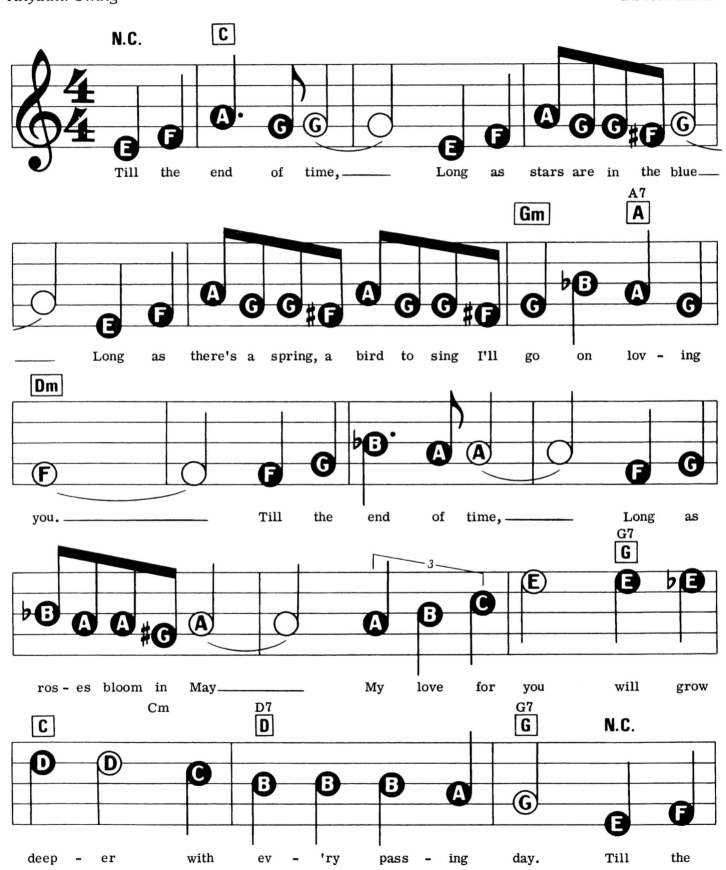

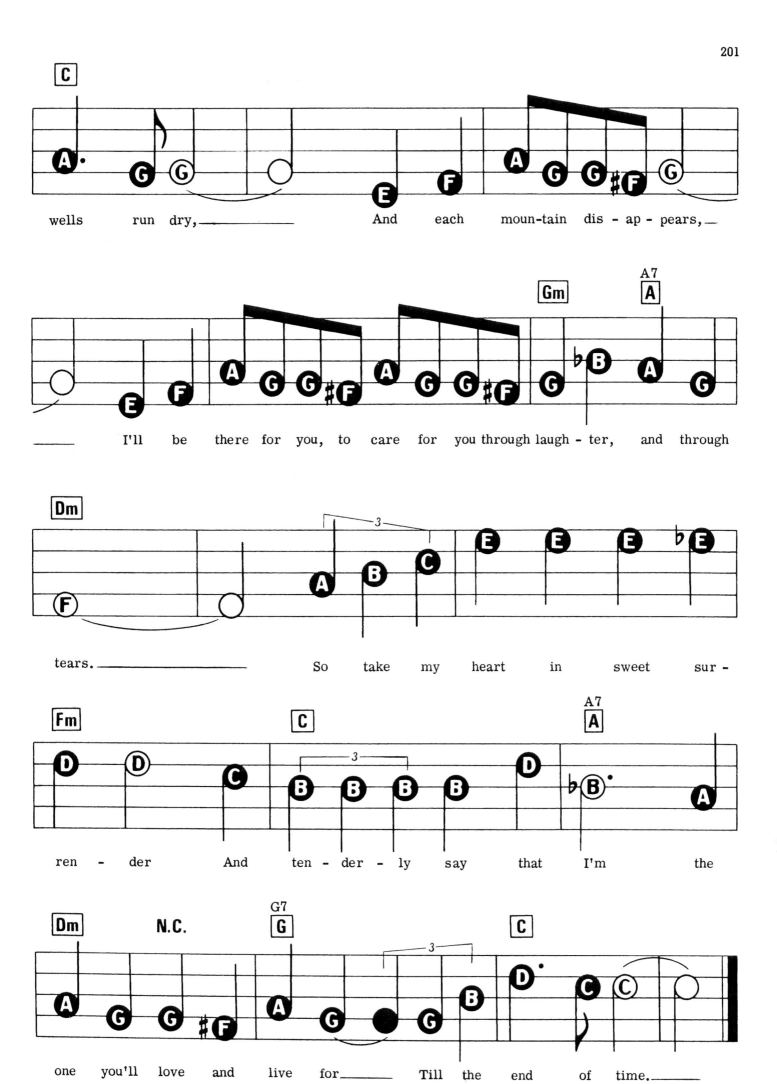

Walkin' My Baby Back Home

Registration 2
Rhythm: Fox Trot

Words and Music by Roy Turk
and Fred E. Ahlert

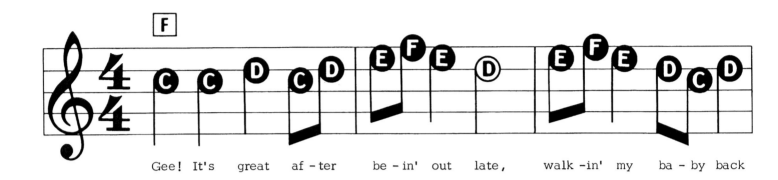

Gee! It's great af-ter be-in' out late, walk-in' my ba-by back

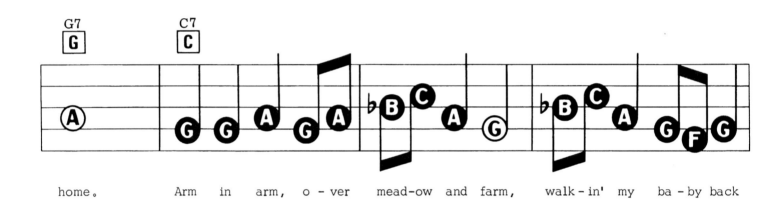

home. Arm in arm, o-ver mead-ow and farm, walk-in' my ba-by back

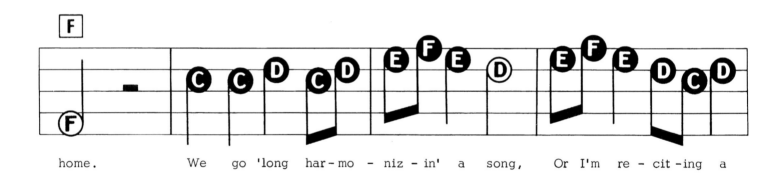

home. We go 'long har-mo-niz-in' a song, Or I'm re-cit-ing a

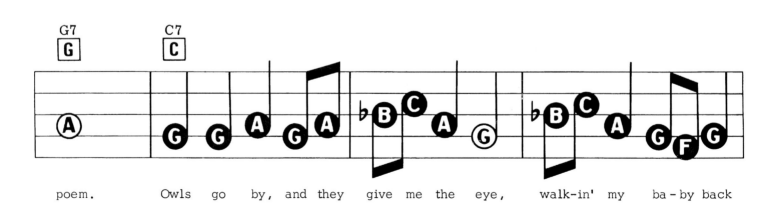

poem. Owls go by, and they give me the eye, walk-in' my ba-by back

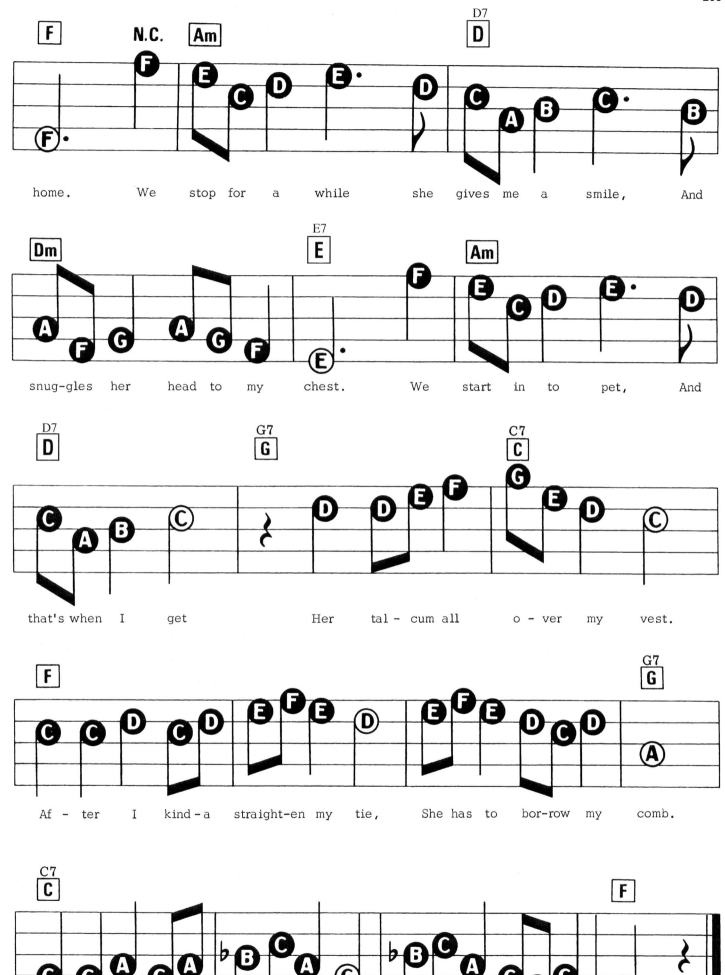

The Way You Look Tonight
from SWING TIME

Registration 1
Rhythm: Fox Trot or Ballad

Words by Dorothy Fields
Music by Jerome Kern

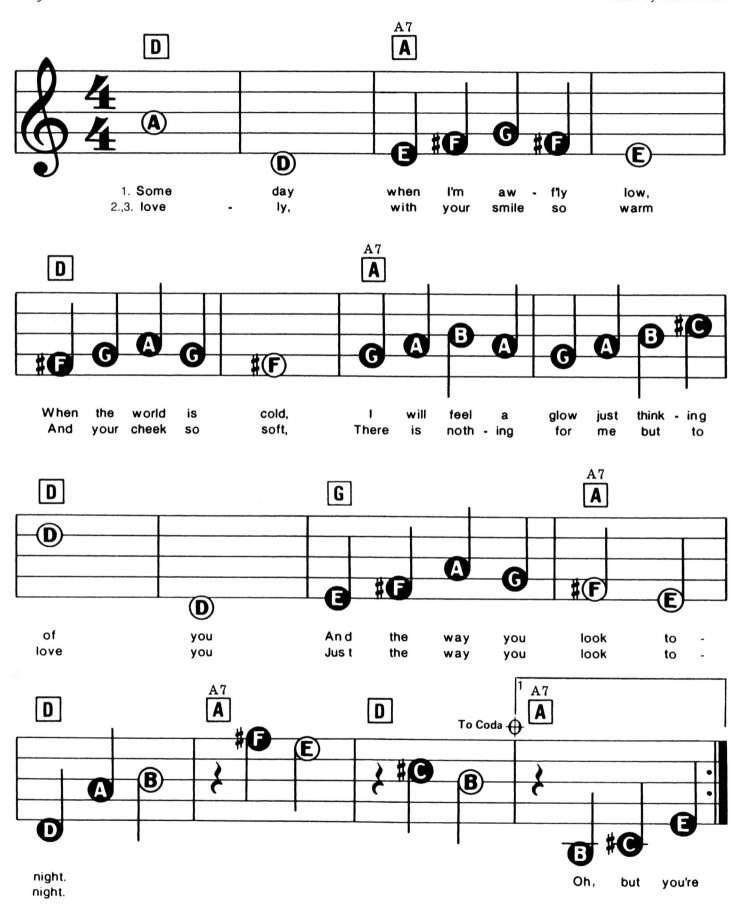

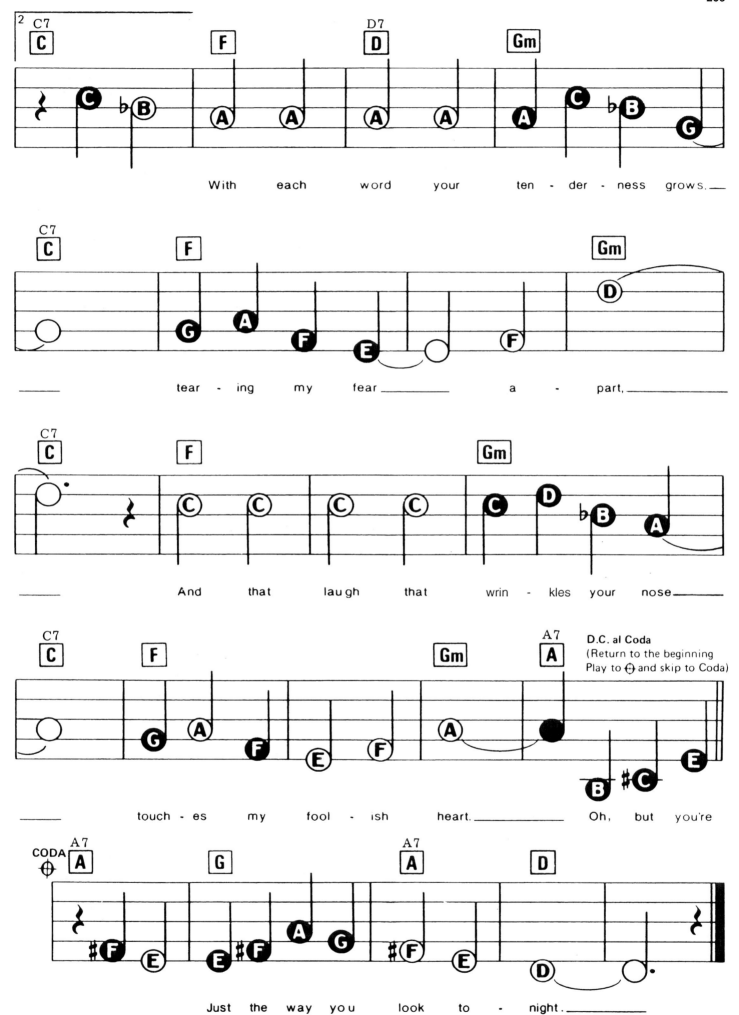

What Kind of Fool Am I?

from the Musical Production STOP THE WORLD – I WANT TO GET OFF

Registration 2
Rhythm: Fox Trot

Words and Music by Leslie Bricusse
and Anthony Newley

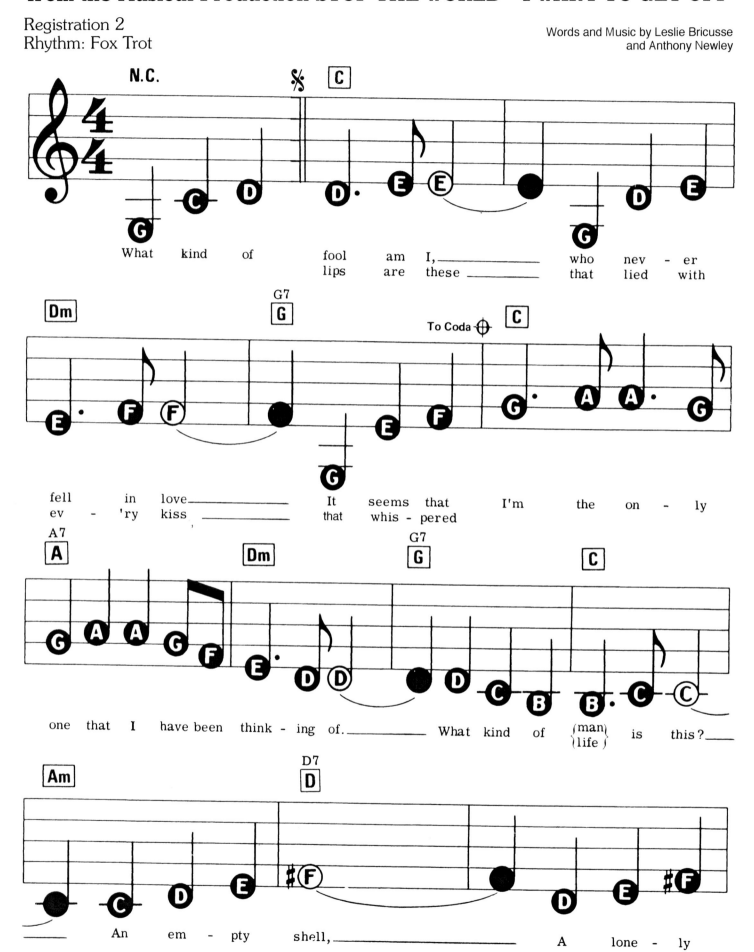

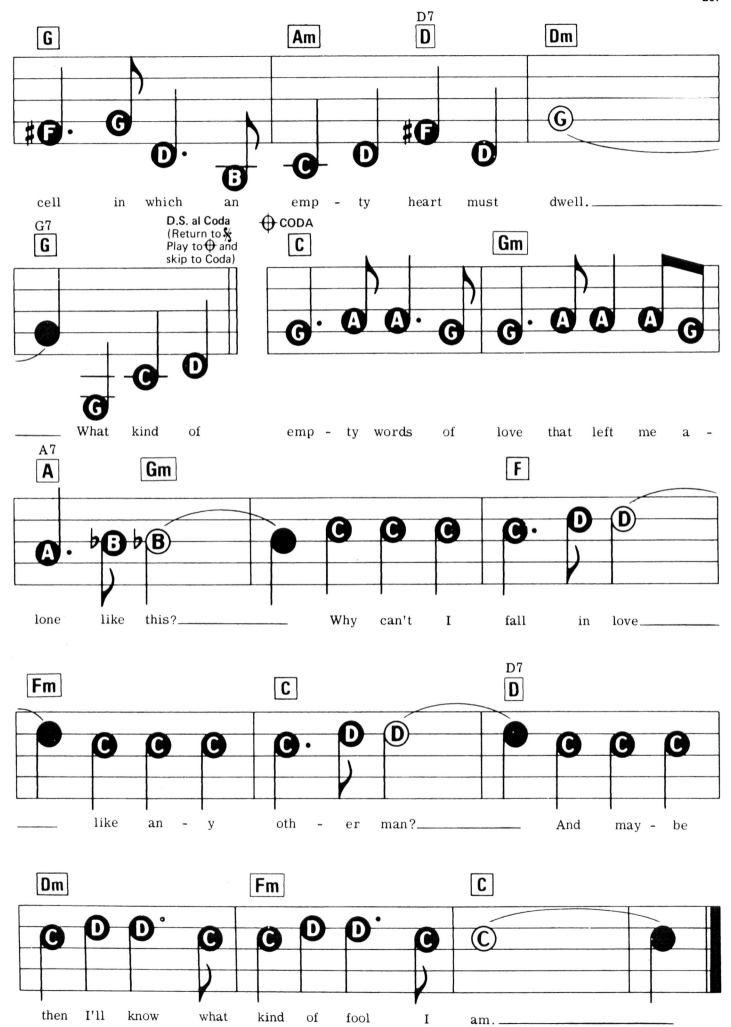

When I Fall in Love
from ONE MINUTE TO ZERO

Registration 10
Rhythm: Ballad or Fox Trot

Words by Edward Heyman
Music by Victor Young

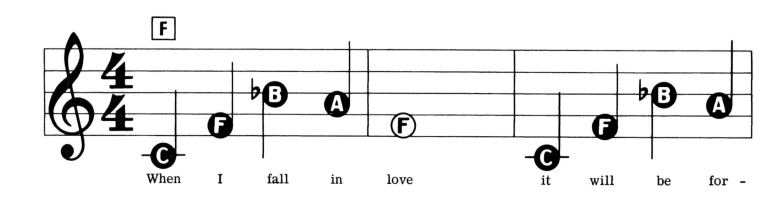

When I fall in love it will be for-

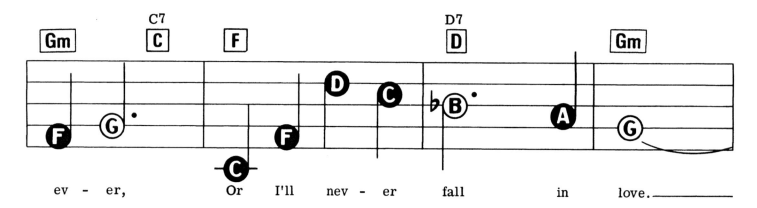

ev - er, Or I'll nev - er fall in love.

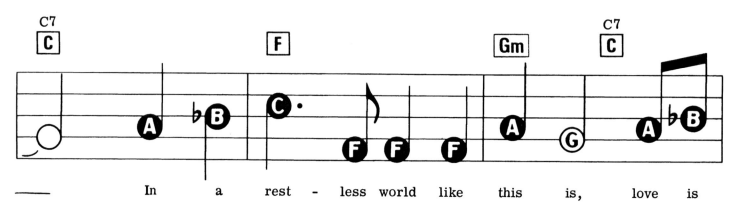

In a rest - less world like this is, love is

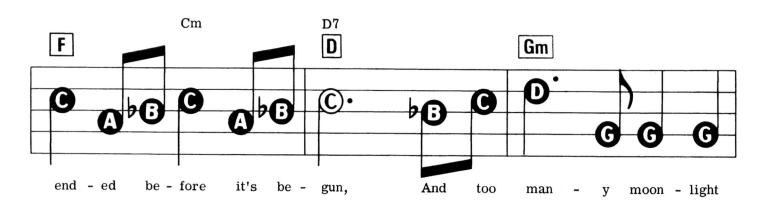

end - ed be - fore it's be - gun, And too man - y moon - light

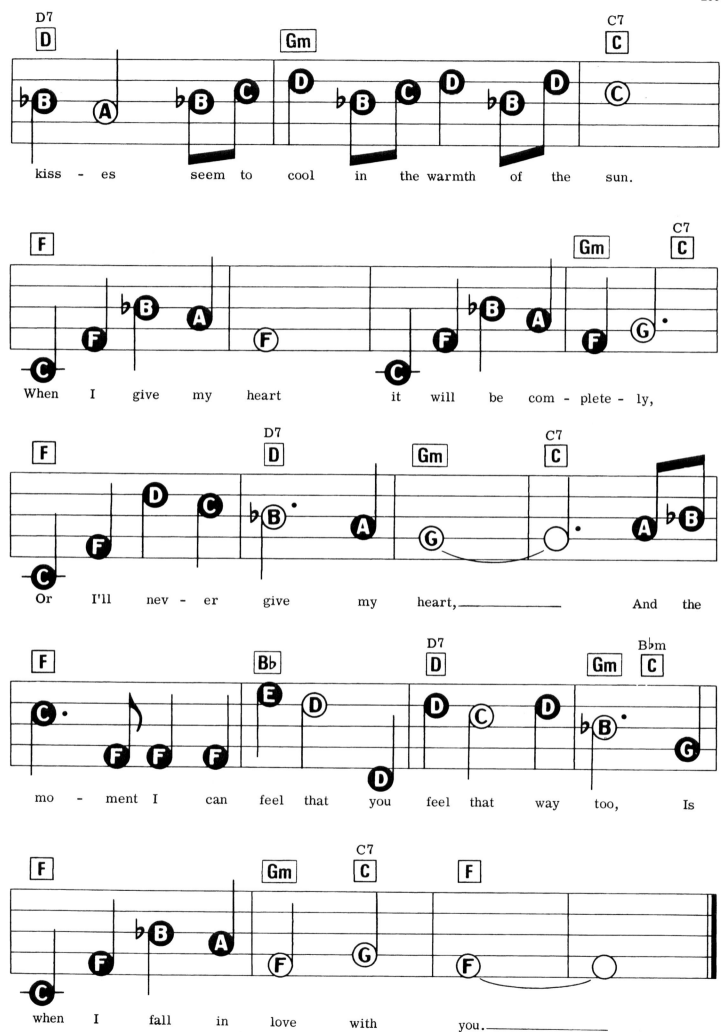

Wish You Were Here
from WISH YOU WERE HERE

Registration 5
Rhythm: Beguine or Latin

Words and Music by
Harold Rome

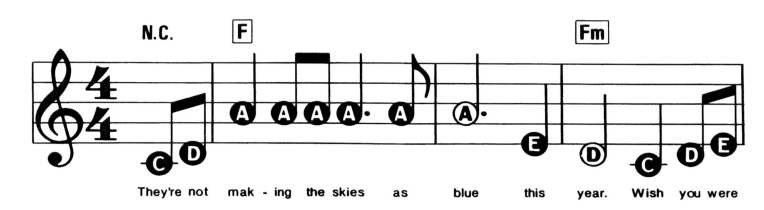

They're not mak - ing the skies as blue this year. Wish you were

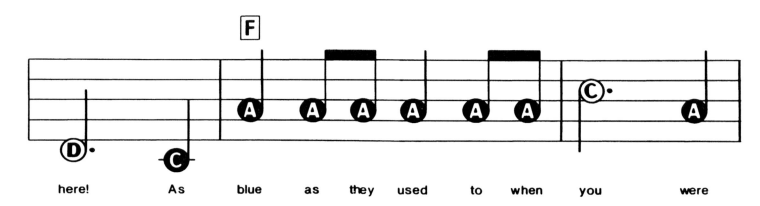

here! As blue as they used to when you were

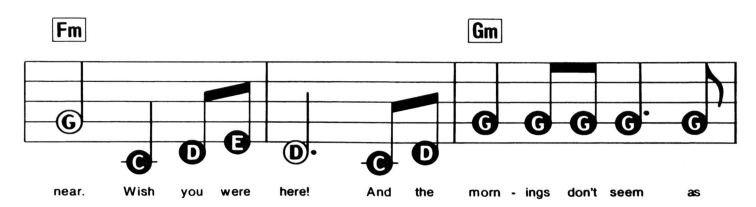

near. Wish you were here! And the morn - ings don't seem as

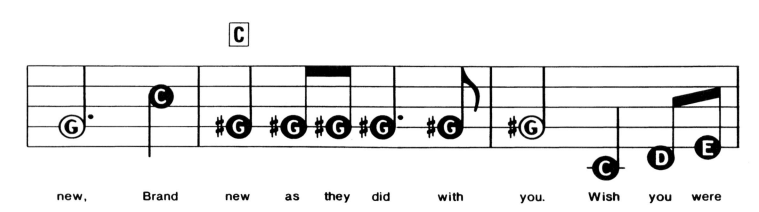

new, Brand new as they did with you. Wish you were

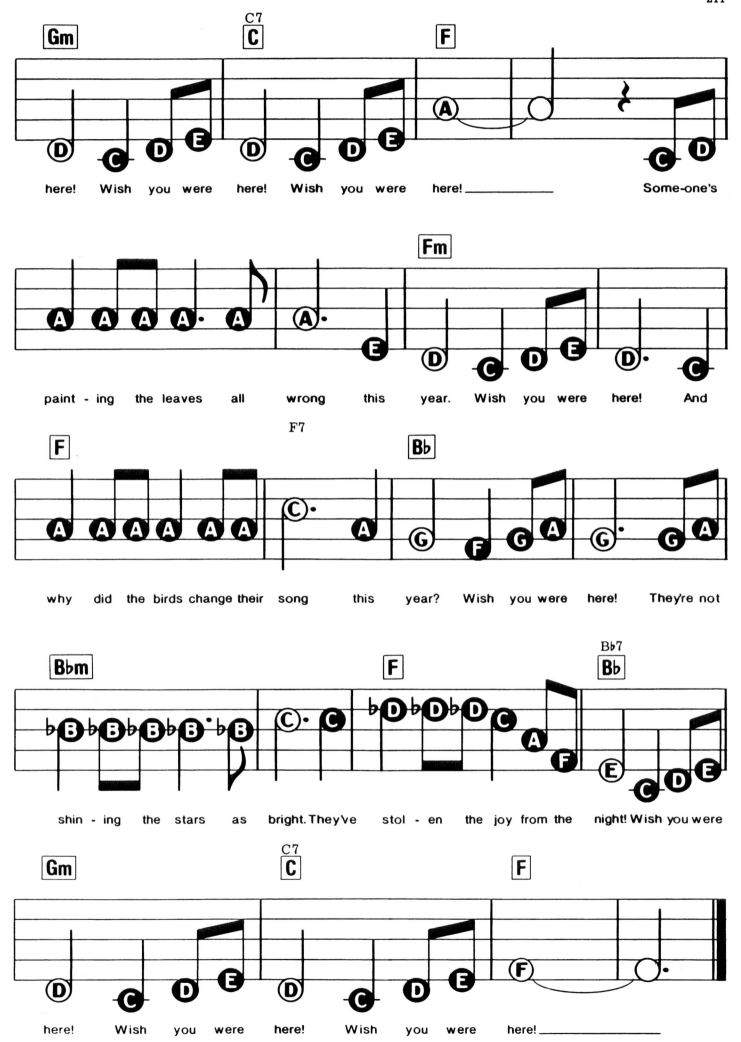

You're Breaking My Heart

Registration 5
Rhythm: Fox Trot

Words and Music by Pat Genaro
and Sunny Skylar

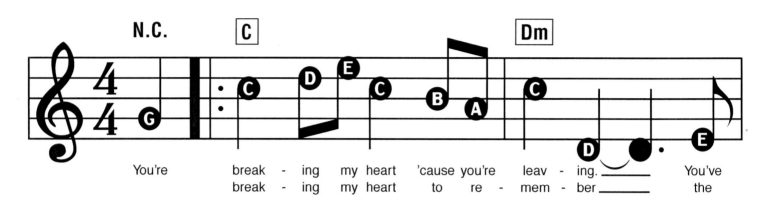

You're break - ing my heart 'cause you're leav - ing. _____ You've
break - ing my heart to re - mem - ber _____ the

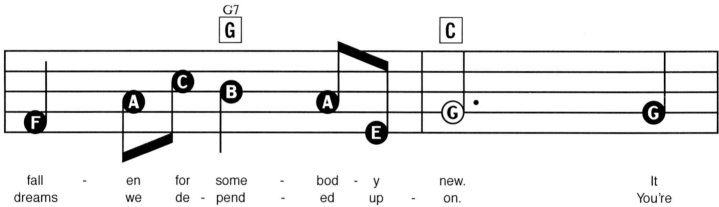

fall - en for some - bod - y new. It
dreams we de - pend - ed up - on. You're

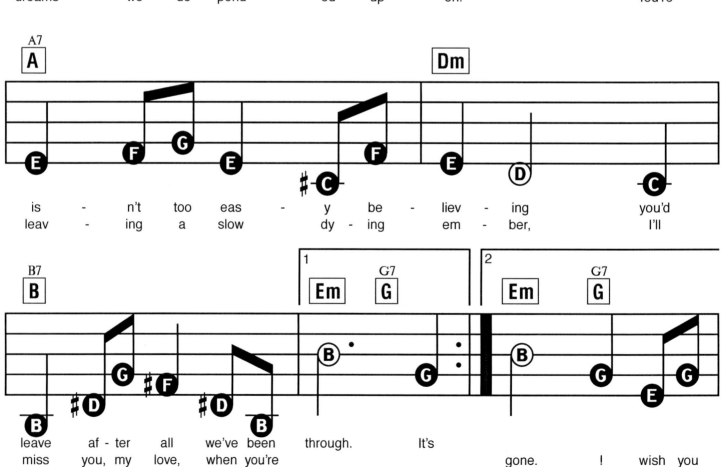

is - n't too eas - y be - liev - ing, you'd
leav - ing a slow dy - ing em - ber, I'll

leave af - ter all we've been through. It's
miss you, my love, when you're gone. I wish you

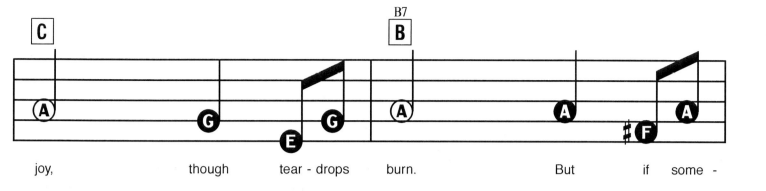

joy,   though   tear - drops   burn.   But   if   some -

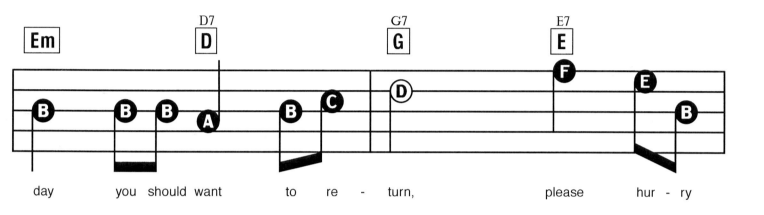

day   you should want   to   re - turn,   please   hur - ry

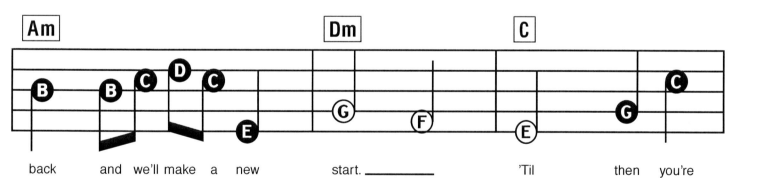

back   and we'll make a new   start. _____   'Til   then   you're

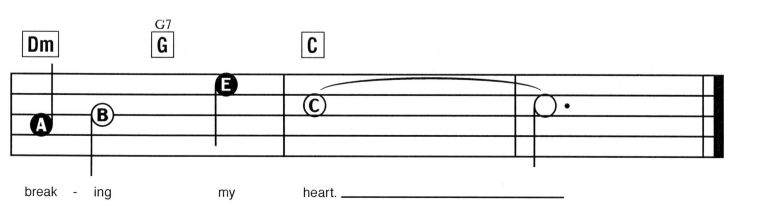

break - ing   my   heart. _____

You're Nobody
'til Somebody Loves You

Registration 2
Rhythm: Swing

Words and Music by Russ Morgan,
Larry Stock and James Cavanaugh

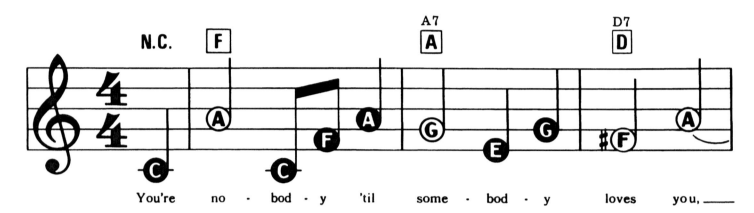

You're no - bod - y 'til some - bod - y loves you, ____

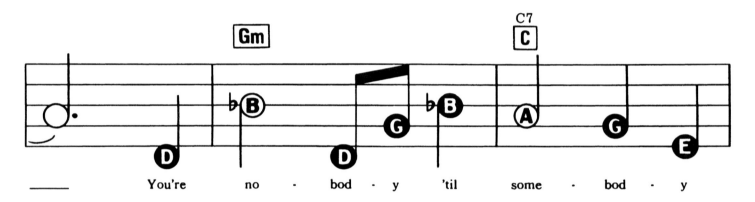

____ You're no - bod - y 'til some - bod - y

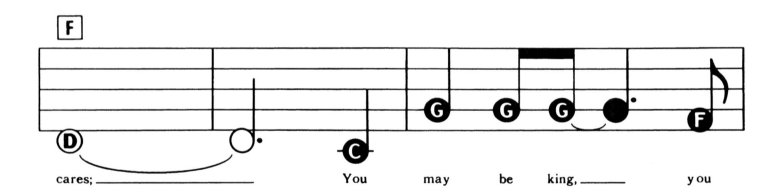

cares; _____ You may be king, ____ you

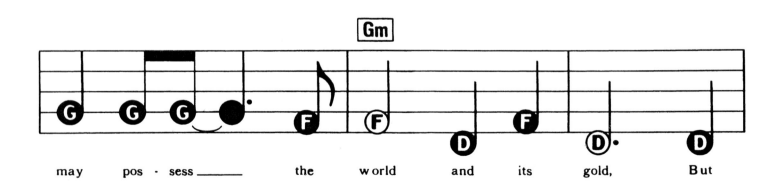

may pos - sess ____ the world and its gold, But

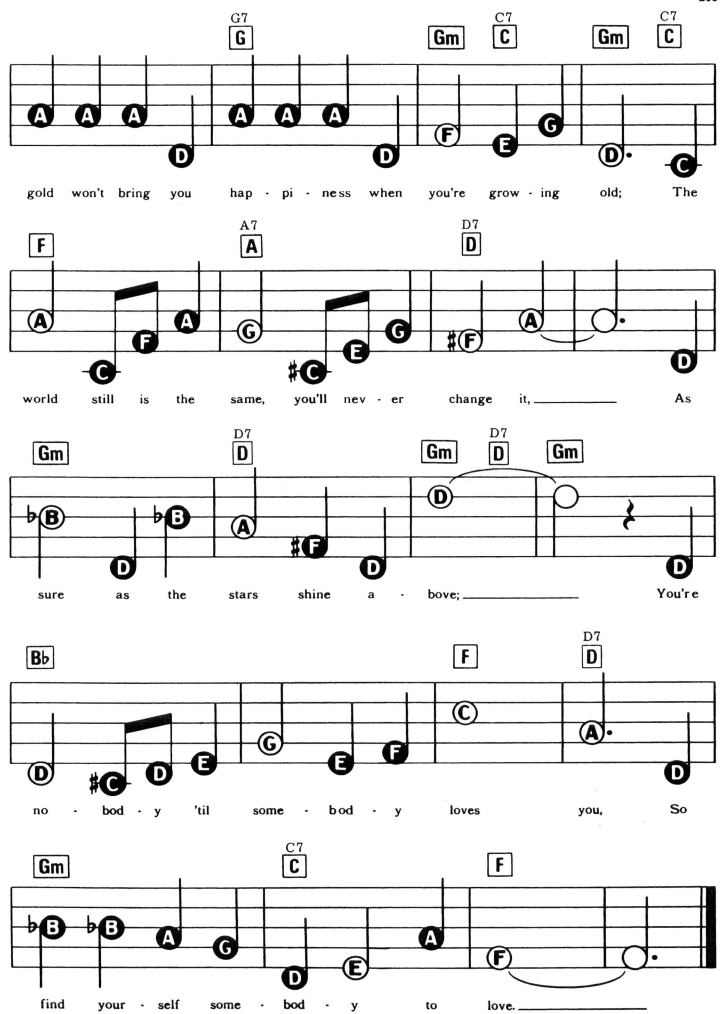

Zip-A-Dee-Doo-Dah
from Walt Disney's SONG OF THE SOUTH

Registration 8
Rhythm: Fox Trot or Swing

Words by Ray Gilbert
Music by Allie Wrubel

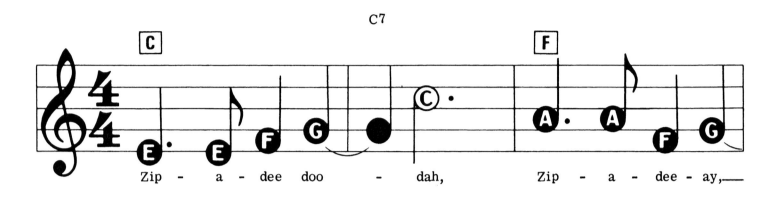

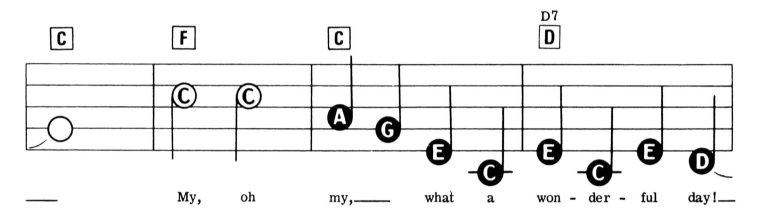

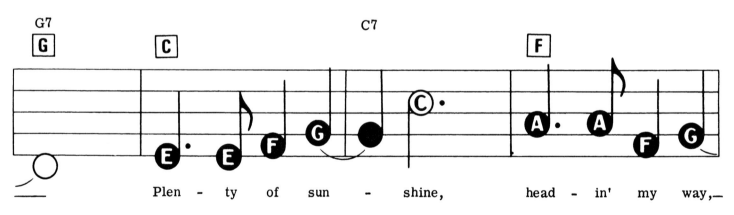

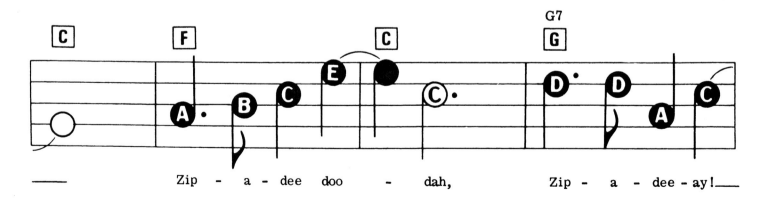

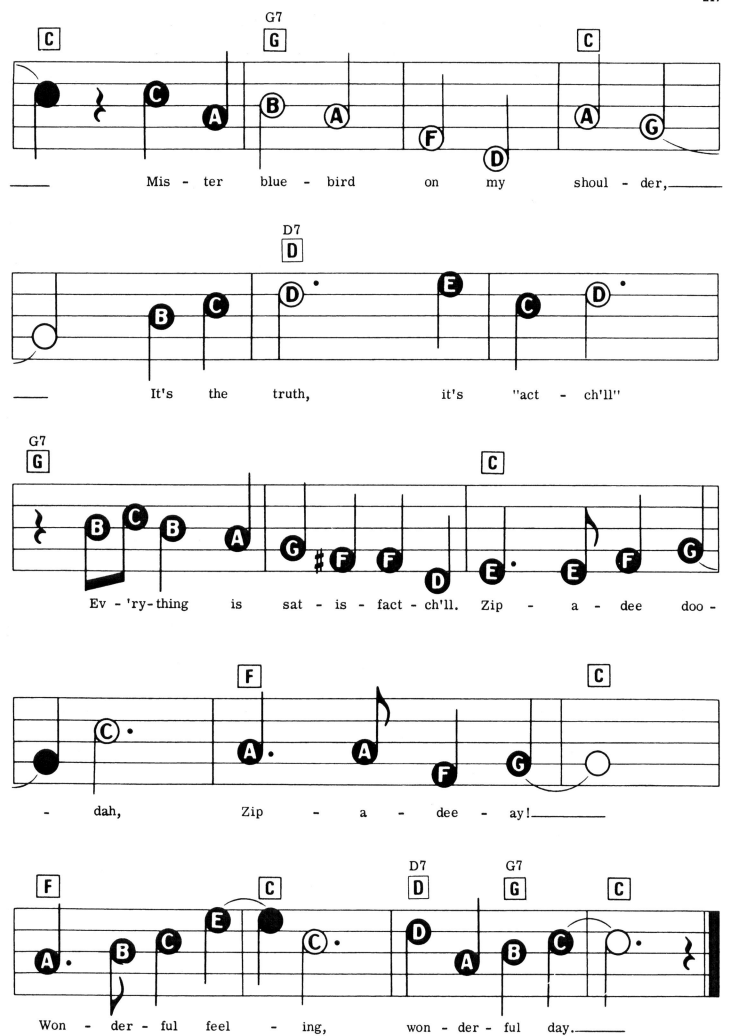

Sway
(Quien será)

Registration 2
Rhythm: Rhumba or Latin

English Words by Norman Gimbel
Spanish Words and Music by Pablo Beltran Ruiz

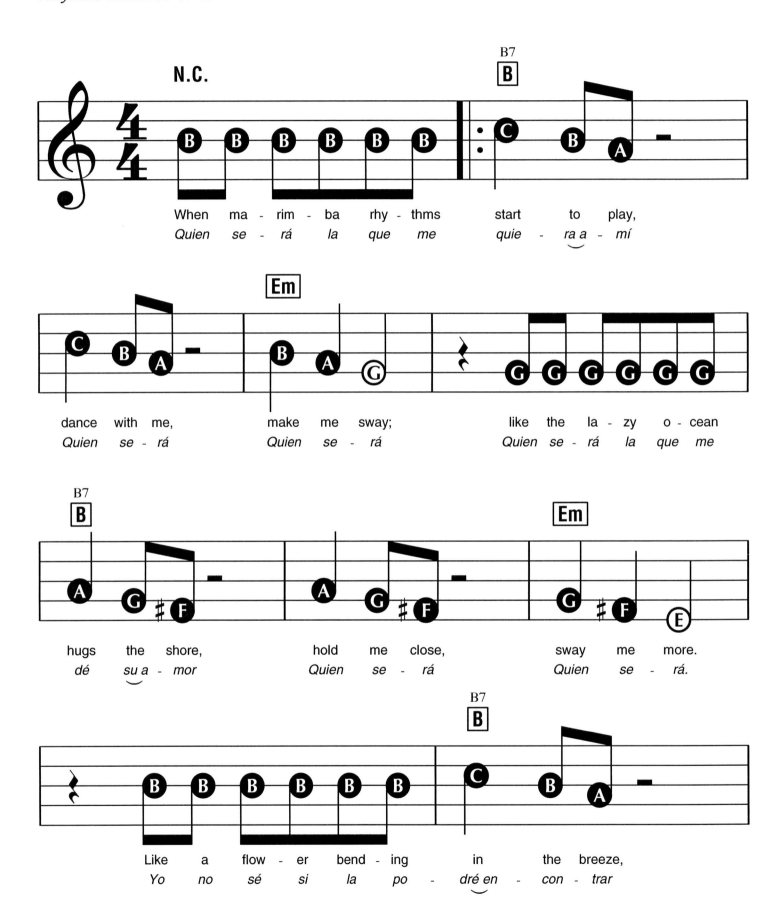

When ma - rim - ba rhy - thms start to play,
Quien se - rá la que me quie - ra a - mí

dance with me, make me sway; like the la - zy o - cean
Quien se - rá *Quien se - rá* *Quien se - rá la que me*

hugs the shore, hold me close, sway me more.
dé su a - mor *Quien se - rá* *Quien se - rá.*

Like a flow - er bend - ing in the breeze,
Yo no sé si la po - dré en - con - trar

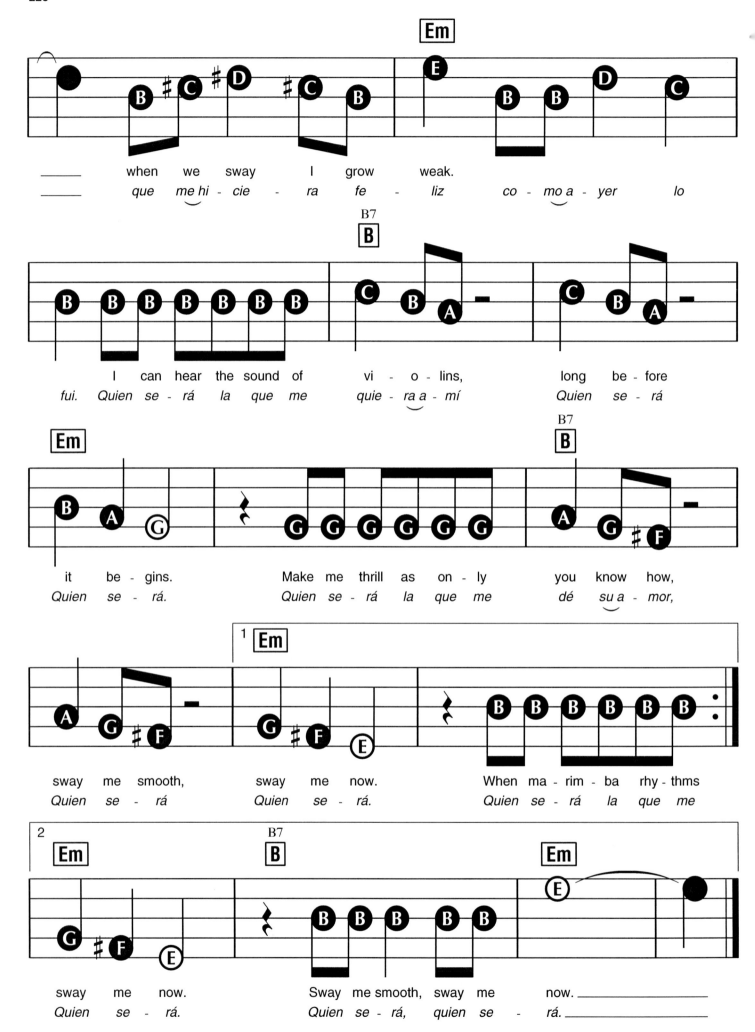

Registration Guide

• Match the Registration number on the song to the corresponding numbered category below. Select and activate an instrumental sound available on your instrument.

• Choose an automatic rhythm appropriate to the mood and style of the song. (Consult your Owner's Guide for proper operation of automatic rhythm features.)

• Adjust the tempo and volume controls to comfortable settings.

Registration

1	Mellow	Flutes, Clarinet, Oboe, Flugel Horn, Trombone, French Horn, Organ Flutes
2	Ensemble	Brass Section, Sax Section, Wind Ensemble, Full Organ, Theater Organ
3	Strings	Violin, Viola, Cello, Fiddle, String Ensemble, Pizzicato, Organ Strings
4	Guitars	Acoustic/Electric Guitars, Banjo, Mandolin, Dulcimer, Ukulele, Hawaiian Guitar
5	Mallets	Vibraphone, Marimba, Xylophone, Steel Drums, Bells, Celesta, Chimes
6	Liturgical	Pipe Organ, Hand Bells, Vocal Ensemble, Choir, Organ Flutes
7	Bright	Saxophones, Trumpet, Mute Trumpet, Synth Leads, Jazz/Gospel Organs
8	Piano	Piano, Electric Piano, Honky Tonk Piano, Harpsichord, Clavi
9	Novelty	Melodic Percussion, Wah Trumpet, Synth, Whistle, Kazoo, Perc. Organ
10	Bellows	Accordion, French Accordion, Mussette, Harmonica, Pump Organ, Bagpipes